The Quality of Mercy

The Quality of Mercy

AMNESTIES AND TRADITIONAL CHINESE JUSTICE

Brian E. McKnight

THE UNIVERSITY PRESS OF HAWAII
Honolulu

Library of Congress Cataloging in Publication Data

McKnight, Brian E
     The quality of mercy.

     Bibliography: p.
     Includes index.
     1.   Amnesty—China—History.   2.   Criminal justice,
Administration of—China—History.   3.   China—Social
life and customs.   I.   Title.
LAW   345.51'05   80-26650
ISBN 0-8248-0736-7

Manufactured in the United States of America

Contents

Preface   vii

Introduction   xi

1. *Ancient China*   1

2. *The Early Empire*   12

3. *Acts of Grace in Medieval China:* A.D. 220–907   37

4. *Acts of Grace in Sung China*   73

5. *Late Imperial China: The Significance of Change*   94

6. *The Uses of Amnesty*   112

A Note on Previous Studies   128

Notes   130

Bibliography   155

Glossary   163

Index   167

Preface

THIS work touches on both social and legal history. It is concerned with problems of the law. But as a historian I am myself less concerned with the law than with the role of things legal in Chinese social life. This volume is addressed first and foremost to those interested in the history of China. But because it focuses on the law I have also tried to write it so that it would be understandable to those working on the legal histories of other peoples. Therefore at some points I recite elementary facts about Chinese history. I hope my sinological readers will bear with me when I repeat the obvious.

The bulk of this book is a description of a historical phenomenon—the system of amnesties in premodern China. I think I have brought forward enough materials to reveal the scope and nature of these amnesties and also to demonstrate that they were actually enforced in practice. But historians who content themselves with description have finished only half their task. In the last chapter I offer a group of hypotheses about the amnesty system, and about general traits of Chinese historical development. Some parts of my argument are widely accepted by historians (for example, that late imperial rulers were in general more autocratic than their predecessors in middle China). Others are unarguable (for example, that the population increased greatly between the mid-Sung and the mid-Ch'ing). I have taken these pieces and assembled them in a novel way. Without so doing I could not adequately explain to myself the information I had gathered about amnesties. If my explanation provokes discussion I will feel adequately rewarded. Since this is the first attempt to deal carefully with the materials, tentative hypotheses are inevitable. Certainly more questions are raised here than can be fully answered.

The study of Chinese legal history is in its infancy. Few works have been written on the role of law in Chinese life. Those studies that have been made have concentrated almost exclusively on formal and traditional topics—the analysis of codes or the recitation of original materials with little analysis. Such studies are necessary. Integrating and analytical work must build upon them. As the notes to this volume indicate, I am much indebted to the compilations of Chinese scholars such as Shen Chia-pen, Ch'eng Shu-te, Hsüeh Yun-sheng, and others. I have been much aided by studies and translations of the codes, such as the works of Wallace Johnson and Tai Yen-hui on the T'ang.

A few studies of the legal systems of certain dynasties, studies built on codes and on other materials, have appeared. Most of these deal with Ch'ing China, but a few touch on earlier periods. In this regard I am most especially indebted to A. F. P. Hulsewé's *Remnants of Han Law:* without this work my chapter on the Han could hardly have been written in its present form. The Han chapter is in fact largely a rearrangement and reanalysis of materials originally noted by Professor Hulsewé. His work forms the basis of the chapter. He was also kind enough to read the material I had prepared and offer many valuable suggestions.

Many others have helped me immensely by reading and commenting on sections of the work. I would like to thank Professors H. G. Creel, Harry Lamley, John Langlois, and T'ien-yi T'ao for their many useful comments; Joseph Cheng of the Center for East Asian Legal Studies who noted several points that deserved clearer explanation; Professor James Liu who read the whole manuscript and offered a number of thoughtful suggestions; and Dr. Chen Fu-mei who went through the manuscript with great care, pointed out a number of flaws, and offered particularly valuable criticisms of the closing chapters. Finally I would like to thank Professor Jerome A. Cohen of the Harvard Law School, both for his suggestions and for having made possible my two year-long visits to the Center for East Asian Legal Studies. In short I am indebted to many for their advice about this study. Since I put their suggestions to my own uses I am responsible for whatever flaws remain.

Introduction

A description of what criminals suffer, and nothing more pretentious, is what we should mean when we speak of punishment. Books of law tell only half the story. They are a dirge of penalties, of feet cut off, of servitude, of beatings, of executions. But from the point of view of society and of criminals the real issue is the punishment they are in fact likely to undergo. How probable is it that they will be caught? And if caught, convicted? And if convicted, what penalties will really be inflicted on them?

In the modern world, where we have begun to collect statistics on crime, we can make tentative judgments on the first two questions and reasonably accurate estimates on the last one. For those interested in social problems prior to the twentieth century, the first two questions are almost wholly unanswerable and evidence bearing on the third is largely anecdotal and impressionistic. Historians turn to codes of laws and, where available, collections of cases; many vital questions are thus put aside because the material bearing on them seems too limited to be worth exploiting. The question of punishments actually inflicted is often ignored due to limitations in the evidence. Yet a recognition of the treatment accorded criminals is as important as a grasp of the preceding steps in the judicial process. The tone of a civilization, the character of relations between the groups that compose it, the quality and sophistication of its political institutions, the pervasiveness of a common ethos among its members—all are reflected in the actual treatment of deviants.

Fortunately historians dealing with traditional China, particularly from the Sung dynasty (960–1279) onward, have available an enormous volume of materials on criminal law. A beginning has been made in the study of traditional Chinese law codes. A few pioneering studies such as A. F. P. Hulsewé's *Remnants of Han Law* have begun modifying our view of Chinese justice by using other sources. However, one vital type of information about the actual treatment of Chinese offenders has been largely ignored. The Chinese records recount thousands of instances of the amnestying of criminals, yet even when historians have mentioned amnesties or pointed out in passing their importance, they have failed to explore their implications for the judicial system as a whole. With the exception of the masterful chapter in Hulsewé's work there are no adequate descriptions in any language of the amnesty practices of any period in Chinese history. And yet, as the following pages will show, an understanding of this system of acts of grace compels a reevaluation of traditional Chinese criminal justice.

This system has a few parallels outside the area influenced by Chinese culture.[1] Asoka says in the fifth pillar edict that in the twenty-six years since his consecration the release of prisoners had been ordered twenty-five times.[2] But in the absence of other evidence we have no way of knowing how thoroughly such orders were carried out. Were all prisoners released or only some? Prisoners everywhere or only in certain areas? Were they wholly released or did they still have residual penalties? Probably such questions can never be answered.

An even closer parallel to the Chinese system is to be found in the Eastern Roman Empire. The Theodosian Code mentions thirteen amnesties granted between A.D. 332 and 413. These acts are strikingly reminiscent of Chinese practices. Most often they were issued at Easter and had strong religious and redemptive overtones. Those who benefited from them, like their Chinese counterparts, were being given the chance to "renew" themselves. Like the Chinese great acts of grace, the grants were general in that all were to be freed with certain exceptions—those guilty of sorcery, homicide, and adultery are most often mentioned as excluded from coverage. In some cases criminals already serving sentences were not freed.[3] (Mommsen tells us that at other times in Roman history amnesties were only issued in times of disorder and civil war and were confined to territory under enemy control.)[4]

Such general amnesties were rare during the European middle

ages, but the idea that the sovereign could pardon offenders lived on, to be embodied either in modern criminal codes (as is the case in Switzerland, Turkey, and Italy) or in state constitutions.[5] In all these instances the use of that power has generally been sporadic or confined to individual cases.

The traditional Chinese case was quite different. From the founding of the empire in the third century B.C. general amnesties and acts of grace were granted frequently. Some of these acts were concerned solely with reducing or forgiving the penalties of criminals—such acts we may properly label amnesties. Many others, however, in addition to their criminal provisions, also provided benefits—tax remissions, gifts of money or rank, and so on—to a wide variety of social groups. Such acts ought to be called acts of grace.

In imperial China the same word, *she,* was used for both sorts of edicts. Since the majority of empirewide *she* in imperial times seem to have contained some noncriminal provisions, I will generally translate *she* as "act of grace" when it is a noun. When the word might mean simply an amnesty, or when the word *she* is being used as a verb, I will translate it "amnesty."[6] The sources themselves frequently distinguish between levels of acts of grace. The most extensive grants in terms of the scope of their benefits were called *ta-she,* a term I translate "great acts of grace." (The word *ta* in this term does not refer to the geographical coverage of the acts. *Ta-she* did apply to the whole empire, but so did many ordinary acts of grace.) Ordinary acts of grace, in discussions of the system, are sometimes referred to as *ch'ang-she.* In the edicts themselves this term rarely appears. There such ordinary grants are merely called *she* or, in some dynasties, *te-yin.*

Acts of grace had been granted occasionally prior to the founding of the empire. Our information about them is meager, but does suggest that the preimperial era was a distinct period in the history of the amnesty system. Under the empire, despite a superficial appearance of continuity, there seem to have been two distinct periods with different traditions of grace, one from the Han through the Sung (960–1279) and one originating under the sino-foreign Liao state (907–1125) and continuing through the Chin, Yüan, and Ming to the last imperial dynasty, the Ch'ing, an era I have here called the late imperial period.

Since the two subperiods within the imperial era differ primarily in terms of the numbers of amnesties granted, they are a clear example of the truth of the old saw that for some things quantity of change becomes quality of change. The value of much research on premodern China has been reduced by the tendency of writers to focus on superficial continuity and ignore underlying evolution. The cocoon may look the same from the time of its spinning until the moment of the moth's emergence. Within it one world has given way to another.

The Quality of Mercy

chapter 1

Ancient China

PEOPLE, ancient and modern, have struggled to impose order and system on a world that is always changing—to create regularity, persistence, and predictability and to suppress the unpredictable, the irregular, and the idiosyncratic. Disorder inspires feelings that are closely linked to feelings about deviance and lawbreakers. Those who violate the codes, written and unwritten, that govern people's lives, are threatening the order so painstakingly created. Their actions provoke anger and fear and hence are punished.

By their actions the deviants have separated themselves from what is proper and orderly. In archaic societies (and to an unacknowledged but considerable extent in modern societies), violation of norms is associated with ritual impurity. If the delicts are serious, their perpetrators may be chastised by being permanently outcast from the body of people clean enough to participate in group ritual life. The ultimate expression of this sanction is capital punishment. Even on a lesser scale deviants may be punished in ways that leave them unfit for group activities, by having their physical wholeness impaired through mutilation or by being made to bear some outward symbol of their state.[1]

Yet no one is perfect. All people occasionally break the rules. Without some mechanism for reintegrating deviant individuals into the group society would collapse. The devices used are manifold, varying from culture to culture, from group to group, and from delict to delict, but many of them share one key goal: the recreation, at least approximately, of the status quo ante. If we can just get back to the way things were before, then we can begin again and hopefully avoid a repetition of the violation. Measures for achieving this goal may be quite formal in their structure, incorporating various ritual elements which are themselves expressive of the maintenance of order; they often include elements that display a fund of political, social, and psychological common sense.

Ritualized devices for the forgiveness of sins are as necessary to a society as the punishments which precede or accompany them. It is in this light that we must view the system of amnesties which was so prominent a feature of traditional Chinese justice. For two thousand years, Chinese imperial rulers issued a bewildering host of amnesties and acts of grace. In frequency, scope, and elaborateness this Chinese practice has no parallel outside the area of Chinese cultural influence. These acts not only freed or reduced the sentences of criminals but also granted benefits to other groups such as soldiers, officials, and ordinary taxpayers. Central to them were the redemptive clauses in which the ruler exercised his power to cleanse the wicked so that they might have the chance to begin afresh.

As a regular practice this system of acts of grace arose under the empire; its roots go much farther back into Chinese history. Many of the underlying beliefs and even specific facets of the individual acts can be traced as far back as the founding of the Western Chou (ca. 1027 B.C.). In our earliest written references to the problems of punishment and forgiveness the Chou founder King Wu speaks to his younger brother about the propriety of dealing leniently with those guilty even of great crimes, provided they were committed through mishap or inadvertence. For the deliberate malefactor the penalty should be death without pardon.[2] Strict and implacable justice to those deliberately guilty with knowledge aforethought no matter how minor their offense, full and complete pardon for those guilty through mishap or mistake no matter how grave the crime—this became the main doctrine on judicial grace. First enunciated by King Wu, it remained current doctrine and was reaffirmed in the late, forged sections of the *Book of Documents*. Given in an epigram in the "Counsels of the Great Yü," it was spelled out at greater length in the "Canon of Shun," where it was said that Shun "gave delineation of the statutory punishments, enacting banishment as a mitigation *(yu)* of the Five Great Inflictions. . . . Inadvertent offenses and those caused by mis-

fortune were to be pardoned *(she)* but those who offended presumptuously or repeatedly were to be punished with death."[3]

The ancient Chinese gave this widely shared attitude toward justice
and mercy a Chinese twist by focusing on the central role of the ruler
and the power of his example. If the king is careful to make known
his aversion to tyrannical executions, then his example will cause
those around him, his officers and subordinates, to extend a like forgiveness to those under their powers. Thus the authority of the king,
his capacity to set things aright, to bring people back into the social
group, will reverberate down the social ladder and bring about the
good ordering of the whole. His grace may even be extended to those
guilty of heinous crimes, to "former traitors and villains and killers
and torturers." Such acts of grace might even lead to the ideal state in
which punishment became unnecessary.[4]

The centrality of the king in this matter was a specific facet of his
key place in the proper order of things. The early Chou leaders attempted to buttress their rule by promulgating to conquered peoples
the set of ideas known as the Decree of Heaven theory. Heaven had
instituted rule among mortals to promote their welfare. It had given
its mandate to rule to the man most able to promote this welfare. The
mandate was not a free gift, however. Should the ruler fail in his appointed tasks, Heaven might withdraw the mandate and pass it to another. The signs of a ruler's failure were various, but injustice was always among them. A ruler who had lost the mandate no longer was
capable of standing in his proper place as the intermediary between
Heaven and man. He could no longer be guided by Heaven's commands. One sign of this failing was his unwillingness to be just and
merciful. He had lost the ability to bring order out of disorder, to
cleanse those who had separated themselves from propriety so that
they could again participate in the general life. It was for such faults
as these that Heaven had withdrawn the mandate from the last ruler
of the Shang and given it into the hands of the Chou.[5]

Hence the Chou founders constantly exhorted their followers and
relatives to act with great care in the conduct of government—to
weave together the warp of justice with the woof of mercy. The king
must be strict and fair. And yet, "being king, he should not, because
the small people go to excess and use irregular [practices], likewise
dare rule the people by exterminating [that is, capital] punish-

ments."[6] Chou success in holding northern China must surely be credited, at least in part, to their having lived up to their own admonitions.

The succeeding centuries of the Western Chou (1027–771 B.C.) and the early part of the Eastern Chou (771–256 B.C.) are little known. Records are few and brief. But with the beginning of the Spring and Autumn period (722–481 B.C.) information grows in quantity and becomes more various. Historical annals appear, greatest among them the detailed and vivid record called the *Tso Chuan*. This work reveals a society changed from early Chou times, but in the matter of justice attitudes appear much as they had been. There is the same emphasis on the distinction between inadvertent crimes in which disorder and pollution seem almost accidental and therefore pardonable, and deliberate and therefore unpardonable crimes such as patricide, the killing of a ruler by a minister, or the harboring of those guilty of crimes against the state.[7]

The ruler may forgive crimes committed through inadvertence and thus restore order. His power to do so—to clean the slate so that offenders can begin afresh—might be expressed by the issuing of an act of grace on his accession to the throne. Such acts reflect how inextricably interwoven were the threads of belief about the proper order of things and the dictates of commonsense policy. By issuing an amnesty at the beginning of his reign, a ruler was declaring his ability to wipe the slate clean and to restore order. He was also reassuring potential enemies within his state that their previous acts were forgiven if not forgotten.[8]

This marriage of the practical and the sacred is again reflected in the frequency with which acts of pardon are associated with military mobilization. In readying their forces for war, rulers of this age repeatedly displayed their benevolence by remitting taxes, giving largess to the people, and issuing pardons to offenders.[9] Viewed through the eyes of common sense, such pardons seem calculated to lift morale and generate popular support. They may also be seen as restoring order, making pure the impure, and reuniting to the people those previously outcast.

The scarcity of records and their character, both in the Spring and Autumn and in the Warring States (403–221 B.C.) periods, limit our understanding of who benefited from these acts of grace and to what extent. A few passages from works of the Warring States period indicate that some criminals in pre-Han times served sentences of servitude and were freed by amnesties. To those who had suffered permanently mutilating punishment, unless they were additionally serving sentences of servitude, a subsequent amnesty must have seemed a cruel joke. Probably grants of grace affected mostly those currently under adjudication, those serving as laborers (who might be freed not only from their labors but also from the visible symbols of their status), and possibly those not yet caught.

With the close of the Spring and Autumn period the brilliant historical panorama painted by the author of the *Tso Chuan* gives way to a shadowy landscape. Romances replace histories. During this era the great crisis through which Chinese society was passing pricked consciences, provoking an unprecedented outpouring of speculation on human nature, society, and the universe. Thinkers comment occasionally on the problem of grace as one minor aspect of their general views. Earliest in time, and predictably on the side of mercy, was Confucius (551–479 B.C.), for whom the art of government involved "pardoning *(she)* small faults."[10] This brief admonition speaks volumes. There is no call for a strict and rigid justice which would punish anyone guilty of any offense. Yet Confucius is not suggesting a mercy as broad as that advocated by King Wu, who had spoken of pardon for "traitors and villains and killers and torturers." Clearly the position of King Wu on this point and that of Confucius are not congruent. As Confucius remarked, if we repay evil with kindness, with what will we recompense kindness? Underlying the general Confucian position is the premise that penalties may relieve symptoms, but the radical cure consists in building a society in which punishments will no longer be necessary. But in general the Confucians did not deny that wrongdoers should be punished. Their attitude is epitomized in the attitudes of Mencius (372–289 B.C.), for whom the ideal ruler was the man who never punished the innocent, was sparing in his use of penalties, but did not draw back from chastising the refractory and the willfully evil.[11]

This Confucian attitude reaches its greatest elaboration in the *Rites of Chou,* a text by an author or authors of strong Confucian leanings.

This text purports to describe the institutions of the Chou founders, though the work as we now have it probably comes from the Warring States period. The *Rites of Chou* is written as a list of offices with appended descriptions of their duties and functions. It is remarkable among all early works in advocating a wide decentralization of the power to grant grace. Other works arguing for or against granting pardons clearly focus on the role of the ruler. In the *Rites of Chou* six separate officers are described as having the authority to pardon or reduce punishments.

At the top of the official pyramid the Grand Minister *(ta-hsiang)* wields as one of his prerogatives what is called "the power to let live." The commentary tells us that "there are those guilty men who have been condemned to die. They are allowed to live."[12] (This same power appears again under the office of the Annalist of the Interior, as an attribute of the Emperor.)[13] At least two officers, the Grand Director of the Multitude and the Chief of Bandit Control, were credited with the authority to reduce punishment. In the case of the former we are told that this was done in times of disaster, such as famines, epidemics, or invasions.[14] The Censor might pardon minor misdemeanors committed by villagers. The Executioner might treat with indulgence major crimes—if committed unknowingly, involuntarily, or through negligence or forgetfulness—or grant pardon if the crimes were committed by the young, the aged, or the mentally incompetent.[15]

Even the people were given a voice in granting pardons. We are told that the Lesser Overseer of Brigands, in deciding capital cases, "listens to the voice of the people asking for execution or pardon *(tz'u)*." The commentaries elaborate on this: "If the people say 'Kill,' the Lesser Overseer of Brigands kills; if the people say 'Pardon' *(k'uan)*, the Lesser Overseer of Brigands pardons."[16] Despite this broad distribution of powers to grant pardons or mitigate punishments, the Emperor still plays a central role for the writer of the *Rites of Chou*. If someone was to be pardoned, the ruler intervened to pronounce the decision—in person for cases in the interior districts, through the agency of subordinates in outlying areas.[17]

This thoroughly utopian vision of the merciful face of Chinese justice tells us little about the actual practice of granting grace in early

China. It is nonetheless important. Authors in later traditional China frequently cite these passages in writing about the amnesty system. Moreover it provides us a fascinating glimpse into the fantasies of a Confucian thinker of late Chou times. His Shangri-la is as ordered as a bureaucrat's diagram of offices, but touched with humane concern.

The Confucian willingness to overlook offenses was not shared by thinkers of other persuasions. The world of their time seemed to be collapsing around them. The old beliefs were scoffed at. People did things to one another that would have been unthinkable in times past. Everywhere the worst were full of passionate intensity. Order became the paramount goal for those committed to helping the world they knew. The first major thinker after Confucius, the philosopher Mo-tzu, is typical of this law and order attitude. He was driven by his agonized pity for the sufferings of those around him to advance a profoundly authoritarian philosophy in which mercy had no place. The need for order overrode other concerns. Though great care was to be exercised in judging cases, the guilty were to be punished without pardon:

> This is to say that upon discovering either good or evil the ancient feudal lords always hurriedly drove to the emperor and represented it to him. Therefore rewards fell upon the virtuous and punishments upon the wicked. The innocent were not prosecuted and the guilty were not pardoned *(wu she)*.[18]

This line of thinking is pushed to its limits by members of that group of thinkers commonly called the legalists. Mercy was anathema. "Kindness and benevolence," says the *Book of Lord Shang*, "are the foster mother of transgressions."[19] The legalist sage was different from the sage of the Confucians. He was "not indulgent with transgressions *(pu yu kuo)* and did not pardon crimes *(pu she hsing)* and so villainy did not spring up."[20] If even minor offenses were punished heavily, the people would be deterred from great crimes. Disorder arose not because of a deficiency of the ordering of the laws but because the authorities shied away from a strict enforcement of them. Harsh penalties applied to all—without distinctions of rank, without pardon or mitigation—were the only road to order and power.[21]

This kind of thinking came to fruition during the Warring States period as the guiding ethos of the state of Ch'in, which in 221 B.C. destroyed its last rival and unified the empire under its rule. Even followers of Confucius were touched by the prevailing legalist doctrines. The most famous was the great Confucian Hsün Tzu (340–245 B.C.), who said: "If anyone is found acting or using his talents to work against the good of the time, condemn him to death without pardon *(wu-she)*. This is what is called the virtue of Heaven and the government of a true king."[22] And in a later chapter Hsün Tzu quotes with approval a section of the *Book of Documents* which says that the government statutes of Chou prescribed death without pardon for all officials who were either dilatory or impetuous in the execution of their duties.[23]

Ambivalence about mercy and severity is also reflected in the book *Kuan tzu*. Some of its sections appear to have been written by Confucians under strong legalist influence, who tried, often unsuccessfully, to blend Confucian leanings with legalist doctrines. In the section "On Establishing Government" there are recurring admonitions not to pardon a variety of offenses, such as disobedience to orders, delaying the communication of orders, failure to act in accord with the laws, or deleting or adding to statutes. Officials are to be treated with legalist severity. In the same section we are told that the common peoples' minor trepasses might be treated indulgently *(yu)* on first or second occurrences. Only the third infraction was not to be pardoned *(pu-she)*, a benevolence toward the people that accords ill with the general legalist tone of the piece.[24]

The same curious mixture of incompatibles recurs in the section "On Conforming to the Law":

> If the people do not commit serious crimes it is because they have committed no major errors. If people have committed no major errors it is because their superiors grant no pardons *(wu-she)*. In general the granting of pardons is of little benefit and great harm. Therefore in the long run nothing can surpass its felicitous consequences. Therefore the granting of pardons is the same as releasing the reins of a runaway horse, while not granting them is the same as [probing] a festering boil with a stone lancet.[25]

Then, before going on in the same vein, this section says: "In civil affairs one may be lenient *(yu)* three times but in military affairs not a single pardon *(she)* should be granted."[26] Some sections lean toward the purely legalist: "If punishments and killings are carried out without pardon then the people will have the excellence of not being careless."[27] Others are idealistically Confucian: "Lighten the collection of taxes, relax punishments *(shih hsing-fa)*, pardon criminals *(she tsui li)*, and be lenient with small faults."[28] At times the writers approach a harmonious blending of the two ways of thought, as when the ruler is advised to lighten taxes and lighten punishments *(ch'ing hsing fa)*, to make the laws practicable and uncomplicated, punishing with incorruptible fairness but not pardoning offenders *(pu-she)*.[29] Deterrence, always a goal of punishment in traditional China, is to be supplemented but not subverted by benevolence.

Ambivalent attitudes also mark the *Book of Rites,* a collection of writings by various hands compiled in its present form in the first century B.C. but containing some pre-Han material. In the "Royal Regulations" section we have an elaborate and idealized description of judicial process—from judges who interrogated the dignitaries, officials, and people in all capital cases, to a king who fixed his punishments only after assessing the mitigating circumstances of ignorance, mistake, or forgetfulness. Great stress is laid on treating doubtful cases leniently. There is also a list of unpardonable crimes, with a heavy emphasis on seditious behavior or destruction of custom, on "splitting words so as to break [the force of] laws; confounding names so as to change what had been definitely settled; practicing corrupt ways so as to throw government into confusion." Those guilty were to be put to death, along with those who used licentious music, strange garments, wonderful contrivances, and extraordinary implements. Such behavior, like "teaching what was wrong" or "giving false reports about [appearances of] spirits" or other phenomena, might bewilder and perplex the multitude. The penalty was death without pardon *(pu she kuo)*. The rule was laid down that voluntary offenses, no matter how insignificant, were not to be forgiven. It is said that the officers in charge of enforcing the rules did not have the power to pardon transgressors. The attraction of legalist teachings was felt here also.[30]

The eclectic tendency revealed in these passages is also reflected in another important development in the thought of the last part of the Warring States period: the increase in cosmological-numerological speculation and its marriage with Confucianism. Beginning as speculation about natural phenomena, cosmological-numerological thinking quickly became invested with political and social overtones. It came to be believed that the acts of the rulers affected natural phenomena; therefore, to preserve the proper rhythms of nature, the government had to match its behavior to the seasons. Thus the season of germination and growth called for different treatment of criminals from that accorded them in the season of decay and death. Several passages in the *Kuan tzu* prescribe the proper behavior for the springtime, which includes among other acts of benevolence and mercy the pardoning of offenders and the freeing of those detained for investigation. When autumn came the state showed its other face, executing capital criminals, forgiving no one, refusing to grant reprieves.[31]

A more elaborate calendar is preserved in the *Book of Rites*:

In the second month of Spring [the Son of Heaven] orders the appropriate officials to visit the prisons, to stop the use of fetters and manacles, to forbid the inflicting of arbitrary beatings, and to put a stop to criminal accusations and trials. . . .

In the first month of Summer . . . they decide cases for which the punishments are light; they make short work of small crimes, and liberate *(ch'u ching hsi)* those who are in prison for small offenses. . . .

In the second month of Summer . . . leniency should be shown to prisoners charged [even] with great crimes *(t'ing chung ch'iu)* and their allowance of food be increased. . . . The various magistrates inflict no punishments. . . .

In the first month of Autumn . . . there should be no excess in copying that severity [of Heaven] or in the opposite indulgence. . . .

In the second month of Autumn . . . beheading and [the other] capital punishments must be according to [the crimes] without excess or defect. . . .

In the second month of Winter . . . if there be among [those hunting or gathering in the forests] those who encroach on or rob the others, they should be punished without fail.[32]

By introducing a cycle of time the authors of this work were able to encompass both mercy and severity. The legalist position, that the offending eye should be plucked out to maintain the health of the body, was proper, but only in its season. The problem of the disorderly and the impure could be dealt with permanently by eliminating the offender, but only when such harshness was in accord with the larger pattern of nature. During the forgiving seasons, by contrast, the ruler could display his prerogative to cleanse and reintegrate offenders.

The contrast between the two extreme positions seems clear, but one must not lose sight of their shared beliefs. All the authors of the major philosophical tracts of the classical period shared a concern about the disorder of their times. All sought to reestablish a proper ordered society in which irregular impure practices had been eliminated or at least drastically reduced in scope. The two schools most prominent in the struggle for political influence, the Confucians and the legalists, agreed on many of the crimes that should be unforgivable—particularly those which thwarted standard social practices or violated proper relationships. They differed in many ways, of course. The legalists' list of unpardonable crimes was longer. Furthermore they would not recognize the role of inadvertence and mishap. If society had been disordered, the problem should be permanently solved by destroying the deviant individual. By contrast the sociologically and psychologically more sophisticated Confucians recognized the basically incidental nature of the disorder that followed inadvertent delicts, as well as the dangers inherent in too harsh a system of exclusion.

The arguments which fill these various works were not divorced from their times. Words, ideas, and theories were weapons in the war that raged between Confucian ideals and legalist practice. The last half of the third century B.C. must have been a grim and frightful time for the Confucians as they saw the forces of the enemy, embodied in the state of Ch'in, swallowing up the other states of China. Who could foresee that governments founded on legalist principles would have need for Confucian acts of mercy?

chapter 2

The Early Empire

DURING the last half of the third century B.C. the western state of Ch'in invaded eastern China, destroyed its rivals, and emerged in 221 B.C. as the unifier of a new empire. Its First Emperor's attempts to impose centralized authority on all of China fed growing discontent which exploded into open insurrection in 209 B.C. Within a few years his imperial armies had been destroyed or dispersed. The civil war that then broke out between the aristocratic general Hsiang Yü and his peasant counterpart Liu Chi (Liu Pang) dragged on for years before Liu Chi finally destroyed his rival and ascended the throne as Kao-tsu, the first emperor of the Han dynasty (206 B.C.–A.D. 220).

Traditional Chinese historians have deplored the brutality of Ch'in rule, but many have acknowledged its great contributions to the later Chinese empire. Han Kao-tsu modeled his administration on Ch'in patterns and staffed his offices with Ch'in officials. It could hardly have been otherwise. He had spent all his adult life living under the Ch'in. The influences of his firsthand experiences of Ch'in rule can only have been reinforced by his experience in the central region of Ch'in power, Kuan-chung, which he captured in 207 B.C. and which became and remained the center of his power from 206 B.C. Thereafter he rarely left this region, steeped in Ch'in tradition, except during military campaigns and during a few later visits to the east. When he first captured the imperial capital in 207, he collected the political and administrative documents housed in the royal archives and made political contacts with local leaders, themselves the bearers of Ch'in traditions.

In light of this background it is hardly surprising that Han rulers depended heavily on their predecessor's legal traditions. When, around 200 B.C., a code was being drawn up, Liu Chi's chief legal advisor, Hsiao Ho, "gathered together the laws of the Ch'in, and choosing those that were suitable for [current] times, made the statutes in nine sections."[1]

But Liu Chi's use of the First Emperor's laws obviously did not wait on this compilation. During the preceding period he also used a modified version of the imperial code in his administration. This Ch'in Code has been proverbial in traditional Chinese historiography for its harshness. Supposedly no mitigation was condoned. The rule was severe punishment mechanically applied.

And yet, in February 205 B.C., Liu Chi, the future Emperor Kao, "amnestied criminals *(she tsui-jen)*".[2] From where did this man, so heavily in debt to Ch'in patterns, draw the precedent for his act of mercy? Almost certainly he found his justification in the history of the Ch'in itself. In the middle of the fourth century B.C. the legalist Shang Yang had reformed Ch'in political institutions. The writings attributed to him are the most extreme expression of law and order thinking in traditional China. His reforms remained current Ch'in practice to the end. But in 249, a century after his reforms and only twenty-eight years before the final victory of the First Emperor, the Ch'in king issued a great act of grace *(ta-she)*, only the second such grant of which any record has been preserved. Here, in the heartland of legal severity, we find an example of the most comprehensive act of judicial mercy used in later China.[3]

This act was no isolated aberration. Amnesties in Ch'in can be traced as far as the reign of Duke Mu (r. 659–621 B.C.). The *Historical Records* say:

Once the Duke Mu had lost a fine horse. The rustic men who lived at the foot of Mount Ch'i together seized it and ate it; there were more than three hundred men. The magistrates arrested them and wanted to deal with them according to law. Duke Mu said, "The sage does not harm men over the question of a beast. I have heard it said than when a man has eaten the flesh of an excellent horse, if he does not drink wine, he will suffer." Then he gave wine to all of them and pardoned them. When the three hundred men learned that Ch'in was fighting [the state of] Chin they all asked to be allowed to follow [the duke in his service].

When, in following him, they saw that Duke Mu was in a critical situation they gripped their lances and fought to the death in recognition of the grace given them in the affair of the excellent horse.[4]

This anecdote epitomizes amnesty as an act of pure grace—guilty men, a benevolent ruler, and the debt of loyalty incurred by the saved.

Amnesties reappear during the third century, when Ch'in was supposedly following the "legalist" policies that contributed in 221 B.C. to its final victory. On four occasions between 286 and 279 King Shao-hsiang "amnestied criminals and transferred them *(she tsui-jen ch'ien chih)."*

In 254, one year after the Ch'in forces had destroyed the remnant of the Chou empire, the Ch'in king performed the imperial sacrifices, thus making explicit Ch'in's claim to the empire. Five years later, when King Hsiao-wen ascended the throne he "pardoned the condemned, honored the subjects who had gained merit under his predecessor, granted ranks and dignities to his ancestors, and reduced the size of his parks and gardens." When Hsiao-wen died within a few days of assuming power, his son Chuang-hsiang ascended the throne and immediately "proclaimed a great act of grace *(ta-she)* pardoning criminals, honoring subjects who had gained merit under his predecessors, raising the honors of his ancestors, and extending benefits to the people." These men reinforced a precedent widely followed in later imperial China—that of making accession to the throne an occasion for grants of grace.[5]

Chuang-hsiang was succceeded by the man destined to oversee the reunification of China. The rule of this unifier and his descendants was to be never ending, so he merely called himself the "First Emperor." By the time he died in 210 B.C. he had done much to ensure the continued existence of the Chinese empire, but he had in the process created many enemies. It is perhaps worth noting that he deliberately abstained from issuing acts of grace. The *Historical Records* say:

[Ch'in] Shih-huang caused the Five Virtues to advance in their proper sequence. Knowing that the Chou had Fire as their Virtue, and the Ch'in had displaced the Virtue of Chou, he adopted [as his virtue] that which could not be overcome [by fire]. Therefore there was at that time the commencement of the Virtue of Water. . . . Being strong and of great severity he treated all affairs according to law, punishing without using benevolence or righteousness, [so that] afterward it would accord with the configuration of the Five Virtues. Thereupon the laws were quickly applied and for a long time there were no amnesties.[6]

The death of the First Emperor was soon followed by open revolt against the Ch'in. The Second Emperor saw his inheritance rapidly crumbling away. In 208 B.C., facing military defeat, he enlisted the aid of the criminals condemned to servitude by granting "a great act of grace throughout the empire."[7]

Han Kao-tsu and his successors inherited this tradition of acts of grace and molded it into a shape it was to maintain for the next millennium. The materials from which they built the imperial system of acts of grace were ready to hand. Historical examples could be found in the acts of Chao, Ch'in, Ch'u, Lu, and Chou. No doubt early Han rulers could have had firsthand reports on Ch'in practices, and quite possibly they had records and written examples to guide them. Since we know that Han Kao-tsu had available a copy of the Ch'in Code, it seems probable that among the materials he saved were those dealing with the law, presumably including acts of grace.

The Han founder provided for his heirs a fountain of precedents. In 205 B.C. he ascended the throne. In accordance with the patterns of Ch'in he issued an amnesty of criminals. He followed this by

showing his virtue and bounty and granting aristocratic ranks to the people. Because the people of Shu and Han had been heavily burdened in furnishing the armies with supplies he exempted them from the land tax and from contributions in kind for two years.[8]

Han Kao-tsu thus reinforced a precedent of mercy and grace which was to be followed for more than two thousand years. Even in those periods when acts of grace were rarely granted on other occasions, an accession to the throne was often followed by the freeing of the condemned and the making of grants to other groups.

Several years later, however, when Liu Chi was formally installed as the first emperor of the Han dynasty he did not issue an act of grace. Perhaps following this precedent the emperors during the early reigns of the Former Han tended not to make such grants on accession. Rather, as is remarked by Shen Chia-pen, they tended to make grants associated more closely with the death or burial of the preceding emperor.[9]

Eight more times during his ten-year reign Han Kao-tsu issued amnesties that touched the whole empire—and created precedents for granting amnesties on the naming of an heir apparent, on the coming of peace, on the establishing of a new capital city, and on the appointing of a new king. In addition he issued some empirewide amnesties —not to mark any specific occasion but for more restricted political ends. In 202 B.C. he declared (for the second time) his forgiveness of all those who had become outlaws during the disorders of the just completed civil war. In 196 (following the example of the second Ch'in emperor) he pardoned criminals so that they could serve in the armies. He set the pattern for forgiving criminals belonging to specific groups by pardoning all officials guilty of undiscovered crimes (in 199); he set the pattern of forgiving criminals in limited areas by pardoning those living in Yüeh-yang when his father died in the palace there. Finally, in the last year of his reign, he amnestied the populace and officials living in a region whose king had plotted rebellion.[10]

His successors honored most of Han Kao-tsu's precedents and added a few of their own. Some of these precedents, like most of those stemming from the Han founder, were connected with imperial family affairs. An amnesty accompanied the capping (coming of age) of the Emperor Hui in 191 B.C., a precedent frequently followed during the later part of the Latter Han (A.D. 25–220), when rulers were enthroned while still young. The Emperor Wu (r. 140–81 B.C.) began a practice, followed by many of his successors in the Former Han and the first emperor of the Latter Han, of granting an act of grace when establishing an empress. Other precedents reflect the increasing hold of certain religious ideas on the rulers of Han times. Amnesties frequently accompanied major cult sacrifices, and followed the appearance of omens, earthquakes, eclipses, visitations by phoenixes, supernatural lights, and so on. To this list might be added amnesties granted on changing reign titles.[11]

Both good and evil signs might occasion acts of
108 B.C., the Emperor Wu sacrificed to Sovereign
of Earth in one night manifested three flames of
upon the altar for sacrifice." An amnesty was grar
areas through which the emperor had passed.[12] A
great-grandson, Emperor Hsüan (r. 73–48 B.C.), sa

> Recently phoenixes have perched in T'ai-shan and
> mandaries] and sweet dew descended in the Wei-yar
> not yet been able to manifest the excellent and glor
> imperial predecessors, in harmonizing and giving re
> serving Heaven and obeying Earth, and in temperii
> four seasons. [Yet We] have obtained and received t
> ages and have been granted this [supernatural] fa
> . . . Let an amnesty be granted to the convicts of th

The converse side of these beliefs is reflected i
peror Ch'eng (r. 33–6 B.C.) blaming himself fo
total eclipse of the sun:

> [Ever since] We secured the [opportunity of] pro
> ancestral temples [We] have trembled with resy
> have not been worthy of [Our] title. . . . The I
> therefore] lies upon Us Ourself. . . . [Let] Ou
> pointed out without keeping silent about anythi
> grace *(ta-she)* [be granted] to the empire.[14]

This statement highlights the connections
events touching the imperial role. The sacred
are reflected in the phraseology. The emper
sponsibility are symbolized in his duty to pr
ples. Nature herself had already made mas
task, and the emperor acknowledges his u
same time he reasserts the prerogatives of th
grating into society those currently excluded
and cleanses others, perhaps Heaven will b
faults.

1 this instance the grant was clearly connected with an unpropi-
s event, but the amnesty evidence as a whole suggests that in
1y instances such events were merely the occasions on which the
were issued. The temptation to go beyond this and say that the
1esties were issued because of certain occurrences may be strong,
the grounds for so doing are weak. Several things indicate that we
1ld be cautious in talking about causes. First, for a clear majority
mnesties granted in Han times we know of no associated event.
y half the empirewide amnesties under Kao-tsu, the Empress Lu
94–179) and Wen-ti (r. 179–156) are associated with noteworthy
1ts. Only one of the five amnesties under Emperor Ching (r. 157–
and only eight of eighteen under Emperor Wu (r. 141–87) are
·ly connected with other occurrences. The list could be continued
would only add similar examples. Clearly, in a great many cases
annot match an amnesty with another event.

1ould we assume that the problem is in our records? That affairs
1e kinds described above were the *causes* for all amnesties? That if
records were fuller we would find such causal events in all cases?
ibly. And yet we would then have to explain the times when
1quakes, or imperial deaths, or enthronements, or eclipses oc-
·d without being followed by amnesties. The annals of the *His-
of the Former Han* mention seventeen earthquakes, but in
four cases were these followed by general amnesties. Fifty-nine
ses are recorded; only six were followed by general amnesties.
1g Mang [r. 9–23] seems to have been particularly disturbed by
ses. Four of the five eclipses that occurred after he came to domi-
the government were followed by amnesties.) The same pattern
s for major sacrifices: dozens are noted in the annals, but only ten
ioned general amnesties. All ten of these cases involved sacrifices
·eaven or Earth performed in the capital suburbs; in seven of
1 the rites had been marked by the appearance of supernatural
s. But not all sacrifices to Earth, or Suburban Sacrifices, or sacri-
that were accompanied by visitations of lights were followed by
·sties. The story is the same if we examine the acts that followed
· events in the imperial family. Empresses were nominated on
ty-six occasions, but in only six cases were general amnesties
ed. Even accessions to the throne, the most important political-

imperial events in Han times, were not always followed by amnesties. In short, no event was inevitably followed by amnesty during the Han.

Nor do there seem to be any internal criteria that determine when a certain event would be followed by an act and when it would not. It seems to have been largely a question of personality and style. Wang Mang's fear of eclipses would seem to be a clear example of the effects of personal conviction on these governmental acts. Wang Mang took these occasions to indicate his personal unworthiness to fill the imperial role. At the same time he reasserted the power of the person filling that role to cleanse the wicked and return them to the group, and thus highlighted the difference between the person of the emperor and his functional authority.

The personalities of the emperors led some of them to be more generous than others in granting grace and to be more attuned to evil portents; the historians who gave us our evidence no doubt also played a role. The compilers of the *History of the Former Han* had available to them a mass of data far in excess of what they chose to include in their work. Not all fortunate or unfortunate portents or occasions were recorded. For that matter we may feel confident that not all acts of grace were noted in the *History*. Given this selectivity we have to say that the presence in the *History* of amnesties without associated events (and of portentous events without associated amnesties) suggests but cannot prove that political or natural occurrences did not cause the issuing of amnesties.

The conclusion that rulers did not feel compelled to respond to fortunate or unfortunate events by issuing amnesties is also strongly supported by another characteristic of Han amnesties—their distribution in time. Han emperors promulgated acts of grace at remarkably regular intervals, in some cases finding in the events of the day a rationale for their actions. But if no such pretext was available they still issued the amnesties. Perhaps we have here a general judicial policy, albeit one with strong religious overtones.

This policy does not appear until the reign of the Emperor Ching, becomes more fully developed under Emperor Wu, and continues under Wu-ti's successors. During the early years of his reign the Emperor Wu was under the influence of his uncles. After he took personal control of the administration in 131 B.C., he instituted direct and active imperial rule. Any policies found are presumably his policies. Beginning in 128 B.C. he issued amnesties with striking regularity—thirteen during the last forty years of his reign, one every three years. This figure is not just an average. It is also the mode for the distribution. In no case did more than five years separate general amnesties during this period. Only four of these amnesties can be connected with events.

The distribution of Wu-ti's general amnesties by time of year is even more striking. With a single exception they were all issued in the third through the sixth months. If fortunate or unfortunate events were the "causes" for the issuing of amnesties, we must assume that under Emperor Wu such natural happenings were trained to occur only in late spring or summer. Is it not clear that we are faced here with a mixture of policy and religious-philosophical beliefs? The months named are those of germination and growth. They are uniquely connected in Chinese thinking (particularly Former Han thinking) with life, not death. If amnesties are to be granted, these are surely the months for so doing. Within them occasions can be found or manufactured. The timing of certain occasions frequently associated with amnesties—naming of empresses or heirs apparent, the performing of certain sacrifices—is at the discretion of the emperor. They can be scheduled in these months of growth, and thus the amnesty that may accompany them comes at the appropriate religious moment. The dates leave no room for argument. Only events completely beyond the control of the emperors such as deaths and accessions are sometimes accompanied by unseasonal amnesties. This monthly distribution is not characteristic of the opening reigns of the Han. In its rise we can read the spreading grip of the synthetic Han philosophy. To Kao-tsu, not so addicted to the ideas of natural-human interconnections, the seasons for declaring amnesties were irrelevant. To Wu-ti, a child of his own times, they were crucial.

This monthly distribution remains characteristic of Wu-ti's successors until the reign of Ch'eng-ti. Only half the amnesties in Ch'eng-ti's reign occurred in the third through sixth months. The deviation from the previous pattern is not random, however. The amnesties not falling in the late spring or summer almost all were granted in the early spring (the first and second months of the year, corresponding roughly to February and March). Here also the impact of ideology is clear. The seasons for decay and death, fall and winter, are scrupulously avoided. Rarely do we read of amnesties occurring after the sixth month, a general pattern that remains characteristic in the Latter Han.

This distribution is explicable as a reflection of Han "Confucianism"—a Confucian extension and elaboration of the cosmological-numerological thought discussed in the last chapter. Han Confucianism postulated that the human and natural worlds interact. Inappropriate acts, especially those of the ruler and his ministers, could disturb the natural rhythm of the world and bring on natural calamities. To be appropriate a human act had to conform to the general character of time, role, and place. In particular each season of the year was thought to be marked by a general character to which human actions should conform. Thus spring was the season of growth, associated with the color green, the element wood, and the burgeoning of new life. Preeminently this was the time of mercy and kindness, of the loosening of the rigid bonds of winter. This seasonality is embodied in the calendars described in the first chapter. Its underlying philosophical rationale is set forth in a work called the *Book of Changes (I ching)*. In this composite work the oldest stratum seems to be a set of mnemonic notations designed to aid soothsayers in interpreting divination patterns in groups of milfoil stalks. To this stratum later writers added expanded prose descriptions of these hexagrammatic patterns, and then, probably in the Han, a final layer of philosophical interpretation, heavily Confucian in content. Under Hexagram Forty, symbolic of lenience and loosening and associated with the season spring, the (Han) Confucian explanation says that the trigram "for thunder and that for rain, with these phenomena in a state of manifestation, form [the hexagram] 'loosening' *(chieh)*. The Superior Man, in accordance with this, pardons errors *(she kuo)* and deals gently with crimes *(yu-tsui)*."[15]

Closely related to these ideas in which spring was associated with benevolence was the Han practice of sometimes reducing the capital sentences of those fortunate enough to have lived through winter, the proper season for executions. Most Han reports touching this problem are ambiguous. They imply no more than a stay of execution for those surviving till spring, though such men could no doubt hope for some form of amnesty before the next season for executions arrived. In the biography of the prince of Ch'u-yuan, however, it is implied that re-ductions of sentence were a regular practice in such cases. This prince, because his brother had distributed liberal bribes, "was able to pass through winter and had his death sentence reduced." The commen-tators appear to differ somewhat on the meaning of this passage. Fu Ch'ien (A.D. 125–195) says, "If one passes through winter and reaches the spring, practices are expansive, and death sentences are reduced"—implying an automatic reduction of sentence. However, Ju Shun (fl. 221–265) remarks that "criminal cases ought to be decided before the end of winter, but if [a criminal] passed through the win-ter, perhaps he would meet with an amnesty or have his sentence reduced"—implying that reductions were neither regular nor univer-sal.[16] In any case it is clear that in many instances such reductions were granted.

By the time of the skeptic Wang Ch'ung (A.D. 29–109) most edu-cated people believed that such acts of grace could actually affect the environment. In his essay "On Heat and Cold," discussing the belief that death or other evil happenings caused cold and benevolence warmth, Wang says, "when one man is put to death the air becomes cold, but when a man is born does the temperature become warm then? When an amnesty *(she)* is granted to the four quarters, and all punishments are remitted at the same time, the fluid of the month and the year does not become warm thereby."[17]

Wang Ch'ung's skepticism was his badge of eccentricity. The tradi-tion he scoffed at, though its hold on most people's minds weakened during succeeding centuries, long retained its fascination for some thinkers. In later works representative of this type of thought, the granting of amnesties and even their time limits were connected with or determined by natural rhythms.[18]

Closely related to this view of acts of grace were ideas connecting them with astrological and other natural phenomena. In the *Histori-cal Records* we are told that:

When the White Emperor [associated with the Five Forces as the sym-bol of the spring and the west] exercises his influence, [if] in the first month on the twentieth and twenty-first days there is a lunar halo, this will always be a year of a great act of grace. . . . When the Yellow Emperor exercises his influence, the Heavenly Arrow thereby arises. The wind comes out of the northwest, always including the days *keng* and *hsin*. If during one autumn this has happened five times then a great act of grace will be issued. If during one autumn it happens three times then a regular act of grace is issued. Commentary: the Yellow Emperor is the central emperor who embodies the pivot. The season being summer the ten thousand things flourish greatly. Then respond with a great act of grace to embody nourishing the people.[19]

In a similar vein, the astronomical treatise in the history of the Chin (280–42 B.C.) says:

[The constellation called] the String [is composed of] nine stars. [It is] the prison of the poor. One [name for it is the] Garland. A third [name] is the Heavenly Prison. It has jurisdiction over the laws and the suppression of violence. One star [near the mouth] makes the gate. It is desirable that it be opened. When the nine stars are all clearly shining then criminal cases are numerous and troublesome. When seven appear then a regular act of grace [is issued]. When five or six stars [appear then] a great act of grace [is issued].[20]

And in the *Divinations of the Yellow Emperor* we read:

[There are] three [situations with regard to] stars being within the Heavenly Prison. The stars should be viewed at evening on the days A, B, C, D, etc. When one star is outside, carry out felicitous undertakings. . . . When all three are outside, the ruler virtuously orders that an act of grace be granted to the world. If the day is A [or] B [the amnesty] should have a time period of eighty-one days. If the day is C [or] D [the amnesty should have a] time period of seventy-two days.[21]

Long after such beliefs had ceased to be a major preoccupation of educated men their echoes reverberated in the pronouncements of the rulers. More than a millennium later during the Ming dynasty (1368–1644), at a time of judicial review with an accompanying grant of grace, we are told:

The connections of the Seven Stars are like the stringing of beads and jewels; in their completeness their form is that of the Heavenly Corral.

When the center is empty then punishments are equitable, officials are not corrupt or biased, and therefore the jails are empty. If within the compass there are one or several stars, then punishments are numerous and the punishing officials are acting incorrectly. If there is one bright star, that indicates that there is a virtuous man guiltless and yet imprisoned. At present we pattern ourselves after the Way of Heaven [in] setting up the legal offices. The various offices genuinely having business will conduct it according to the Way of Heaven.[22]

Such religious elements may have determined the times at which amnesties were granted; they did not necessarily determine that amnesties be granted at all. The Han founder, who does not seem to have been so fully under the spell of these conceptions as were most of his successors, issued amnesties with great frequency. In the Latter Han the frequency of amnesties increased over the years while the grip of Han Confucianism on educated thought was steadily weakening. We are left with the pieces of a puzzle. How are these frequent grants to be explained, and how are the variations to be explained away? True, the Han inherited a tradition of granting amnesties, but not of granting them every few years. No doubt our lack of records minimizes the numbers of amnesties before the Han. Still we have no reason to assume that they were granted frequently or regularly during these earlier times.

Then the Han begins, and in ten years Kao-tsu issues nine empire-wide amnesties. His example was not followed by Empress Lü (under whom four amnesties were issued in fifteen years) or Emperor Wen (with only four amnesties in twenty-three years, almost six years between acts), but from the accession of Emperor Ching (157–141 B.C.) the pattern of Kao-tsu reappears. Emperor Ching averaged one grant every 3.2 years, Emperor Wu one in three years. And the last emperors of the Former Han granted grace even more frequently—once every 1.2 years in the case of the Emperor P'ing (A.D. 1–6). Wang Mang continued the pattern with nine amnesties in his seventeen years of power.

The Latter Han opens as a continuation of the preceding period. During the first six years of his reign the Emperor Kuang-wu (r. 25–58) issued eight general amnesties. Then suddenly he stopped.

Twenty-five years passed before his next amnesty. During the remainder of the first century A.D., Kuang-wu's successors issued amnesties with some restraint. Ming-ti (r. 58–76) issued only three great acts of grace in an eighteen-year reign; Chang-ti (r. 76–89) issued three in thirteen years; and Ho-ti (r. 89–106) issued five in seventeen years. Still, as these figures show, there is a progressive decline in the length of time between acts, and after the accession of Shang-ti (A.D. 106) the pattern of the late Former Han reappears. Under one Latter Han emperor (Hsien-ti) great acts of grace came on average once every three years; under two others (An-ti and Shun-ti) every 2.3 years; under two others (Chih-ti and Huan-ti) once every year or so; and under three others (Shang-ti, Chung-ti, and Shao-ti) less than one year. Between A.D. 167 and 196, great acts of grace were promulgated in every single year but 170 and 185.[23]

The patterns are crystal clear. Han emperors granted empirewide amnesties with great frequency. Why did they do so? And how are the exceptions to this practice of frequently granting amnesties to be explained? Amnesties cannot be tied to their occasions. Neither omens, nor sacrifices, nor events touching the imperial family are peculiar to those reigns in which amnesties were frequent. They occurred under the Emperors Wen and Ming as well as under the Emperors Huan and Ling. Some later dynasties repeat the pattern of frequent amnesties and some do not, though the events that might mark amnesties are the same. Emperors died, the earth quaked, comets appeared, men came to the throne, yet the granting of amnesties varied enormously.

In the Han the frequency might be traced to the peculiarly strong hold that religious-philosophical views favoring amnesty had on Han emperors. This cannot have been the case in later dynasties when the grip of the peculiar Han worldview on educated opinion had weakened. A policy of frequent amnesties, fraught with social consequences, could only have continued because in some way it was thought necessary or highly rewarding.

Shen Chia-pen, and others, have pointed to the use of frequent amnesties in troubled times.[24] The opening years of the reign of Kuang-wu are an example of this pattern. No doubt rulers sitting on precarious thrones were tempted to issue many acts of grace. Such amnesties are clearly tied to day-by-day politics. But this alone cannot account for the general phenomenon. How could it explain the plentitude of amnesties under Wu-ti and most of his successors, irrespective of political circumstance? No doubt at times the granting of amnesty was an expression of imperial weakness, the act of a man on a shaky throne; we must not lose sight of the fact that the converse was also true: the granting of an amnesty was also an expression of an emperor's power. The keys to the kingdom were given into the hands of the emperor. To him belonged the power not only to bind but to loose. In stable periods both the binding and the loosening, the casting out and the bringing back, were revelations of his authority.

The emperors themselves speak of amnesties as ways of redeeming those capable of being saved. An edict of the Emperor P'ing says, "Verily an ordinance of amnesty is [an instrument] for the purpose of giving the empire a new beginning. It is sincerely hoped that it may cause the people to correct their conduct, purify themselves, and preserve their lives."[25] In the Chinese idiom the emperor is not only the father of the people, stern and just, but their mother as well, nurturing and kind.

The obvious influence of ideological and short-range political considerations should not cause us to overlook the role of underlying situational factors—if not in the issuing of an individual act, then in the policy of issuing them with great frequency and regularity. Perhaps the roots of this policy are to be traced to the fact of empire itself. From the unification by Ch'in, China was potentially a society under tight rein. But the reins were fragile. Behind the figure of rigid control stood the specter of collapse. Given the disparity between the superb bureaucratic mechanisms for rapid political action and the limited methods of transport and communication, means had to be devised to prevent regional discontent from reaching the point of insurrection. In dealing with the grievances of the common people, the emperors relied on policies combining tax relief in hard times, periodic grants of goods and ranks, and attempts to police the administrative conduct of local officials.

The explosive potential represented by the convict and criminal population posed a different problem. Fugitives were natural leaders for local uprisings—if they were uncaught and unforgiven. And thousands of convicts, set apart from the general population by their iron collars, their distinctive clothes, and their shaved beards, were always a threat—if they felt they had little to lose. But to give such men hope was to free them from desperation. A convict who knows that an amnesty will come soon, perhaps in a matter of months, at most in a few years, faces his choices very differently from a man who, set apart from the people, confronts only a future of grinding labor. A fugitive might hesitate to commit desperate acts which would endanger his life and jeopardize his chances for pardon.

Institutional factors are also the keys to understanding the exceptions to the rule of frequent amnesties. At the beginnings of dynasties, once full military control had been established and dangerous enemies eliminated (not until nearly the end of Kao-tsu's reign and nearly a decade after the success of Kuang-wu), emperors were able to abandon the expedient policy of granting amnesties which had been forced on them by the instability of their positions and adopt a more "natural" position of strict justice. Since their military machine was battle-hardened and in full readiness, and the number of convicts small, the danger of unrest among prisoners was slight. As the decades passed, and the number of convicts increased, a commitment to strict justice became ever more difficult to maintain. The implications of reunification and centralized control became increasingly evident. Gradually, perhaps reluctantly, the emperors issued amnesties with greater frequency. Thus the pattern of frequent amnesties was reestablished.

This pattern of empirewide amnesties, with its striking implications for the feel and tone of Chinese justice, actually understates the role of grace in Chinese law. In the preceding discussion I have focused mostly on general amnesties *(she* or *ta-she)*—empirewide acts which affected most if not all classes of the guilty and accused. This focus was required if the periods were to be comparable. But in addition to these general amnesties there were large numbers of special amnesties. These might result in amnestying men from a certain region, as exemplified by Han Kao-tsu's pardoning of criminals in the place where his father had just died. Such local amnesties were frequently granted in Han times, most commonly to convicts in areas through which the emperor had passed while on tour.[26] Or special amnesties might pardon a particular category of persons, as when Kao-tsu forgave officials their crimes. Followers of men involved in treasonous acts or deserters from the army were sometimes spared by such amnesties.[27] Sometimes pardon was extended to all those undergoing penal servitude, thus limiting the group affected. On still other occasions penalties were reduced rather than pardoned, or those guilty were granted permission to redeem their punishments for cash.[28]

Another Han practice of limited grace that in later times became a part of the system of judicial mercy was the "inspection of cases" (lu-ch'iu). The term was ordinarily used for the annual tour by the Regional Inspectors. Hu Kuang (A.D. 91–172) reported that "the incarcerated convicts in the prefectural settlements are all reviewed and inspected; the records of their depositions are checked to verify what is true and false. Cases of unjust treatments are immediately adjusted."[29] And the *History of the Former Han* notes that whenever Ch'üan Pu-i, the Regional Inspector of Ching-chou, returned home from his tour his mother questioned him closely on the number of men he had spared. In his commentary to this biography Yen Shih-ku defines *lu-ch'iu* as "to inspect [cases] so as to know the circumstances [and if] there has been injustice to suppress it and eradicate it."[30] In the Latter Han the same term was used for those occasions when the emperor personally went to a prison in the capital to inspect prisoners being detained in light cases. Hulsewé has shown that in Han times this practice, which resulted in the liberation of numbers of prisoners, was always taken in an effort to alleviate a drought.[31]

Irregular in the Han, the inspection of cases became fixed policy under some later dynasties and resulted automatically in reductions of sentence or liberation for the affected prisoners. Since these inspections closely resemble the annual investigations which the *Book of Rites* says were carried out each spring by the emperor, we may have here a direct effect of utopian writings on practice.[32]

Han sources do not give us a very clear picture of how acts of grace were promulgated. In most cases it seems that decrees of amnesty were issued after the event with which they were associated (when they were in fact associated with an event). In some examples the emperor mounted a high place, in the Han frequently a tower, to issue the order.[33] (This ceremony is a foreshadowing of the practice of later

dynasties.) He would promulgate a decree which began with an expression of the general rationale for the act and then spelled out its
terms. In A.D. 126 the Emperor Shun issued a typical order:

> The former emperor was of sagely virtue but he did not long enjoy his
> throne. He soon lost his illustrious [task]. Evil people have taken ad-
> vantage of this. The common people murmur angrily, which above dis-
> turbs the harmonious ethers [and below] causes disastrous plagues. I
> have received the Great Undertaking, and have not yet been able to re-
> lieve [this situation]. In general the root of the highest principle is in
> broadly bestowing virtuous benevolence, and in cleansing old evil to
> give men a new beginning. So [let us] Greatly Amnesty the world, giv-
> ing to males two grades of rank, [and] to heirs, [and] those who are
> styled the Three Elders, the Filial and Pure, and the Skilled Farmers
> three grades. Landless migrants who on their own accord wish to report
> [to the authorities may be given] one grade. Widows, widowers, the
> solitary and afflicted who are not capable of supporting themselves
> [should be given] five measures of grain per person. Chaste wives
> [should be given] three lengths of silk per person. Those who, being
> tried according to law, would be liable for exile are not to be exiled.
> Those serving penal servitude who have fled, and so are liable for re-
> capture, are not to be seized again. Members of the imperial clan who
> because of their crimes have been cut off [from the lists of imperial clan
> members] may again be registered. Those who have had communica-
> tion with [the seditious] are not to be investigated. [Officials] should
> be urged to cultivate their duties in order to benefit my people.[34]

When such an act had been issued, according to Wei Hung (fl. A.D.
25–57), messengers from the capital carried it to the kingdoms and
the commandaries, from which it was then passed on to the prefectures under their control.[35] These decrees for amnesties in Han times
were called *chih-shu* or ordinances.[36]

What types of people could hope to benefit from these acts? And
what benefits might they expect? Although most persons accused or
convicted of criminal acts received some grace at the time of an amnesty, the degree of benefit varied with the nature of their original
crime, with their situation at the time the act was issued, and with the
kind of amnesty.

The criminal's situation was of great importance in determining eligibility for benefits. Under both sorts of general amnesty it seems to have been true that fugitives were in most instances freed from further prosecution. Hulsewé cites several examples of men who came out of hiding after the declaration of an amnesty and apparently were allowed to return to ordinary life. These incidents occurred both in the Former Han and in the Latter Han, and they happened after both ordinary and great acts of grace.[37]

The crime committed also affected the benefits a criminal might receive. Specific statements in the amnesty decree could exclude or include particular crimes, but there appear to have been certain general expectations about the coverage. Certain crimes seem to have been covered by all amnesties, while others apparently were excluded in many amnesties. The coverage seems to have differed chiefly according to the kind of amnesty issued. This point brings us to a most difficult question: What distinction existed between ordinary amnesties (she) and great acts of grace (ta-she)? At no point do the sources define clearly the differences between the sorts of acts. We can only sift the meager and sometimes contradictory evidence to reach some tentative conclusions.

Perhaps great acts of grace customarily did, and ordinary amnesties did not, preclude the prosecution of legal cases stemming from events prior to the issuing of the act in question. The evidence is ambiguous but suggestive. Late in the Former Han, when great acts of grace had become commonplace, emperors repeatedly warn officials against raising old cases; we do not find such warnings in the earlier part of the dynasty when ordinary amnesties were more common. The earliest clear example dates from 32 B.C. when Wang Tsun was punished for having discussed a case that had occurred prior to a great act of grace. The later clear examples of this same sort all stem from the closing years of the Former Han, when almost all empirewide amnesties were great acts of grace. In 1 B.C. the Emperor P'ing spelled out the current policy:

Verily an ordinance of amnesty is [an instrument] for the purpose of giving the empire [an opportunity of making] a new beginning. It is sincerely hoped that it may cause people to correct their conduct, purify themselves, and preserve their lives. In the past the high officials have frequently brought up in their memorials matters which occurred prior to an amnesty, including them [with their present charges in order to] increase [the severity of peoples'] greater or lesser crimes. [As a result] they have executed or ruined guiltless [people, which practice] is almost opposite to the intention of emphasizing fidelity, being careful about punishments, [and inducing criminals] to purify their hearts and renew themselves. . . . From this time and henceforth high officials shall not be permitted to present matters which occurred prior to an amnesty and put them into a memorial to the emperor. If anyone acts contrary to this written edict, he is acting against the [imperial] favor and shall be sentenced for impiety.[38]

Earlier in the Han an ordinary amnesty was issued which included specific instructions barring prosecution of some prior legal matters, but the circumstances of this act itself suggest that this was an irregular stipulation, not a customary one.[39]

Thus it seems possible that in the Han period ordinary amnesties *(she)* did not prevent prosecution for prior crimes whereas great acts of grace *(ta-she)* did. This interpretation at least fits our evidence. We must, of course, be careful to separate the people who would benefit from this policy—especially those whose crimes had not yet come to light or against whom judicial actions had not yet begun—from fugitives who benefited from both ordinary and great acts of grace.

Great acts of grace and ordinary amnesties may also have differed in the benefits they gave to those being held in jail for crimes previously committed. Hulsewé has assembled examples of acts which freed men held in jail. All his examples are great acts of grace. None are ordinary amnesties.[40]

Great acts of grace and ordinary amnesties may also have differed in the benefits they extended to men guilty of capital crimes. Various sorts of evidence indicate that both types of general amnesties usually included capital as well as lesser criminals; but ordinary amnesties merely reduced their penalties whereas great acts of grace forgave them entirely.

In later times most ordinary amnesties reduced death sentences; great acts of grace forgave them completely. We cannot assume from this alone that the Han system was similar in this regard. Since the

Han system did resemble its later counterpart in many other ways, however, this evidence at least suggests that the pattern of benefits for capital criminals may have remained the same.

These later documents also prove something we might otherwise only surmise—that amnesties were lengthy pronouncements. In our Han sources many have been reduced to a few words. The brief notations now found in the Han annals may not mention capital criminals; this in no way indicates whether or not such criminals were mentioned in the original documents. The abbreviated remnants only prove that capital criminals were pardoned by the acts in which they are mentioned—not that they were not pardoned in amnesties in which no mention of them now occurs.

Moreover, there are many instances where Han capital criminals were spared death so that they might be sent to serve in the armies.[41] Apart from cases in which men were specifically spared death to join the armies, there are many records of men serving on military expeditions whose "punishments had been relaxed (ch'ih-hsing)."[42] Possibly such men had originally been sentenced to penal servitude, but it seems at least equally plausible that they were men spared death by amnesty.[43]

Finally the assumption that capital criminals were covered (though not fully pardoned) by ordinary amnesties makes it easier to explain the large number of amnesties specifically limited to those undergoing penal servitude. (During most of the Han this category would have included the bulk of those not sentenced to death.) Hulsewé has compiled a long listing of acts of grace, not called ordinary amnesties, which freed such persons. Ordinary amnesties that did not benefit capital criminals would have resembled such pardons of those at hard labor. But different terms are used to describe these two sorts of acts. One explanation is that ordinary acts of grace did customarily bring some benefits to capital criminals.[44]

If ordinary amnesties reduced death sentences to exile at hard labor or to service in the army, how did they affect those already sentenced to penal servitude? Hulsewé argues that such persons were not freed completely by acts of grace, great or ordinary, unless the act so stated. They were relieved of the outward symbols of their condition—their iron collars, their red clothing, and their shaved beards. Thereafter they remained to serve out their terms of labor, but as commoners working for the government. Thus the amnesty removed the ritual symbols of their outcast state, leaving only labor as a residual penalty.

Such people were called *fu-tso*. Meng K'ang says that this term referred to convicts

> who are freed from punishment. There was an imperial edict granting amnesty, and their iron collars, the iron rings for their legs, and their red [convict] garments were taken off. They were changed [from] cases of transgression and were not [treated as] convicts. They were added to the common people. This was the established rule. Thus, they again work for the government to complete [the term] for their original crime to the year, month, and day.[45]

Several edicts specifically refer to the freeing of such *fu-tso*.

There seems little doubt that Hulsewé's view is correct, but perhaps only for ordinary amnesties. All the citations which specifically mention *fu-tso* can be dated from the reigns of the Emperors Ching (r. 156–140 B.C.) and Wu (r. 140–87 B.C.), during which great acts of grace were uncommon.

Hulsewé has shown that ordinary amnesties did not completely free those undergoing penal servitude; whether such persons were freed completely by great acts of grace is unclear. In later times great acts of grace did free men sentenced to penal servitude; they even reduced the sentences of men sent into perpetual exile. Furthermore, we do not find mention of *fu-tso* in those eras of the Han when *ta-she* were common. But all these pieces of evidence remain suggestive, not conclusive.

There is also evidence that great acts of grace regularly extended their coverage to crimes excluded from ordinary amnesties. Ordinary amnesties seem not to have included criminals guilty of plotting rebellion, those found guilty of Great Sedition *(ta-ni)*, or those jointly adjudicated for rebellion which their relatives had planned. To my knowledge there are no examples of such persons benefiting from ordinary amnesties.[46] There is some evidence though, that they may have benefited from great acts of grace. All our Han examples of amnesties that merely "pardon capital criminals or less" are ordinary amnesties. All the examples that extend coverage to "those guilty of plotting rebellions or of great sedition" are great acts of grace.[47]

This of course merely suggests that ordinary amnesties never, and *ta-she* sometimes, benefited such criminals. However, Wei Hung (fl. A.D. 25–57), who lived in an era when *ta-she* were the rule, said that after every solar eclipse, enthronement, or appointment of an empress or heir apparent, an amnesty was issued which pardoned those guilty of rebellion and great refractoriness.[48] He is not correct in saying that amnesties were always granted on such occasions. Still, his error is suggestive. The emperor under whom he flourished, Kuang-wu, did grant amnesties on accession, on appointing an heir apparent, and on naming his empress. Finally a number (though not all) of the eclipses of his reign were associated with amnesties. Wei Hung thus seems to have been describing occasions for amnesties as he knew them from his personal experience, not as historically true for earlier times. Should we not presume that in describing the groups who benefited he is in the same manner describing things as he knew them to be in his own time from personal observation?

In summary, during the Han ordinary amnesties *(she)* and great acts of grace *(ta-she)* differed systematically neither in their geographical coverage, nor in the grants they made to noncriminals, nor in the occasions on which they were issued. Indeed, the distinction between them during this era is not wholly clear. However, there does seem to be some evidence that great acts of grace extended their mercy to criminals not covered by ordinary amnesties and also provided greater benefits.[49]

Great acts of grace had been proclaimed even in preimperial times, but they become more common under the Han. About one-third of Kao-tsu's and more than one-half of the Empress Lü's empirewide amnesties were *ta-she*. Then the pattern changes and they remain rare until the reign of Hsüan-ti (r. 73–48 B.C.). About a third of the empirewide acts of grace in his reign and that of his successor Yüan-ti (r. 48–32 B.C.) were *ta-she*. Under the last three emperors of the Former Han a majority of such acts were *ta-she*. Under the Latter Han, ordinary acts of grace were far less common than great acts of grace. Most general amnesties were *ta-she*. Other empirewide acts of grace were limited in their coverage or benefits. If it is true that *ta-she* were wider in scope and gave greater benefits, then the overall trend in Han times was toward a more lenient penal policy—one with more extensive benefits conferred more often.

Beginning in the late Former Han the system of grace embodied in these amnesties was frequently attacked, largely on practical grounds; it was rarely defended, although it fitted well with the systematic syncretic Confucianism of Han China. In 42–41 B.C., after the appearance of a series of omens, the Erudite K'uang Heng submitted a memorial to the emperor which noted that although great acts of grace were promulgated year after year, crime did not stop. Such wrongdoing was rooted in improper morals and distorted values, he argued, and without rectification of these fundamental flaws the granting of frequent amnesties was of no use.[50]

This cautionary note was echoed by the general Wu Han. In A.D. 44 when he fell ill the emperor paid him a personal visit to ask his desires. The old soldier replied, "I understand nothing. I only desire that Your Majesty be careful not to issue amnesties and that is all."[51] His critical attitude is reiterated by three later writers: Wang Fu (ca. 90–165), Ts'ui Shih (ca. 110–170), and Hsün Yüeh (148–209). Wang Fu devotes the sixteenth section of his *Ch'ien Fu Lun* to a discussion of amnesties. He begins by likening curing the ills of the state to ministering to the body and remarks that under the conditions of his time nothing was more hurtful to the people than the excessive number of amnesties. Such acts, and the similarly motivated grants of permission to commute crimes, were of benefit only to the evil, not to the good. Good people after all did not commit crimes and therefore had no need to be forgiven. But if amnesties were frequent then devious and evil people, knowing they would soon be spared by acts of grace, would not hesitate to slander virtuous and upright officials.[52]

Ts'ui Shih, in his *Essay on Government*, echoes the idea that people come to expect amnesties if they are given too frequently, so that criminality increases. He compares his own era unfavorably with the times of Han Wen-ti (r. 179–156 B.C.) when amnesties were few, and he repeats the adage from the *Kuan tzu* comparing refusal to grant amnesties to the lancing of a boil: painful but beneficial. Since people have come to expect an amnesty every spring, however, one last amnesty should be granted with clear warning to the people that no more would be issued. If that should prove too stringent, he concludes, then they should be issued no more than once in ten years.[53]

This same railing against amnesties as regular measures of government is heard from Hsün Yüeh. "Someone said, 'Are [amnesties] systematic?' I answered, 'They are expedient measures and not systematic. There is system in their righteousness but not in their administration'."[54] The Han penchant for amnesties arose, in his view, because of the need to escape from the evil effects of Ch'in legalism. Like the system of the "Three Laws" inaugurated by Kao-tsu, the system of great acts of grace was designed to permit the world to renew itself. Its continuation into later times was an unfortunate historical accident.[55]

In these attacks, as in the current practice of the system itself, the men of Han times set the pattern for later ages. The few articulate defenders of amnesty attempted to confine the issue to the highest possible level of ethical and philosophical abstraction. The multitude of detractors repeatedly attacked what they saw as the practical outcome of the system. Through it all, despite the commentary of the chorus, Chinese emperors continued to issue acts of grace with great liberality.

chapter 3

Acts of Grace
in Medieval China:
A.D. 220–907

BY the third century the Han government was nearing collapse. Real authority rested with generals who had grown powerful during the suppression of uprisings in the second century. Finally in 220 one of them ended the charade by forcing the last Han emperor to abdicate. The state that succeeded to the Han, called Wei, failed to seize the whole empire. Rival regimes emerged in Szechuan and in the lower valley of the Yangtze River. This division was both symptomatic and symbolic of the disorders of the age. Within the chrysalis of the old Han empire a new economic and social order had developed. Now it emerged fully. Great aristocratic families had grown strong even as the general economy declined. With their economic strength drawn from control over large, tax-privileged, manorially operated estates, and their social position dependent on bloodlines rather than on bureaucratic position, these families were naturally hostile to the meritocratic, centralizing ethos of the Ch'in and early Han. Their emergence as the dominant force in society was accompanied, perhaps inevitably, by a decentralization of power which brought with it military weakness in the face of foreign threats. Increasing numbers of tribesmen spilled across the northern frontiers, coming first to raid or to serve, and then to stay and to dominate.

For a brief period at the close of the third and opening of the fourth century, China was loosely reunited by the state of Chin (265–420); but whatever power Chin might have had to stem the advance of the barbarians was dissipated in fratricidal struggles among the imperial princes. By the 320s, northern China had been overrun by tribal armies and southern China had become the refuge for tens of thousands of Chinese in flight from the north. The division born of these wars was to last for more than two hundred and fifty years.

The legal and historical records preserved from this troubled age are uneven in quality and in many respects inferior to those for the preceding Han period. The legal landscape is obscure, yet a remarkable number of features can be seen if only dimly and in outline. What is perhaps most striking is their familiarity. Many features echo Han practices or foreshadow the practices of later times.

From this dark age come the first evidences of the elaborate set of ritual acts performed during the granting of acts of grace in T'ang and Sung times. In reading materials from this age of disunion through to the rise of the Mongols in the thirteenth century, there is no sensation of witnessing the changing of practices, but rather of watching a darkened scene slowly being flooded with light.

The proclamation of acts of grace from elevated places, prefigured in some Han acts, appears again under the Northern Wei (386–535). In 529 and again in 531 the emperor mounted a gate and from there "[proclaimed] a great act of grace to the world."[1] The ceremonies involved are first described under the Northern Ch'i (550–581). We are told that "when there is an act of grace the Commandant of the Military Storehouse *(wu-k'u ling)* sets up a [pole surmounted by] a golden cock and places a drum to the right outside the gate to the imperial palace. The prisoners are assembled there, and after the drum has been struck one thousand times they are released from their fetters."[2] During the T'ang (618–907) identical procedures were followed; the common people, the officials, and the imperial guard, as well as the prisoners, assembled facing to the north. After the emperor had mounted the gate tower for the ceremony, the proclamation of amnesty was read to the assembled multitude.[3]

The earliest complete description of what must have been an impressive as well as joyous ceremony records the rites used during the Sung period (960–1279) for acts of grace issued on the occasion of the Suburban Sacrifices. On the day of this triennial event the emperor and his attendants rose in the dark predawn hours. Dressed in special robes the emperor rode in his carriage through the late night quiet to the altar in the southern outskirts of the city, where he performed the solemn sacrifices to Heaven and Earth.

Then he reentered his carriage and returned to the city. In a tent set up for the occasion inside the Gate of Imperial Virtue he changed back into the robes he wore at regular audiences. Now, as sunrise approached, he was ready for the second great act of the day. With his retinue standing in their assigned places, he mounted the gate tower and sat on the throne erected there. The Commissioner of Military Affairs *(shu-mi shih)* and the Commissioner of Imperial Pennants *(hsüan-hui shih)* stood by him in attendance. The Imperial Guards were in their places.

Below the tower a multitude was waiting, and had been waiting, during the hours of darkness. They stood in ranks facing north: the officials of the civil service, the imperial princes, foreign dignitaries, the tribute commissioners from the prefectures, units of the army, Buddhist and Taoist clergy, the elders from among the commoners of the city, the prisoners in their chains. On the preceding day the Director of the Court of Imperial Sacrifices had arranged a great bell and drum outside and to the right of the gate. The Presenting Official led the assembled officials as they lined up in rows. After bowing to the emperor they returned to their places to stand again in readiness. The attending official called out, "The Drafting Officials who are to receive the decree may come before the tower." When they had done so he intoned the order to establish the golden cock. After the Drafting Officials had moved to their assigned places, the head of the Bureau of Music stepped forward to beat one thousand strokes on the great lizard-skin covered drum as a signal for the prisoners to be made ready.

The head of the Directorate of Imperial Workshops then moved to the southeast corner of the tower where he oversaw the setting up of the seventy-foot-long wooden staff surmounted by a small square platform on which stood the four-foot-high gilded cock. On the silken banner that hung from the cock's beak were the words "Let a Great Act of Grace Be Granted to the World." After this banner had been rolled up and placed on the platform, skilled acrobats contended in climbing up the four rough silk ropes which hung from the platform's sides. The successful one helped bring the pennant to the emperor. Then a red rope was used to fasten the edict of amnesty to a wooden carving of a crane surmounted by an immortal. This carving, with its precious burden, was lowered from the tower on a rope run over a pulley, to be received by officials who stood waiting on a magnificently decorated tower. They laid it on a table from which it was taken by still other officials. Only after it had been read aloud, and transferred, with accompanying prostrations, through the hands of several groups of officials were the prisoners finally freed of their fetters and their sentences. The ex-prisoners, for whom the vigil had begun in darkness, had been transformed into free men at the moment of the rising of the sun with all its associations of benevolent renewal, "washed clean" in the Chinese idiom, so that they might begin again.[4]

The whole ceremony was drenched with symbols. The elevated position of the emperor, a characteristic of amnesty granting from the Han on, symbolized the imperial role as intermediary between human below and heaven above. The role of heavenly grace, mediated by the emperor, is again reflected in the use of an immortal riding on a sacred crane as the agent bringing the letter of amnesty to earth. But the central meaning of the ceremony is made especially clear in the joint presence of three traits: the timing of the act, its use of color, and the presence of the golden cock. By scheduling the ceremony to coincide with sunrise, and by using the color red, the ritual specialists made unambiguously clear the dominant position of the *yang* tendency. Warmth, light, color—all revealed how closely the act was tied to conceptions of life and growth, lenience and renewal. As the ultimate symbol there is the figure of the golden cock. From very early in Chinese history the cock was a *yang* symbol, useful in exorcism. Not only were evil specters warded off by the *yang* force of the cock but its blood could be used to revivify those who had suffered "sudden death." Moreover, it was the celestial cock whose crow awoke the cocks of this world and thus created the new day. No wonder it played a key role in a ritual by which people were to be washed clean.[5]

Great acts of grace were thus promulgated amid scenes both impressive and joyous. Lesser acts of grace were given less grandiose treatment. For most of the Northern Sung ordinary acts of grace were proclaimed in the Hall of Literary Virtue. During and perhaps after the reign of Hui-tsung (1100–1126) they were announced in the Hall of Light *(ming-t'ang)*. The edicts were then carried out to the palace gate where they were received by the Palace Postern Commissioners *(ko-men-shih)* who placed them in a box and transmitted them to the chief minister. He read the decree before the assembled ministers, who called out "Ten Thousand Years!" The act of grace, written on silk, was then dispatched to the prefectures by horse post.[6]

Upon receipt of such a letter of amnesty the Prefect assembled the military and civil officials, the Buddhist and Taoist clergy, and the commoners, and read the decree aloud. Reports on the decree were then forwarded to the subprefectures for action. The Prefect meanwhile composed a letter of congratulation which was sent to the emperor. In the Sung these local officials, Prefects and Subprefects, were expected to follow up the receipt of such a letter of amnesty by offering sacrifices to local mountains and rivers, former rulers, meritorious former officials from their area, and great scholars.[7]

Like the ritual that marked the original proclamation of the act of grace in the capital, the ceremony of reading it in the prefectures was a most solemn act. The Japanese monk Ennin has left us a striking description of the prolaiming of a T'ang edict. Since the reception of letters of amnesty differed only in minor details from the reception of edicts, Ennin's description suggests the reverence with which imperial orders were received:

An Imperial Rescript by the new Emperor has arrived from the capital. Two carpets were spread in the court in front of the gate of the mansion inside the city walls, and above the steps on the north side of the great gate was placed a stand, on which was spread a purple cloth, and on this was placed the Imperial Rescript, written on yellow paper. The Administrative Officers and Secretaries of the prefecture, the Subprefect and the Superintendents of Registers of the subprefecture, the Commissioner of Troops, the military officers, the military officials, the common people, and the monks, nuns, and Taoist priests stood in ranks according to their posts on the east side of the court facing west. The Magistrate came out from within [his mansion], preceded by twenty military officers, ten each leading the way on the left and the right. When the Secretaries, the subprefectural officials, and the others saw the Magistrate come out, they bowed their heads almost to the ground.

The Magistrate called out, "The common people," and they chanted a response all together. The Magistrate stood on one of the carpets and an Administrative Officer stood on the other, both of them facing west. Then a military officer called out the titles of the various officials, and the row of Secretaries and subprefectural officials chanted their response in unison. Next he called out to the row of Military Guard Officers, Generals, and Commissioners of Troops, and the row of military men chanted their response in unison. He also said, "The various guests," and the official guests and clients chanted their response. Next he said, "The common people," and the common people, both old and young, chanted their response together. Then he said, "The monks and Taoist priests," and the monks, nuns, and Taoist priests chanted their response all together.

Next, two military officers brought the stand with the Imperial Rescript and placed it in front of the Magistrate, who bowed once and then picked up the Imperial Rescript in his hand and lowered his head, touching it to his forehead. A military officer knelt and received the Imperial Rescript on his sleeve and, holding it up, went into the court and, standing facing north, chanted, "An Imperial order has arrived." The magistrate, Administrative Officers, Secretaries, and the military, all together, bowed again. A military officer called out, "Let the common people bow," and the people bowed again, but the monks, nuns, and Taoist priests did not bow. They had two Assistant Judges spread out the Imperial Rescript. These two men wore green coats. Two other Assistant Judges read it alternating with each other. Their voices were loud, as when government decisions are announced in our country. The Imperial Rescript was some four or five sheets of paper long, and it took quite a long time to read, while no one sat down.

After the Imperial Rescript had been read, the Magistrate and the others bowed again. Next a Secretary and a military officer came out into the court and voiced their thanks to the Magistrate and then hastened back to their original posts and stood there. The Magistrate announced to the officials, "Let each be diligent in his charge," and the Administrative Officers and the others all chanted their response. Next a general representative called out, "The monks and Taoist priests," and the monks, nuns, and Taoist priests chanted their response. Next he said, "The common people," and they chanted their response. Then the Commissioner who had brought the Imperial Rescript walked up in front of the Magistrate and bowed again, whereupon the Magistrate stepped off his carpet and stopped him with his sleeve. Several tens of officials and guests went up in front of the Magistrate and stood with their bodies bowed toward the ground. A military officer called out, "You may leave," and they all chanted their response in unison. The officials, the military, the monks and Taoist priests, and the common people thereupon dispersed.[8]

To take advantage of these acts of grace, fugitives had to surrender and confess their guilt within a fixed time limit. Although such limits probably were established early in the history of the amnesty system, the earliest extant record of them dates from A.D. 420 under the Liu Sung dynasty. Almost all the records of actual grants of pardon set a hundred-day time limit. This was the practice under the Liu Sung (420–479), the Southern Ch'i (479–502), and the Liang (502–550), as well as the T'ang and later dynasties.[9]

Prior to the T'ang those who did not come forward to confess by the deadline were "considered guilty as before." According to the T'ang Code those who had fled were expected to surrender to the authorities and confess. If they did not do so and were captured during this period, they might still be tried, but only for the act of having fled, not for their original crime. However, if those who are called "current criminals" (hsien-tsai), presumably those currently held and undergoing adjudication, did not confess within the hundred days they again became liable for their original crime.[10]

Those guilty of certain crimes committed prior to an act of grace but first discovered by the authorities within the hundred-day grace period could not be treated as if they had deliberately concealed their acts (even though they had not come forward to confess at the time their crimes were uncovered). The lawmakers seem to have reasoned that until the end of the hundredth day the opportunity for a change of heart and a confession still existed. Until the criminal had gone through that last day without confessing, his determination to evade acknowledgment of his acts could not be proved.[11]

In form and content, as in rites and practices, the records from the Han to the T'ang provide tantalizing glimpses of the system of acts of grace. In both incidental references and partially preserved decrees the most striking characteristic is continuity rather than change. Whole phrases are passed from dynasty to dynasty. At least by the Sui (581–618), the phrases and format for the criminal provisions of great acts of grace had become largely standardized. A decree of 609 can serve as a typical example of the tenor of such acts. For six centuries and more, with some variation in the groups included or excluded, most great acts of grace contained criminal provisions much like the following:

[Sui Yang-ti, Ta-yeh], eighth year [A.D. 612], fourth month, the day *ping-shen*. The decree said . . . the world may be granted a great act of grace. . . . From dawn and before, all those guilty of capital crimes or less, whether already discovered or not, whether already judged or not, [including] prisoners and current convicts, without distinction as to the seriousness of their crimes, are to be pardoned and released. Those not covered by ordinary amnesties *(ch'ang-she),* those guilty of Plotting Rebellion, of Great Sedition, or of Heresy which has misled the multitude and has touched on the state, are not to be covered by this grant.[12]

Though the records from Sui times reveal the continuity of amnesty provisions affecting criminals, it is only from the T'ang that one finds decrees of grace which seem to be complete. Encyclopedic collections have preserved hundreds of T'ang acts of grace. Most have obviously been abbreviated; some are only a column or two of print. But among them are others that appear to have escaped major alteration. The tenor, scope, and flavor of a traditional Chinese *ta-she* come through with full clarity in a decree issued by the Emperor Hsüan-tsung in A.D. 729:

K'ai-yüan, seventeenth year, eleventh month, the day *wu-shen.* [The emperor] had visited the various Imperial Tombs. Upon his return he issued a great act of grace. The edict said, "Nothing is more important in the conduct of sacrifices than that they be offered with proper solemnity. As regards the highest form of virtuous behavior nothing can be added to filial reverence. . . .

Now, imperial Heaven has cared for my T'ang. With a worshipful heart I seek to make it prosper for my descendants. As to this good fortune in the receiving of blessings, how could I confine the benefits of such grace to me, the one man? [Such grace] ought to be extended to the whole world. Let a great act of grace be proclaimed to all under Heaven. Let all those liable for crimes committed prior to dawn of the twenty-second day, eleventh month, seventeenth year of K'ai-yuan, without distinguishing whether [their crimes] were serious or not, whether [their crimes] have already been discovered or not, whether [their cases] have been decided or not, including those who would not be freed by an ordinary amnesty, be completely freed. Those men who, for miscellaneous crimes, were sentenced to exile from the Hsien-t'ien period [A.D. 711] or later and who have already been transferred to nearby jurisdictions, and all those registered at Ch'i-hsi or Kua-chou, we forgive their past evil and solely consider how they may renew themselves. All such ought to be freed to return. Those who were jointly adjudicated for rebellion and perpetually exiled, as well as 'city slaves' *(ch'eng-nu)* may be transferred in a measured way to nearer jurisdictions and registered there as ordinary citizens. Demoted officials may be transferred in a measured way to nearer territories. Among those officials who have lost their offices or grades of nobility those not yet decrepit from age may in a measured way be given salaries."13

This act of grace then goes on to provide tax relief to the common people, awards to the virtuous, promotions to officials, ceremonies for the illustrious dead, gifts to royal princes and other members of the royal household, advancements and transfers to some worthies, aid to families that had lost members in wars, and a promise of a separate decree to specify the grants to be awarded soldiers. Almost every group in T'ang society received some benefits. The absence of any grants to Buddhists or Taoists is therefore all the more striking. Very few acts of grace gave benefits to these religious groups. Perhaps it was felt that such gifts would not be fitting, since acts of grace were already thoroughly expressive of indigenous religious concepts embodied in the state cult. The ideological dress of such acts was wholly Confucian. Filial reverence of the imperial ancestors played counterpoint to royal concern for the sufferings of the people.14

The document also makes it possible to begin to answer two critical questions: Who benefited? And to what extent? First, it is clear from this and many other examples that, as in the Han, and indeed throughout imperial times, great acts of grace were general amnesties —they covered all the empire.15 They were also general in that they benefited all criminals, freeing most of them completely and giving lesser benefits to those guilty of certain serious crimes. Few crimes were regarded as so heinous that their principals were by statute denied all benefits. (Crimes could of course be excluded from benefits by specific statement in the text of the act of grace.)16

As was true from the emergence of the system during the early years of the empire, a great act of grace included all people guilty of capital crimes or less. Though there had been minor changes in penalties after the fall of the Han, the basic character of the punishment system had remained much the same. Most criminals were sentenced to death, to some form of servitude at a place removed from their homes, to degradation of status (if they were members of the elite), or to beating. Thus under the T'ang system an amnestied criminal might be escaping from (1) decapitation, (2) strangulation, (3) several degrees of permanent lifetime exile, graded according to the distance from the jurisdiction of conviction and all entailing forced labor, (4) penal servitude, graded according to the time involved, (5) degradation of status or loss of position, (6) beating with the heavy rod, or (7) beating with the light rod. With the exception of certain groups to be discussed in more detail, all criminals sentenced to any of these punishments were completely freed by a great act of grace.

These benefits were available whether or not the crime had been discovered at the time of the act of grace. This phrase made clear and explicit one implication of the rule that affairs which had occurred prior to the amnesty were no longer subject to prosecution. In one sense such provisions might be traced back to 199 B.C. when Han Kao-tsu pardoned officials whose crimes had not come to light, but as a general stipulation the oldest extant example of this provision occurs in a document from the southern dynasty of Liang, during the reign of Wu-ti (502–550). A nearly contemporaneous example is recorded for the period 534–550 under the Eastern Wei located in northern China and for the state of Ch'en in 558. The phrase was adopted by the Sui, the T'ang, and later dynasties.[17]

The freeing of those whose cases were still under investigation or in process of trial was presumably covered by the phrase "whether or not their cases have been completed." (In T'ang times a serious case was "completed" if the Imperial Secretariat had already passed judgment and the Ministry of Justice had returned the case to the original unit of jurisdiction. For minor cases it would seem that they were considered complete after the circumstances had been determined and the matter investigated).[18] Like the explicit stipulation concerning cases not yet discovered, the phrase concerning cases not yet completed goes back at least to the southern dynasty of Liang, where it appeared in a decree of the year 508.[19]

No distinction was to be made "whether the case was light or heavy"—that is, the seriousness of the circumstances of the crime was not to be taken into account. No extant document seems to establish clear guidelines for defining "heavy" circumstances. Possibly the meaning was not closely circumscribed in order to afford the judges in a theoretically rigid system the flexibility necessary in any working legal order. Within undefined but generally understood boundaries set by the accepted values of the elite, a judge could thus mesh law and equity in his treatment of a case. But the grace of the amnesty overrode such distinctions. This provision, which can be traced back to the Liu Sung dynasty in the year 420, became a regular part of the rulings of later states.[20]

When the document says that all are to be "pardoned and freed," it means pardoned in the most complete sense. Not only were criminals to be be spared their punishment, but their criminal record, for legal purposes, was expunged. Although for certain crimes the investigations had to be completed, the accused was not to be punished; and if he later committed another criminal act the crimes committed prior to his liberation could not be counted in classing him as a recidivist. A great act of grace cut off all legal concern with the prior acts of criminals forgiven under its terms. (An ordinary act of grace, by contrast, although it might spare men punishment, did not erase the legal fact of their crimes.)[21]

This expunging of the record by great acts of grace went back at least to the Southern Ch'i (479–502). In the first year of that dynasty a decree said that "those guilty of offenses against good morals and public opinion, of crimes of corruption, luxury, and theft, all are to be washed clean. Their former records are to be expunged so that they can begin anew."[22]

The related practice of not permitting the raising of matters that had occurred prior to an amnesty, a practice which had begun in the Han, was also continued during later times. In 558 an emperor of the Northern Chou issued a decree which said in part:

Frequently in recent times we have received from officials [reports concerning] matters which took place prior to an amnesty. As to this, even though [such officials] were thinking about [suppressing] the evil, still

exile on the contrary is treated more seriously? If light and heavy punishments are not properly categorized, there will be doubts concerning
their meaning.

Reply: Those under a death sentence send up a memorial and permission is by imperial edict. But those under a sentence of life exile
remain at home because of this article. Remaining at home thus necessarily follows the ordinary principle, whereas the imperial edict is an
expression of special grace. How then is this grace allowed to a person
condemned to death to be equated with the judgement made by an official? In view of this difference, the applicability or nonapplicability of
the amnesty is not due to the punishment being heavy or light.[26]

Another form of residual punishment was designed to promote social stability and respect for law by forestalling private vengeance.
Murderers spared capital punishment by acts of grace were not permitted to continue living in the area where they had committed their
crime. The state, fearing that the relatives of the victim might be
tempted to take the law into their own hands, transported the killer a
fixed distance from the location of the crime. The problem of private
vengeance in such cases was noted specifically in the Chin period
(265–419), when it was said that people "are not permitted [privately
to seek] vengeance [on the murderers of their relatives]."[27] The system of transporting the killers seems to appear for the first time during the succeeding Liu Sung dynasty (420–479). During this period
those affected were said to have been "transported" (hsi-sung).[28]
During the T'ang, although the name was changed to "shifting the
residence" (i-hsiang), the practice remained the same. The T'ang
Code says:

> All those who, having killed men, are liable for the death penalty but
> on meeting with an act of grace are spared [are to] shift their residence
> one thousand li or more. Commentary: if the victim has relatives with-
> in the mourning degree system [the killer] must be shifted in resi-
> dence. [The same rule] applies to those especially spared.[29]

Residual penalties might also include payments of restitution. The
T'ang Code spelled out in detail a system that apparently also existed
in earlier times: those who committed crimes involving booty such as

robbery, theft, fraud, bribery, or rapacity were required to pay back the amounts involved. In some cases thieves had to make double restitution. Although the general rule was that intervening acts of grace or reductions of sentence would not spare them repayment of the principal booty, such acts might under certain circumstances decrease, eliminate, or in some cases increase, their payments. If the booty from robberies or thefts had been seized prior to the act of grace, the criminals could avoid double restitution, though the original amount had to be repaid. What was called the "single booty" was also ordinarily exacted from the other types of criminals mentioned above, even though an act of grace had intervened. But when the booty had already been expended and an act of grace intervened before restitution had been made, the criminal would be spared some or all of the payment. (The same provision governed the sending in of commutation monies—with the added stipulation that if the time limit for commutation had passed, the criminal was not to be spared payment.)

Although in most cases acts of grace either reduced payments or left them unaffected, in one set of circumstances they might actually increase them. If the criminal had been sentenced to death or exile and the booty had already been expended, no restitution was required. But if an act of grace or reduction of sentence intervened to spare the culprit, the booty was exacted according to law, provided that the case had not been memorialized. If it had already been memorialized, the criminals were forgiven payment. (Men who owed restitution for one crime and were exiled for another, and the families of criminals who died, were also spared payment.)[30]

Rules similar to those governing booty applied when sumptuary laws had been broken and forbidden materials had been used in the making of goods—carts, clothing, houses, and grave monuments. Although the culprits might be spared a beating because of an intervening act of grace, they still had to replace the improper materials. They had one hundred days, the regular amnesty time limit, in which to rectify their fraud—either by replacing the offending materials with materials that met state specifications or, in some cases, by selling the goods. This rule could not cover materials in graves, since replacement would involve desecration. If the situation was not corrected within the time limit, the criminals were to be tried according to statute.[31]

Acts of grace also provided an opportunity for the rectifying of false representations without fear of penalty. Those who had entered false information concerning landownership or the ages, relationships, numbers, or statuses of household members—facts which might affect taxes, levies, or questions of inheritance—might correct the misrepresentations within the amnesty grace period. (A wife might have been listed as a concubine, or a concubine as a wife, for reasons of inheritance. An illegal adoption might have occurred. Someone might have entered the Buddhist or Taoist clergy without permission. Ages or property holding might have been registered incorrectly to avoid tax burdens. All such frauds could be set straight without fear of punishment.) This provision seems to have been aimed particularly at members of the local clerical staff or officials, those who had to connive if such frauds were to succeed. The opportunity to correct such frauds was linked with a threat—if they were not rectified their perpetrators could be accused after the expiration of the amnesty time limit, even though this action technically constituted discussing an affair which had occurred prior to an act of grace.[32]

Acts of grace might also legitimate errors in judgment, provided the error had led to an act of mercy. Under the T'ang Code (and later codes) if a judge had ruled erroneously prior to an act of grace his decision was to be reversed if it had resulted in a heavier sentence than was proper for the case; his decision was to be confirmed, however, if it had resulted in a lighter sentence. The commentary cites a case in which a man killed his elder cousin from his paternal uncle's family in a fight but was tried for having killed a blood brother—that is, for an offense classed as Contumacy (o-ni). After the act of grace the error was corrected and the case was reclassified as one of Discord (pu-mu), a lesser crime though still one of the Ten Abominations. Since the act of grace specified that it did not cover crimes not forgiven by ordinary amnesties, the criminal was still exiled to two thousand li (the penalty for Discord) but escaped decapitation (the penalty for Contumacy).[33]

Medieval Chinese lawmakers were also very concerned about preserving the proper social order among the people. In particular marriage and adoption were regulated by a host of laws. The authorities

strictly prohibited relationships that crossed class lines between commoners and the servile classes or those which involved marriages between certain close kin.

Those who were married (or betrothed) contrary to statute were to
be separated. Marriages or betrothals might be illegal because of the
kinship relations of the parties, because the woman involved was a fugitive from justice, or because one of the partners was of servile status.
In all such cases, apart from whatever criminal penalties attached to
the acts, the parties were divorced. The servile were returned to their
original status. An intervening act of grace might spare those involved
from criminal punishment. It could not prevent a rectification of status and a separation of the parties. The same held true for divorces
mandated by the state because of the presence of the causes of "appropriate separation" (i-chüeh).[34]

In cases of adoption the lawmakers were concerned because boys of
servile status who were adopted by commoners would become heirs
and thus might be called upon to perform ancestral sacrifices to non-
kindred of a higher status. In such adoption cases the commoner
might be beaten or sentenced to penal servitude. Those who had
given the boy for adoption were also punished. The servile individuals were returned to their original status. An intervening act of grace
might free the commoners involved from criminal penalties. Under
no circumstances would it prevent the servile parties from losing their
fraudulently gained higher status.[35] The emperor had the power to
cleanse a person of impurity. He did not have the power to legitimize
the unclean state of affairs which had arisen as a result of a criminal
act.

The social values of the T'ang ruling elite are also revealed in the
legal treatment of certain groups whose conditions made them objects
of pity or implied diminished responsibility—the aged, the young,
the disabled, the ill, the mentally incompetent, and women. Persons
in these groups might (or might not) be subjected to the trial process,
but they would usually be treated differently after conviction. Persons
over seventy or under fifteen (as well as those who were legally of
diminished competence because of idiocy or physical handicaps such
as blindness or lack of a limb) were allowed to redeem crimes of exile
or less. Those over eighty or under ten were given the further privi-

lege of Petition—the right to have their cases, after trial, submitted to the emperor for his judgment in instances of rebellion or homicide. For lesser crimes they were not adjudicated or were allowed redemption. Those ninety or over, or seven or less, could not be executed.[36]

Age or illness might under certain circumstances change the impact of acts of grace. Most individuals jointly adjudicated for rebellion or sedition were to be exiled even if there had been an amnesty. However, men over eighty or women over sixty (or ill) were permitted to redeem their crimes if they met with an act of grace. Age, youth, or illness might also excuse those jointly adjudicated in cases of black magic poisoning *(ku)* from accompanying the principal criminal into exile.

Women occupied a peculiar place in this scheme. Generally women were not sent into exile; they were beaten and allowed to remain at home in the custody of their husbands. An obvious exception to this practice was the women who had made *ku* poison or taught others to make it. An intervening act of grace would spare them strangulation, but they were still sent into exile (accompanied by the members of their household). Women between fifteen and sixty who were in good health, if convicted under joint adjudication for Plotting Rebellion or Great Sedition, seem to have been sent into exile also.[37]

Status had major implications for the treatment of criminals in traditional Chinese law. For general purposes the Chinese population in traditional times may be divided into three major status groups—the servile, the large mass of common people, and the ruling elite. Under the empire the ruling elite comprised the civil and military officials, some of their relatives, and those related to the imperial house. The officials were divided into nine main grades. Beyond the limits of officialdom itself this ninefold system was extended to encompass other elite groups such as nobles and palace women who were provided with equivalency ranks in the civil service grading structure. Although from the fall of the Han to the fall of the T'ang officialdom was dominated by members of large aristocratic clans, official position was not hereditary. Many members of these clans never took official posts, and occasionally men from outside the charmed aristocratic circle could work their way into the civil service.

Official rank, whether derived from membership in officialdom or from membership in one of the groups holding equivalency ranks, helped insulate its holder from the full impact of the criminal justice system. During the T'ang and the Sung (960–1279), all those with official rank were permitted by statute to commute sentences of exile or less into redemption payments in copper. Those with rank seven or higher also had the privilege of Reduction *(chien)*, which mandated an automatic reduction in penalty of one degree for most crimes bearing penalties of exile or less. The privilege called Petition *(ch'ing)* was granted to all holders of rank five or above. When criminals claimed this right, legal officials had to verify their right to Petition, try the case, and pronounce the sentence. They then submitted a memorial that indicated the grounds on which the defendant had been granted Petition, explained why the crime was a capital one, specified whether the punishment called for strangulation or decapitation, and asked the emperor to concur with their verdict and sentence. (Punishments of exile or less would have been avoided through Commutation, without resort to Petition.) The greatest privilege, Deliberation *(i)*, was reserved for those graded rank three or higher. In the words of the T'ang Code: "If those deserving one of the eight deliberations commit a capital crime, a memorial is sent up requesting authorization to consider and fix a penalty. The officials do not dare decide the case themselves."[38] Certain crimes precluded the use of these privileges. None of the privileges were to be used by someone who committed one of the Ten Abominations. Petition and the lower privileges were not to be extended to murderers or to those who within their spheres of jurisdiction committed rape, robbery, or kidnapping or took bribes to subvert the law.

In addition to these privileges officials were also granted the important right of substituting administrative sanctions for normal penalties. Apart from the minor sanctions that followed petty misdemeanors, those with official rank who could not commute punishments or evade them entirely might replace some or all of their penalties by reductions in title or official rank. The higher the official rank, the heavier the penalty that could be replaced. Those who lost office in this way might resume a lesser rank after a stated period. For certain crimes the state took the initiative in depriving the culprits of their official rank. This process differed from replacement in its compulsory and more punitive character. Such withdrawal of official standing was divided into three grades. Least serious was "resignation from occupied office" *(mien so chü chih kuan)*. Those affected might resume office in one year at a rank reduced by one grade. More serious was "resignation from office" *(mien-kuan)*, which required a three-year wait before the resumption of office with a two-grade reduction. Most serious was "disenrollment" *(ch'u-ming)*, which involved removing the offender's name from the list of those with official rank, depriving him of all titles of nobility, and reducing him to the status of a commoner. But even this grave punishment did not deprive the criminal permanently of higher status. He became eligible to resume office in six years at reduced rank.

Officials had not always had such privileges. Indeed one of the most important themes of Chinese legal (and social) history is the continuing struggle by the bureaucrats to modify the egalitarian law code of the first unifying dynasties to accord with their class interest— to build around themselves a wall of privilege. This drive to transmute political power into legal privilege had by the T'ang succeeded in insulating the officials in large measure from many of the more brutal aspects of Chinese justice. And then, having reached its fullest extent, the wall of privilege began to crumble in the face of increasing despotic power in the hands of the emperors.

In the T'ang, however, this weakening of the system had not yet begun. The full panoply of official privilege was in force. In its details it portrays both the extent of legal privilege and the limits set to it: practical immunity from physical punishment for minor crimes, but a carefully orchestrated set of residual penalties for major offenders.

As a residual punishment following amnesties, Disenrollment is mentioned sporadically in pre-T'ang sources. During the Chin (265–419) officials guilty of Lack of Filial Piety *(pu-hsiao)*, deliberately killing nobles or superior officials, making false accusations, taking bribes to subvert the law, or seizing men for sale and corruptly enticing slaves to desert were to be Disenrolled and registered among the common people even if they met with acts of grace.[39] And during the Latter Wei (in A.D. 513) a functionary notes in passing that officials who stole, accepted bribes, or practiced corruption, as well as those jointly adjudicated for rebellion, were disenrolled after benefiting from acts of grace.[40]

The rules of the Sui (581–618) prefigured those of the T'ang—those guilty of the Ten Abominations, or of intentional homicide *(ku-sha)*, were disenrolled despite amnesty. As under the Latter Wei, the T'ang also disenrolled those jointly adjudicated for rebellion or sentenced to exile with added labor. In T'ang law, however, those guilty of corruption or robbery were treated less harshly than under the Latter Wei. They were not disenrolled but merely forced to resign from occupied office. The latter punishment was also visited on officials who committed the crime of fornication or kidnapping within their sphere of jurisdiction. As had been true in earliest times, officials suffered these residual penalties only if their cases had been completed when an act of grace was issued. Cases still in process were dropped without penalty.[41]

From Han times on, many acts of grace specifically reinstated people expelled from the elite. In the T'ang most great and many ordinary acts of grace reinstated at least some ex-officials. There are even examples of government action to aid those so rehabilitated in the replevin of their illegally seized properties or in the recovery of properties originally confiscated by the state.[42]

The phrase "those not to be spared by ordinary acts of grace" *(ch'ang-she so pu mien che)*, which occurs in the translation of the *ta-she* from the K'ai-yüan period (713–742), has antecedents which can be traced back to the Han. During the Latter Han several decrees of grace explicitly pardoned "all those who ought not to be treated leniently" *(chu pu ying yu she)* or "all those whose crimes are not liable to receive pardon" *(chu fan pu tang te i she)*.[43] The use of different wording suggests that this provision was not at this time a regular part of acts of grace. The stipulation reappears in A.D. 220 under the state of Wei as those "not to be amnestied" *(pu tang te she)*, but the phrase current in Sui, T'ang, and Sung acts of grace seems to occur first in a document from the Northern Chou (A.D. 580).[44]

This phrase, which appears in many of the extant T'ang *ta-she,* raises a host of problems. What was the nature of ordinary acts of grace and how did they differ from *ta-she?* What did it mean to be "spared" or "not spared"? And in practice what sorts of criminals were placed in the category of those "not spared"?

Because of variations in their terms, the character of ordinary acts of grace *(ch'ang-she)* cannot be definitively described even for the

T'ang, but their basic nature is clear. Similar in ritual and administration to great acts of grace, these ordinary acts differed in the scope of the benefits they entailed and might also differ in the geographical scope of their coverage—ordinary acts of grace might be general and affect the whole empire, but they might also be localized *(ch'ü-she)*. It has been suggested for Han times that ordinary acts of grace brought lesser benefits to a more restricted body of criminals. The same pattern holds in the post-Han period. During these centuries the pattern which was to remain standard through the T'ang and Sung periods appeared—an ordinary act of grace usually resulted in the reducing of death sentences to exile (and at times to penal servitude), those sentenced to exile were either freed or reduced to penal servitude, those liable to penal servitude were either beaten or simply freed, and those liable for beatings were released.[45]

The same general pattern was followed in the T'ang, with reductions of one degree for serious sentences and release for those subject only to beating. The grants to noncriminal groups were also less extensive than under great acts of grace. Still, ordinary amnesties played an important role in T'ang times. The encyclopedia *Ts'e-fu yüan-kuei* alone lists more than one hundred such acts for the T'ang; more than sixty applied only to limited parts of the empire, but more than forty others were empirewide.[46]

An example of an ordinary act of grace, albeit with terms considerably more liberal than was usually the case, will indicate the tenor and style of these acts:

K'ai-yüan twenty-fourth year, fourth month, the day *ting-ch'ou* [A.D. 736]. The decree said:

We in our thoughts on the roots of good government consider that teaching is primary and punishment is secondary. And yet convicts who suffer the hardships of being transported and those who have become involved in crimes are still numerous. Sometimes they are held in jails for years. Now [this problem] is spreading like a fog. How can I forget to have a natural pity for them? Moreover I am concerned that those who enforce the law are not careful [and that] among those who are punished some are not deserving of punishment. If I do not investigate this how can I be said to be possessed of mercy?

[As to] the world's current prisoners, those guilty of one of the Ten Abominations where the sentence should be death, and those who have made false [seals], or are the chief culprits in the killing of someone with a sword, should first be beaten sixty blows [and then] permanently exiled to distant evil places in Ling-nan. Other men with capital sentences should first be beaten one blow and then all exiled to Ling-nan. Those guilty of crimes calling for exile where the circumstances [of the original crime] were serious should be beaten sixty blows. Where the circumstances were not serious they should be beaten once. When the beatings have been completed they should all be liberated. Those sentenced to penal servitude or less are all to be freed. Those who have secretly confiscated official goods or practiced fraud with regard to them, or robbers, must in the usual way solicit guarantors and establish deadlines for the paying back of the amounts involved. In accordance with the regulated writings on administrative punishments those officials guilty of rapacity may be released. As usual do not order them to come forward [to the capital].

In the capital order the Secretariat and Chancellery [to handle it]. [In the] capital city assign the responsibility to the Prefect. In the outer prefectures assign the responsibility to the senior officials of that prefecture. Subsequently memorialize on the carrying out of these administrative sanctions.[47]

At several points the T'ang Code gives a straightforward definition of what it meant "not to be spared" by such an ordinary act of grace. At one point the code says that the phrase was to be understood as covering "the class [of those who] even if they meet with a great act of grace (ta-she) are still sentenced to death or exile, or to disenrollment, resignation from occupied office, or shifting of residence."[48]

Clearly the phrase was meant to cover criminals who were to suffer either their original penalty or some residual penalty, despite an intervening great act of grace. It obviously applied to those not totally freed. It did not necessarily mean that those covered by it received no benefits. But the simplicity of this definition is deceptive. When an attempt is made to determine just what persons fit this definition, and what punishments they still had to suffer, the sometimes bewildering complexity of the T'ang Code becomes apparent. Inclusion in, or exclusion from, the group of those not spared might be affected not only by the specific nature of the crime but also by the age, sex, and status of the individual committing it. Moreover, in some cases inclusion was determined by the age, sex, and status of the victim, by the relationship if any between criminal and victim, by the position of the case within the judicial process at the time of the act of grace, and by other clauses of the amnesty letter.

In determining whether or not an individual was to be spared, the nature of his crime was a key factor. Many of the crimes which might exclude a criminal from pardon by an act of grace fell under the rubric of serious crimes called the Ten Abominations—Plotting Rebellion (mou fan), Plotting Great Sedition (mou ta-ni), Plotting Treason (mou-p'an), Contumacy (o-ni), Depravity (pu-tao), Great Irreverence (ta pu-ching), Lack of Filial Piety (pu-hsiao), Discord (pu-mu), Unrighteousness (pu-i), and Incest (nei-luan).

In the T'ang Code the most severely treated of these Ten Abominations was the fourth, Contumacy (o-ni), defined as "to beat or plot to kill (without actually killing) one's paternal grandparents or parents; or to kill one's maternal grandparents, or one's husband, or one's husband's paternal grandparents, or his parents."[49] Although not enumerated here, the actual killing of close relatives (as opposed to merely plotting to kill them) was included implicitly under Contumacy. The unforgivable character of the most serious of the homicides included here—most particularly actual killing of parents or grandparents—was reflected in the law at least as far back as the Chin (265–419). The list of especially frightening homicides was expanded in the Liu Sung (420–479) to include the killing of an elder brother by a younger brother, a husband by his wife, or a master by his slave. The latter crime, although not listed under Contumacy in the T'ang Code, was implicitly included in the list of crimes not to be spared by analogy from the provision that slaves or unfree persons who merely struck or plotted to kill their masters (or raped their master's wives) were not to be spared. Even if these unfree people had killed at their victim's own request they were not to be pardoned.[50]

In the T'ang, Contumacy was punished by decapitation in all cases, but a distinction was drawn between two groups. Those who actually killed their parents or paternal grandparents were to be executed even if they met with an act of grace. Those who merely plotted to kill parents or paternal grandparents—or actually killed more distant relatives such as paternal uncles and their wives, elder brother or sisters, or elder relatives of the *hsiao-kung* degree of mourning—were spared by intervening acts of amnesty, though still subjected to exile. (By implication the group who might be spared also included wives who killed their husbands, or their husband's paternal grandparents or his parents, or their own maternal grandparents.)[51]

No other crime seems to have been so detested as the killing of parents or grandparents. Even rebellion and sedition appear to have been viewed as less frightful, or at least as less unforgivable. This attitude may go back to the Latter Han. Several great acts of grace during that period extended pardon to those guilty of Plotting Rebellion or committing Great Sedition,[52] and in the Chin (265–420) officials complained about the current system, which pardoned rebellion and sedition but not matricide or patricide. By the T'ang this attitude had been enshrined in the code.

These two crimes against the state—Plotting Rebellion and Plotting Great Sedition—comprised the first and second of the Ten Abominations. Plotting Rebellion was defined in the T'ang Code as "to plot to endanger the altars of Soil and Grain"—that is, the ruler and the state he governed. The penalty for Plotting Rebellion was decapitation for the principals, strangulation for the plotters' fathers and their sons aged sixteen or over, enslavement for their minor sons, their mothers, wives, concubines, daughters, paternal grandparents, grandchildren, brothers, sisters, and servile dependents, and exile to three thousand *li* for paternal uncles and male first cousins in the male line including the aged, the young, and the disabled. These relatives were said to have been "jointly adjudicated" *(lien-tso)*. The government also confiscated the properties of the principals and of those persons to be jointly adjudicated who had been dwelling in common with the principals.[53]

No other crime swept into its net such a variety of peripherally involved persons. Common sense would suggest that the law was unlikely to spare the principals involved in rebellion, even if acts of grace intervened. And yet the code indicates that such men were not executed, saying that those guilty of rebellion, on meeting with an ordinary act of grace, were "still to be exiled."[54] There are also a multitude of acts in which rebellion was explicitly included as one of the crimes to be completely pardoned by an act of grace. Of course there are many acts that explicitly excluded from coverage certain named rebels (and at times their immediate followers), but this specific naming of individuals suggests that under ordinary circumstances rebels would be included. They were specifically excluded because otherwise the judicial authorities might treat them as having been pardoned. Finally we know of cases where emperors, intending to issue acts of grace that excluded those currently (or recently) in revolt against the state, were chided by officials on the grounds that such piecemeal exclusions would vitiate the credibility of the whole amnesty.[55] The commonsense assumption, that active rebels would be treated without mercy, seems in many cases to be contradicted by the facts. Certainly it is clear that those who had merely plotted rebellion and those jointly adjudicated very frequently escaped with their lives.

The T'ang Code deals in detail with the fate of these persons "jointly adjudicated for Plotting Rebellion." The most general provision regarding acts of grace was that the treatment of persons jointly adjudicated was to conform to the treatment of the principals. If the principals themselves benefited from an act of grace, then their relatives were to be freed completely, even if they had already been registered as slaves by the government. Although wives of rebels might be freed in this way, they were still compulsorily divorced from their husbands. Adopted descendents were also returned to their original families.

Treatment of the property of the accused depended on the situation. Even if the principals had already been executed, property not yet seized by the government at the time of the arrival of the letter of amnesty was not thereafter to be confiscated. If the principals had not yet been executed, and were spared by the issuing of an act of grace, they were allowed to keep property not yet seized. Property already seized but not yet divided and registered by the government offices was returned to them. Property already divided and registered was not returned.[56]

Plotting Great Sedition *(mou ta-ni)*, the second of the Ten Abominations, included such crimes as plotting to destroy the ancestral tombs of the reigning house. If overt acts had occurred, the punishment (both for principals and for those jointly adjudicated) was the same as that for Plotting Rebellion. If overt acts had not occurred, the punishment for the principals was reduced to strangulation, and those jointly adjudicated could benefit from the T'ang Code provisions dealing with mere accessories. When an act of grace intervened, those who had committed overt acts of Great Sedition, and their jointly adjudicated relatives, were treated like those guilty of, or jointly adjudicated for, Plotting Rebellion.

The third of the Ten Abominations, Plotting Treason *(mou-p'an)*, meant "to plot to betray the country or to serve rebels." The penalty for principals was the same as that for Great Sedition—decapitation if overt acts had occurred, strangulation if the crime had been discovered at the plotting stage. A commentary to one section of the T'ang Code indicates that the crime was viewed less seriously than Rebellion or Sedition even when overt acts had occurred. Although some persons were to be jointly adjudicated with those guilty of Plotting Treason, these relatives were not considered to have violated one of the Ten Abominations. Thus they could benefit from acts of grace which excluded those guilty of one of these ten great crimes. (Those jointly adjudicated for Plotting Rebellion or for Sedition were listed under the Ten Abominations.) Moreover, unlike those jointly adjudicated for Plotting Rebellion or Sedition, those jointly adjudicated for Plotting Treason might be allowed the privilege of Reduction or Commutation and might be spared expulsion from the body of officials.[57]

Only one other crime seems to have frightened the authorities as much as these homicides and crimes against the state—the making of the black magic poison called *ku,* classified under the fifth of the Ten Abominations as Depravity *(pu-tao)*. During the T'ang it was commonly thought that *ku* poison could be manufactured by putting poisonous creatures such as spiders and scorpions in a sealed vessel. As they killed and ate each other their poisons became joined—and in the end were concentrated in the survivor. The T'ang pharmacologist Ch'en Ts'ang-ch'i said that such a *ku* creature

can conceal its form, and seems to be a ghost or spirit, and makes misfortune for men. But after all it's in only a reptile ghost. If one of them has bitten a person to death, it will sometimes emerge from one of that man's apertures. Watch and wait to catch it and dry it in the warmth of the sun: then, when someone is afflicted by the *ku*, burn it to ashes and give him a dose of it. Being akin to it, the one quite naturally subdues the other.[58]

Despite the currency of this and other formulas for curing *ku*, the very possibility of its use was terrifying to the medieval Chinese. It symbolized for them a world of horrible aspect, the dreadful steaming lands of the south, and their supernally gifted sorceresses. Thus the women who made *ku* were to be strangled. Even those who merely raised the animals to be used, or taught the secrets of manufacturing *ku*, were subject to the same penalty. Those living in the same household with the principal criminal were all to be exiled to three thousand *li*. If an amnesty intervened, the sorceress herself apparently would be spared strangulation and be sent instead into exile. Those in her household would still have to accompany her. These jointly adjudicated persons might be spared exile if they were aged (over eighty), under age (under ten), disabled, ill, and lacked a family member to accompany and care for them.[59]

Residual punishments might also be inflicted on those guilty of certain crimes not included in the Ten Abominations. Under the Liang (502–557), bandits who escaped death because of amnesty were to have the character "bandit" tattooed on their faces and were condemned to perpetual servitude as chained workers in the mines. Similar provisions are found in later times.[60] Finally, the unforgivable category also seems to have included all crimes deliberately committed as a result of foreknowledge of an impending act of grace.[61]

Apart from the crimes statutorily excluded from being fully pardoned, it was possible for the authorities specifically to exclude (as well as to include) certain crimes in a letter of amnesty. The Sui dynasty act quoted earlier excluded Plotting Rebellion, Plotting Great Sedition, and Spreading Heretical Doctrines to Mislead the Multitude. Under the T'ang specific crimes were also sometimes excluded, yet it is difficult to assess how common this practice was. Well over a hundred great acts of grace are partially preserved from the T'ang. The most commonly excluded crimes—rapacious corruption among officials and offenses falling under the Ten Abominations—are excluded in less than ten percent of these decrees. In the case of offenses under the Ten Abominations, in almost half these examples the edicts excluded only criminals sentenced to death. Those guilty of one of the Ten Abominations but sentenced to exile were to be freed. Serious homicides are excluded in about five percent of the decrees. Other crimes, including heretically misleading the multitudes, joint adjudication for rebellion, armed robbery, corruption in judicial cases, illegal production of seals, and plotting rebellion or great sedition, are mentioned in only a few scattered acts. This absence of phrases excluding crimes is due partly to the highly abbreviated state of our sources. Nevertheless, it still seems clear that no crimes were systematically and regularly excluded from great acts of grace.[62] (This flexibility thus permitted the emperor to extend his grace to those whose original sentences had specifically stated that they were never to be benefited by acts of grace. Even "perpetual exclusion" need not be perpetual. How could the sovereign bind himself not to overrule his past acts?)[63]

The problem of interpreting these decrees is posed by the vast majority which, in the form now extant, do not mention such crimes, either to include or to exclude them. One obvious reason for the absence of such stipulations is the abbreviated form in which these acts have been preserved. Mid-T'ang examples of great acts of grace often occupy five or more pages of ten columns each. In one version of one decree the text runs to more than sixteen such pages. Yet most of the decrees from the last century of the T'ang, and many from the first century, have been reduced to a few columns of print. Often very little remains beyond the statement that a *ta-she* was issued. For this reason the apparent general rule of interpretation—that the most serious crimes, if not explicitly included or included by obvious implication, were outside the sphere of the grant—is of little use.[64]

Even in their highly abbreviated form these T'ang *ta-she* reflect a change in policy during the course of the dynasty. Early T'ang rulers followed in the steps of their Sui predecessors by frequently excluding those guilty of Plotting Rebellion, Plotting Great Sedition, or committing other crimes among the Ten Abominations. But from the reign of Hsüan-tsung (713–756) the situation reverses itself. Many decrees not only bring such crimes under the scope of the amnesty but permit the principals to be completely pardoned. No T'ang great acts of grace from this era or later specifically *exclude* such criminals, as was so common in the early T'ang.

Most *ta-she* explicitly extend their pardon to all those not yet caught or discovered, to all those in any part of the investigation or trial process, and to all those awaiting punishment. They are frequently less clear concerning the treatment of those already undergoing punishment—in particular, some do not adequately describe the treatment of men already in exile.

The fate of men sentenced to exile but not yet at their assigned location is dealt with in the T'ang Code. Under its provisions (as under the codes of later dynasties) men sentenced to exile were allotted a fixed number of days for their trip to the place of exile; the time varied with the distance to be covered and was calculated from the day the criminal set out on his journey. According to the T'ang Code, echoing policies followed in the Latter Wei (386–535) and the Eastern Wei (534–550):

[As to the cases of] all men being sent into exile who meet with an amnesty while en route, it is necessary that the stages of their journey be calculated. [If] they have exceeded the [permissible] time limits they are not to be freed by the amnesty. . . . The general calculation of whether the journey had exceeded [the limit] begins with the day they set out on the road. Subcommentary: If those exiled to two thousand *li* journey on foot, it should take forty days. If an act of grace occurs before the fortieth day, the criminals should be freed by the act of grace, whether they have covered a long or a short distance. However, if they have exceeded the time limits then they are not covered by the act of grace. . . . If within [the time limits] for the journey the criminal arrives at the place of registration he also is to be freed completely by the act of grace. Subcommentary: If a person is exiled to two thousand *li* and so has forty days [to travel], if before the forty days [are completed] he reaches his place of exile, and then there is an act of grace, he is to be freed.[65]

On first reading, this passage seems to imply that a man who had reached his place of exile would only be freed if an act of grace happened to come before his term for travel had expired.[66] In light of the clear statements in the T'ang Code and the decrees of amnesty, however, this passage must be seen in terms of the policy aims of the state. This ruling was clearly aimed at minimizing delay in the movement of prisoners by giving the convicts themselves a strong incentive to get to their assigned places of exile—if not quickly, at least within the specified time limits. The last clause, about freeing those who arrived ahead of schedule, was obviously inserted to reassure those involved that only late arrival, not early arrival, would be punished. The code also made provision for extenuating circumstances which made it impossible to keep to the appropriate time schedule. As a last measure to promote rapid and effective transporting of prisoners, the code ruled that those who escaped en route were not to benefit from acts of grace (thus setting these men apart from ordinary fugitives).[67]

Despite the apparent implication of this passage from the T'ang Code—that men already in exile were not freed by acts of grace—there is abundant evidence that at least in some cases these men were freed, and in all cases they had the conditions of their punishment improved. The commentary to the T'ang Code says that when "there is an amnesty and exemption from labor, the same principles are applicable to those in life exile as to the general population."[68]

The remaining burden that exiles had to bear was their distant separation from home. In practice such men were frequently "freed to return" (fang-huan) by acts of grace. Thus exile, theoretically a lifetime punishment, might in practice be only temporary. Beginning in the Latter Han there are a number of decrees which speak about "returned convicts" or allowing those sentenced to "long-term servitude" (ch'ang-t'u) to return home. In the Han such men had not been sentenced for life; in the Liu Sung (420–479), Southern Ch'i (479–502), Liang (502–557), Ch'en (557–589), and Sui (581–618) they had been sent into perpetual servitude.[69]

Such a scattering of examples, in the absence of statutes, cannot prove that grants permitting exiles to return were a regular part of great acts of grace in this period. The same problem holds for the T'ang. No general ruling says that permission for exiles to return should form a regular part of great acts of grace. Yet occasionally in the seventh century and rather frequently in the eighth and ninth centuries, the decrees say that those in exile are "freed to return."[70] Grants of this kind seem to have been particularly frequent in the acts of grace which accompanied the enthronement of new emperors. Still, it is clear that, at least during the first half of the T'ang, such provisions were by no means a part of all *ta-she*. When the Emperor T'ai-tsung (627–650) came to the throne, he issued a *ta-she* which among other provisions freed to return all those who had been sent into exile since the beginning of the reign of his predecessor Kao-tsu (618–627). Clearly the three great acts of grace issued by Kao-tsu during the course of his reign had not freed these exiles.[71]

Although we have evidence that during the first half of the dynasty not every great act of grace freed exiles to return, both contemporary commentators and later traditional historians seem to have thought this provision a regular part of late T'ang *ta-she*. The great ninth-century writer and official Han Yü said, "The letter of amnesty in a single day goes ten thousand *li*, those destined to die and lesser criminals all escape the path of death, exiles return to be cleansed."[72] Since we must allow Han Yü a poet's license, his testimony is less impressive than that of his contemporary Wang Shen. In 813, while serving as a high official in the Ministry of Justice, Wang submitted a memorial:

> I have noted that in the various jurisdictions men who have been registered in exile, when they meet with an act of grace, are all freed to return. Only as regards those in exile in the five cities of T'ien-te Military Prefecture and in the various border cities the circuit authorities invariably memorialize asking that such men be detained at the border defense areas, and then it will be ordered that to the ends of their lives they may not return.[73]

Wang asked that these unfortunates be treated like exiles held elsewhere in the empire. A decree so ordered. (Although the compiler notes that "from this decree on, this became a fixed system," we know from a decree of 875 that men from T'ien-te were still being discriminated against. They were ordinarily to be freed to return by amnesties only if they had been in exile ten years or more.)[74]

Whether or not grants of freedom to return became a "fixed system," it is clear that the lot of those "perpetually exiled" was far from hopeless. There was a substantial chance that at some point they would be freed to return to their original homes. Indeed, in 839 it was decreed that exiles having served six years were to be released and allowed to return. Apparently this rule fell into disuse as T'ang power collapsed, but it was revived during the Latter Chin (936–944) and was incorporated in the Sung Code.[75]

Even classes of exiles that the T'ang government did not wish to forgive completely might benefit by being moved from their place of registration to some more congenial part of the empire. Under this type of grant, called "measured transfer" *(liang-i),* those affected were moved to some "nearer place," presumably nearer the capital. Although this measured transfer was most frequently a benefit accorded to officials who had been disgraced and exiled and not to ordinary criminals, there are a number of examples of ordinary exiled criminals being transferred. A *ta-she* from the year 875 says:

> . . . Demoted and exiled officials may in a measured way be transferred to nearer jurisdictions *(tso-chiang kuan liang-i chin-ch'u).* Those who have already been so transferred may again be granted measured transfer. . . . Men in exile [that is, criminals sentenced to *liu*] and men in exile because their original death sentences were reduced [should be] transferred to nearer territories *(liu-jen chi chiang-ssu tsung-liu che i chin-ti).* . . . The various sorts of exiled and demoted men, where within the original imperial order it said "even if there is an act of grace [this individual] is not within the limits of [benefiting from] measured transfers" [but who] after the act of grace of the twelfth day of the tenth month of last year already [were given] a measured transfer to five thousand *li* may again be granted a measured transfer to one thousand *li.* Those previously granted a measured transfer to three thousand *li* may again be given a measured transfer to five hundred *li.*[76]

Criminals who had been transferred might look forward not only to more transfers but eventually to being wholly freed. Degraded officials, after two transfers, might next be "reranked" *(fu-t'zu).*[77]

Lu Chih, in a series of memorials which apparently date from the early years of the ninth century, described the system and its flaws in some detail. He paints a sorry picture of the plight of the families of officials who, on learning of the granting of the grace, rushed to prepare for their return journey, only to find months being consumed by the paperwork associated with the system. He was also critical of the disparity between the moderate practices of earlier times (when men were moved by stages of only three hundred to five hundred *li*) and the lenient practices of current times which led to bitterness and confusion among those clustered near the capital.[78]

The old practices of which Lu Chih speaks may well have been those followed during the reign of Hsüan-tsung (713–756), under whom the system of measured transfer seems first to have become common. During and after his reign, acts of grace frequently included provisions for the granting of measured transfer. The great majority of those eighth and ninth-century *ta-she* which include neither permission to return nor measured transfer are obviously defective, in the sense of being highly abbreviated. Since most of the longer decrees contain such provisions, it seems reasonable to suggest that at least during this era they were a regular if not a required part of *ta-she*.

Compared to the seventh century this practice represented a liberalization of T'ang amnesty policy. This same trend toward liberalization was also reflected in the increasing frequency with which empirewide ordinary acts of grace were issued. The first three T'ang emperors issued relatively few,[79] while the Emperor Hsüan-tsung (r. 713–756) issued more than twenty during his reign of just over forty years. This pattern of frequent empirewide ordinary acts of grace continued into the late T'ang, ending only at a point where the sources clearly become highly defective. The lack of such acts during the last quarter century of the dynasty is almost certainly a result of faulty sources; the lack for the first two emperors may be attributed with equal certainty to deliberate policy on their parts. In particular the Emperor T'ai-tsung (r. 627–650) was noted for rarely giving empirewide amnesties. Early in his reign he said to his attending ministers:

> In this world there are many stupid men and few intelligent ones. The intelligent are not willing to do evil; the stupid love to break the laws. Generally the grace of amnesties should only reach to those not truly evil. There is an ancient saying, "The good fortune of petty men is the misfortune of sagely men. In one year to give repeated amnesties

makes good men cry out." In general to nourish the weeds does injury to the crops; to treat solicitously evil villains injures good men.[80]

His pattern of restricting ordinary acts of grace was rarely repeated in later reigns, though the Emperor Te-tsung (780–805) issued no empirewide amnesties during the last ten years of his reign.[81]

The T'ang distribution of ordinary acts of grace follows an obvious trend: from being very rare to being very common. The T'ang distribution of great acts of grace echoes in striking fashion the pattern of the Han. Given with some frequency (one every twenty-seven months) by the founder Kao-tsu (r. 618–627), they were sharply restricted (one every fifty-five months) by his successor T'ai-tsung (r. 627–650). Under the third emperor, Kao-tsung (r. 650–684), they were issued on average once every forty months—less frequently than under Kao-tsu but more frequently than under T'ai-tsung. Under the rulers that followed Kao-tsung, the T'ang moved quickly to a policy of issuing grants with great frequency, a policy that by and large was continued until the end of the dynasty.[82]

Since between the fall of the Han and the Sui–T'ang reunification (with the exception of the brief interlude of Western Chin) the area of China was divided between a number of competing states all but two of which were short-lived, it is difficult to assess the meaning of changes in amnesty frequencies during the lifetime of an individual state. Nevertheless, taken overall, the frequency with which amnesties were granted is in itself revealing. From the founding of the Chin in 280 to the fall of the T'ang in 907, a great act of grace was issued on the average of once every eighteen plus months. The most liberal states during this era were the southern states of Ch'i and Sung: grants every thirteen months. The most conservative was the northern, barbarian-controlled state of Northern Ch'i: one great act of grace every twenty-seven months.

The contrast between the northern states with their partly foreign ruling groups and the southern refugee states with Han Chinese ruling elites is revealing, particularly in light of later developments under foreign dynasties. The Northern Wei, Northern Ch'i, and Northern Chou averaged one great act of grace every twenty-three plus months. The Sui (twenty-one months) and the T'ang (twenty-two months) should doubtless be included in this northern grouping. By contrast the southern states issued a plenitude of great acts of grace—Chin, Liu Sung, Ch'i, Liang, and Ch'en averaging one grant every fifteen months.[83]

These differences between north and south must not be allowed to overshadow the striking general pattern in which they form mere variations–in medieval China, on the average of once every two years or less, the state opened up its judicial doors, returning to society almost all of the criminals in its grasp and preventing forever the prosecution of those who had succeeded in eluding it. The docket was cleared, the jails were emptied, the open cases were closed–all in a manner without precedent elsewhere in the world. This remarkable system, so well portrayed in the code and decrees of the T'ang, reached its fullest development under the succeeding dynasty, the Sung (960–1279).

chapter 4

Acts of Grace
in Sung China

LIKE its predecessor the Han, the T'ang dynasty ended in political fact decades before it ended in name. Its division into rival power centers dominated by military men preceded by decades the final snuffing out of formal T'ang rule in 907. But unlike the Han, the era of division which followed was relatively brief. China was again divided into a number of competing regimes and short-lived dynasties, but within these states the trend toward recentralization proceeded apace. In 960 a successful general displaced the child emperor of the state of Latter Chou (951–960) and founded the Sung dynasty (960–1279). During the ensuing decades the Sung founder and his successor reunified almost all of China proper, except for a small slice of territory inside the Great Wall held by the sino-foreign state of Liao.

The T'ang and Sung form a fascinating matched and mismatched pair. In some ways the later state was a faithful imitator of its illustrious predecessor. The Sung Code, for example, is virtually a copy of the T'ang Code amended only in minor ways.[1] Thus most of the T'ang provisions concerning acts of grace described in the preceding chapter applied in law during the Sung. And yet in style and tone the dynasties were radically different. The T'ang was brilliant, cosmopolitan, lyric, the great age of Chinese poetry; the Sung was elegant, refined, a culture whose measure may perhaps be indicated by the observation that four of the greatest writers of prose in all of Chinese history lived at the same time, and knew one another, during the last half of the eleventh century.

This new culture of the Sung period was the product of both social and technological change. The late T'ang and Sung periods saw the rise of new urban mercantile groups, conscious of their own identity, and patrons of new cultural innovations. The same era also saw the invention and spread of printing, vastly increasing the possibilities for widespread literacy. One result of the rise of printing is a change in the nature of our source materials for Chinese history. For the T'ang and earlier periods of imperial history we depend to an unfortunate extent on the products of official historiography. For the Sung and later times we can supplement or replace these works with the voluminous products of private scholarship.

Printing, by sharply decreasing the cost of books, made possible the rapid spread of literacy among the growing urban mercantile groups as well as among well-to-do rural landowners. The spread of literacy contributed to the rise of popular literature and to a growing interest in scholarly pursuits, including the study of history. The Sung is considered one of the two great ages of history writing in traditional China. Some of these works dealt with earlier times, but a few dealt with the Sung itself. Describing the Northern Sung (960–1126) we have the voluminous and excellent annalistic history called the "Rough Draft for a Continuation of the Comprehensive Mirror" *(Hsü tzu-chih t'ung-chien ch'ang-pien)*—usually referred to by Sung historians as the *Rough Draft*. For the Southern Sung (1126–1279) the record is far less complete. There are some fine histories dealing with limited parts of the latter period, but nothing to match the *Rough Draft*.[2] This great work, when supplemented by the standard dynastic history of the Sung and other annals, makes possible the compilation of a list of Northern Sung acts of grace that appears to be nearly exhaustive. The statistics derived from this list provide a picture of the traditional system of acts of grace in its classic form. They also raise a host of questions (which they cannot answer) about its impact on the social order.

The various histories, in combination with compilations of official records, encyclopedias, individuals' collected writings, and other miscellaneous sources, also offer a wealth of information on certain aspects of the operation of the amnesty system. In detail this material is of interest only to specialists in Chinese administration and law; in its broad outline it is valuable because it demonstrates conclusively the continued use of T'ang practices by Sung rulers. During the Sung, as under the succeeding dynasties, the same types of criminals were treated in much the same way under the same sorts of acts of grace.[3]

This continuity in the working of acts of grace was made possible by continuity in the punishments inflicted. There had been a number of changes in detail—according to the Sung Code, the penalties classed as penal servitude were replaced by beatings on the back with the heavy rod, and exile was in practice a general term for a variety of punishments which differed somewhat in their conditions. But, speaking broadly, the Sung (and later dynasties) continued the pattern of subjecting criminals to execution, restriction of liberty plus labor, loss of status, and beatings.[4] Thus the statistics on the Sung may be read in the light of T'ang usage.

As under previous dynasties, great acts of grace were the most significant grants. During the three hundred and nineteen years of the Sung (960–1279) great acts of grace were issued on one hundred and ninety-five occasions—once every nineteen months on the average.[5] One hundred and fourteen of these grants were issued during the Northern Sung (960–1126), one every seventeen plus months, and eighty-one are recorded for the one hundred and fifty-three years of the Southern Sung (1126–1279), an average of one every twenty-two months. This difference is due at least in part to the inferior quality of Southern Sung sources.

This poverty of materials is also probably a major reason why the sources record far fewer empirewide ordinary amnesties *(ch'ang-she)* during the Southern Sung: only eighteen for the period 1126–1279 (one every hundred and two months). Few of these come from the last seventy-two years of the Southern Sung, a period for which our records are especially poor, while seven occur during the (relatively well described) reign of the first Southern Sung emperor, Kao-tsung (r. 1127–1163). By contrast thirty-eight such acts are recorded for the Northern Sung (one every fifty-two months).[6]

The weaknesses of Southern Sung sources reduce the value of statistical analysis of acts of grace in the period; the fullness of Northern Sung records makes possible a more suggestive evaluation of the effects of amnesty on the lives of Sung criminals. These effects naturally would have varied with the sentence involved. Those sentenced to death would have been freed by a great act of grace or would have had their sentences reduced by an ordinary act of grace (1) if they had not been caught when the amnesty was issued, (2) if their crimes had not yet come to light, or (3) if they were involved in the judicial process. The first two situations require no particular interpretation; the third raises some problems. If we are trying to evaluate the likelihood that a capital criminal already in custody would be executed (assuming for the moment that the evidence of his guilt was clear), one factor obviously would be the amount of time taken up by the judicial process between arrest and execution. If the process took eighteen months, and acts of grace came every seventeen months, then no criminals (under ordinary circumstances) would ever have been executed. Unfortunately no information seems to be available concerning average process time. We can, however, make an informed guess in the light of an analysis of the trial procedures followed in capital cases.

After the arrest of a suspect on the subprefectural level, he was held in jail until a hearing at which he and any witnesses were interrogated, possibly with the use of judicial torture. The results of this process were recorded as a "preliminary finding" *(chieh-chieh).* This record, and the accused, were then sent to the prefectural level where the case was "reviewed" *(shen-k'an).* If the results of the prefectural authorities' examination agreed with those in the preliminary finding, and they felt the penalty recommended to be appropriate, the materials were then sent to the circuit level. The circuit officials again checked the records and perhaps dispatched special investigators (or went themselves) to investigate the facts. If they were satisfied they wrote a report and forwarded it to the capital. In the capital the case went first to the High Court of Justice *(ta-li ssu),* where after review and approval it was forwarded to the Ministry of Justice *(hsing-pu)* for further review. If the ministry concurred with the high court, the case next went to the emperor for his approval. If he accepted the verdict calling for execution, the officials were required to resubmit the execution order to him several times so that he might have the opportunity to change his mind.

Only when all these formalities had been completed was the death sentence passed back through channels for transmission to the local authorities who would carry it out. Any disagreement at any point in the line would tie the case up in further discussion and review.[7] Sometimes this process could be greatly drawn out. One official (admittedly citing the instance to make his point about delays) noted that a case of a man guilty of homicide had dragged on for a year and a half—and had been reinvestigated and reversed seven times! The man kept confessing, and the higher authorities kept overturning the rulings of their subordinate jurisdiction. (In this case the court finally had to dispatch a special commissioner to bring the confusion to an end.)[8] And one amnesty speaks of the necessity of investigating prefectures having jurisdiction over cases that had "already taken a year or more and have not yet been settled."[9]

No adequate figures exist showing the time consumed in Sung trials, but data based on an analysis of Ch'ing dynasty archives for Tanshui and Hsinchu indicate that three months after the initiation of criminal cases more than half of them had not yet been decided by the court of first instance.[10] In serious criminal cases calling for execution, this first-instance decision would automatically have been followed by review of the case at higher levels, including review at the capital.

Obviously, under both the Ch'ing and the Sung, many months must have passed between the arrest of an ordinary criminal and his execution. This elaborate process can rarely have taken less than half a year—and that only for simple and unambiguous cases. During some later dynasties, such as the Ch'ing (1644–1912), there were circumstances under which local authorities could carry out summary executions, but such swift "justice" appears to have been very rare during the Sung. Some writers on Sung law have suggested that in many instances capital cases could be decided on the local level alone, without the elaborate review process. Although there is some evidence that this happened during some periods, there is a great body of evidence which indicates that during most of the Sung the review process was in force for most cases.[11]

Thus, for a person guilty of a capital crime, the critical span of time was not that between two acts of grace but that between two acts of grace minus the judicial process time (which we can tentatively suggest probably did not average less than six months). Anyone arrested

served this full forty-two months in distant exile our hypothetical (and supremely unlucky) criminal would have had to commit his crime immediately *after* the issuing of the 965 amnesty, been apprehended and seized on the spot, and been interrogated, tried, reviewed, and transported instantly. If we make the assumption that commission of crimes calling for exile was more or less evenly distributed in time, then the average exile in this long barren stretch (still assuming instant arrest and judicial process) would have had to serve only twenty-one months before seeing his lot improved. The mean length between acts of grace under T'ai-tsu was eighteen months, so even retaining the fiction of instant judicial process and assuming the worst possible case (committing the crime on the day after the last amnesty), the maximum sentence before relief would have been eighteen months and the average term nine months. Figure 1, which gives data for the other Northern Sung emperors, indicates that under the least openhanded emperor (Che-tsung; r. 1086–1100) the average exile would have served only nine and a half months before transfer whereas under the most liberal (Hui-tsung; r. 1101–1126) his term would have been a mere four and a half months.

Traditional China had not learned the secret of instant justice, however. Pursuit, arrest, trial, review, and transportation all took time. Cases of exile passed through the same initial stages as cases calling for the death penalty including a limited review at the capital. Because the central review process in cases calling for exile was not elaborate, the total trial time was doubtless shorter than in the average capital case. After trial and review the exile still had to be moved to his destination, a process which during much of the Sung was not carried out during the coldest months of the year.[14] Even during the temperate months exiles were moved only periodically, so that a man might have to wait some time before he was set out upon the road.[15] If we assume that the entire process took four months, then under no emperor would the average exile have actually remained at his supposed place of registration for a full half year.

Those sentenced to the most distant and fearsome places of exile would have had to pass through several amnesties before being freed. But even in their cases the chances of being freed within a few years were good. To return to the worst possible case, a man with the su-

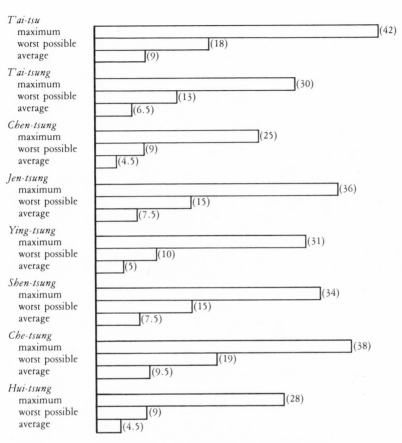

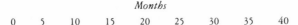

Figure 1. Time Spent at Place of Original Exile

This chart assumes instant judicial process and transport—that is, a man moved from arrest to his place of exile instantly. The maximum figure indicates the longest elapsed time between empirewide amnesties. The worst possible case is the mean length of time between empirewide amnesties and reflects the theoretical fate of a man arrested immediately after the last amnesty, tried, convicted, and transported instantly to his place of exile. The average is an attempt to convey some sense of the probable fate of the average criminal. It assumes that crimes calling for exile were more or less evenly distributed in time—that is, in a stretch between amnesties half the crimes calling for exile would be committed before the midpoint and half afterward. Thus it is this last, and by far the smallest, figure which is probably the best indicator of how much time the average exile actually spent at his place of original assignment—always with the proviso that the judicial process itself took no time at all.

preme ill fortune to have committed a crime punishable by exile at the worst possible point in the Sung dynasty (immediately after the amnesty of May 965), who had been arrested on the spot, tried, convicted, and moved to his place of exile by the time the sun set on that day, would have been a completely free man six and a half years later. During much of the Northern Sung an exile initially sent to the worst places would have been free within two years. Furthermore, we should remember that, except for the truly unpleasant maximum security locations, an exile's "punishment" consisted chiefly in the beating he received before he left for exile and the labor he did there. Except for those serving in the armies, an "exile" who had been transferred from these unhealthy places and whose term of labor was over was being punished in only a nominal way. True, his liberty was restricted. He could not return to his home place or travel about at will. But there is some question (for the Sung period) of how serious a penalty this was. Indeed we have rulings which say that men who have been freed should not be forced to leave the area where they were registered or to give up their army registration if they wanted to remain as they had been.[16]

The lot of those accused must not be romanticized. Life in Chinese jails was grim, and the time spent awaiting trial or transfer was unquestionably unpleasant and often dangerous. No doubt such time in jail was frequently a harsher punishment than life in the place of exile. Many men died before being tried, or perished en route to their places of exile, and in the worst exile locations the death rates were doubtless also quite high. But our figures suggest that in the better-run prefectures the death rate among prisoners was probably not a great deal higher than among the population at large (though in the worst prefectures it might run to ten percent a year). And the Sung authorities did attempt to penalize the jurisdictions with the worst records and reward those that had the best records of prisoner health.[17]

Probably the group least affected by acts of grace were those suffering the lightest punishments—those that merely involved beating with the light or heavy rod. In the Sung the district magistrate could try and punish with up to one hundred blows of the heavy rod on his own authority without submitting the case to review by higher authorities. Moreover, cases of nominal penal servitude commuted to beating did not have to pass beyond the prefectural level, so that the time consumed was probably far less than in serious crimes. Once a beating had been inflicted the arrival of an amnesty would seem merely a grim joke. Thus the punishments most likely to be inflicted under the Sung were the lightest ones.

On first looking at the statistics there is an understandable tendency to wonder whether in fact the system worked. How could a society simply turn loose its serious criminals? And why would it do so? These questions need to be placed in perspective. We in the United States turn loose a very sizable percentage of the small part of our serious criminal population that we manage to arrest, try, and convict. Our society survives despite a penchant for putting criminals back on the street. Why not traditional China? Still, such a perspective does not deal with the major question. Did the Chinese actually enforce these acts of grace? Do we have here a fictive system? Or was this system honored in the observance rather than the breach?

The answer to this last question seems to be a clear, if qualified, yes: the state did free people by means of amnesties. The yes must be qualified for at least two reasons. First, when a document of amnesty arrived freeing men in exile, local officials were required to fill out a report describing the circumstances of the crime and the behavior of the criminal since his arrival in exile.[18] By stressing the seriousness of the circumstances or the convict's bad behavior, officials could in some cases prevent his release. Or they might prevent release irrespective of the crime by stressing the importance of the prisoners to their jurisdiction (if, for example, the convicts were serving as border guards). This power obviously lent itself to abuse by harsh officials.[19] Second, we know of men (such as the father of Ch'en Fu-liang) who remained in jail without being released by acts of grace, and we have reports of cases continuing through several amnesties.[20] And yet there is a great weight of contrary evidence of various sorts which indicates that as a rule acts of amnesty were effective.

To assume that the system was a fiction we would have to believe either that the emperors never intended that their orders be obeyed, or that low-level local officials, career civil-service functionaries appointed and holding tenure at the goodwill of the emperors, had the nerve to ignore solemn and personal expressions of the ruler's will, countermanding by inaction the sovereign's personal expression of grace and benevolence. The first alternative is highly implausible, given traditional Chinese political beliefs. The second possibility seems equally unlikely. We cannot say that open flouting of the imperial will did not happen, but those familiar with traditional Chinese government will recognize that except in times of dynastic decay it was not likely to have been a common practice.

Again, how are we to explain incidents such as the case under the Emperor T'ai-tsung, when that ruler became furious because the case against a corrupt official had not been completed prior to an amnesty? The emperor wanted to issue a special order that the criminal be excluded from grace, but he was dissuaded by a court official who argued that "when the emperor performs the Suburban Sacrifice and hands down grace it reaches to the world." No specific individual ought to be excluded. T'ai-tsung rescinded his order.[22]

Why such concern to keep secret the dates on which amnesties were to be issued? Officials urging secrecy were fearful that men who knew the dates of upcoming amnesties might commit crimes, confident that they would soon be freed. In a typical comment on this problem the administrator of the Bureau of Policy Criticism *(chih chien-yüan)* remarked (in 1055) that "one amnesty per year is called by the people the 'warm grace' *(je-en)* because it always comes in the fifth or sixth month. Corrupt clerks and evil bandits rely on it in committing evil and wait so as to avoid [punishment]." If the system was but a polite fiction, how can such comments and concerns be explained?[23]

Why such specific directives on how to treat certain limited categories of wrongdoers? If no one would be affected, why issue special instructions touching specified groups or barring certain criminals from benefiting?[24] If the system was a fraud, why should officials ask for a rule that criminals be meted out swift justice some days prior to upcoming acts of grace? (Their request was not accepted.) Or why ask that certain crimes (such as violent robbery) committed in the months immediately prior to such a grant be excluded from coverage? Why regulations excluding from grace certain criminal acts committed after the announcement that the emperor was going to offer the triennial great sacrifices but before the arrival of the act of grace which always accompanied these sacrifices?[25]

Why should their more punitive colleagues accuse overly merciful officials of deliberately seeking delays even in simple cases so as to keep them in process until an act of grace occurred? Or of handing down lenient sentences because they knew there would soon be a pardon issued? And why would accused persons seek so stubbornly to delay the proceedings—faking illness, injuring themselves, claiming to be pregnant, falsely claiming to be overage or underage, arguing that they had official status or were protected by the official status of a relative, or refusing to accept judgments where their guilt was clear? Such deceptions could only increase their punishment—unless, that is, they were spared through amnesty.[26]

Why should a functionary complain that minor misdemeanors by officials haunted them for a lifetime while even bandits and killers were absolved by acts of grace? How is one to explain the popular sayings of the 1120s—that to get ahead quickly in the official world nothing beat becoming a bandit and waiting for a pardon or that "if you want office kill men, commit arson, and wait for a pardon."[27] And why should administrators be concerned about the care with which local officials attended to the system of records ostensibly to be used in assessing the status of convicts at the time of amnesty? Or about the system used for distributing the letters of amnesty and recording their proper implementation?[28]

How can we account for the creation of detailed provisions to cover odd cases—as when local amnesty was awarded to a jurisdiction in which the leader of a gang had been captured while his followers were elsewhere? (They were also to be cleared.)[29] How are we to explain the multitude of historical anecdotes—the Sung official Yang Kao, attacked by a murderer he had captured after the killer had been released by an act of grace; or the rich man Li Chia (sentenced to die because of the murders committed by his gang of cutthroats) being exiled following an amnesty; or the man of the Po family who, having killed a man, was spared by an amnesty and became "even more overbearing than before, so that the villagers stood in fear of him"?[30]

Even the abuses of the system are evidence of its general effectiveness. If it was but a fictive system, there is simply no way to explain the actions of those officials who were guilty of summarily trying and punishing prisoners because they knew an amnesty was forthcoming. Their behavior is explicable only if we assume that they knew that the amnesty was going to be enforced and did not want their charges to escape unpunished.

We must also assume that the system was actually enforced if we are to understand the continuing litany of complaints about the frequency with which amnesties were offered. The emperor had expressed his will. If this expression was purely nominal, what conceivable reasons would a career bureaucrat have for flatly disagreeing with his lord, bluntly saying that the emperor was contributing to an increase in the crime rate? There are dozens of such diatribes during the history of the system.

Added to all these reasons is the impression left by the sheer weight of the materials that bear on the detailed functioning of the system. For the Sung there are literally hundreds of rulings that touch on the performance of the system. No one who reads through the voluminous references in the *Sung Collected Documents* can come away without the conviction that the rules were followed with considerable care.

The system worked. It freed people. We know that it did not work perfectly, but even if it worked most of the time it is still an astonishing phenomenon.[31] And it is important to remember that the figures given in the preceding pages represent the minimum level of grace. Not only is it possible that a few general amnesties escaped the eye of the historical compilers, but I have made no attempt here to integrate local amnesties, of which there were over a hundred during the hundred and sixty-six years of the Northern Sung. Many of these affected only small sections of the empire, but others covered a number of circuits and thus affected areas inhabited by a substantial percentage of the empire's total population.

Even when these local amnesties are added to the total the picture is incomplete, for the Sung also witnessed the full development of another facet of the system of acts of grace: the amnesties referred to as an "inspection of cases" *(lu-ch'iu)*. The practice of these inspections of cases began in the Latter Han when emperors personally examined cases from the capital area. During that era the process was avowedly aimed at uncovering abuses of justice and expediting the judgments against the guilty as well as freeing the innocent. In practice the process often led to reductions of sentence or release of prisoners. The procedure was continued under a number of the states of the post-

Han period. At times the emperor himself took part in the inspections; in other cases he detailed subordinates for the task and might even send men out into the prefectures to conduct the investigations. It seems not improbable that such subordinates would lack the emperor's power of discretionary grace, and that when the emperor was absent the emphasis would be on justice rather than mercy, but the sources for this era are so tersely worded that it is not possible to assess the effect of the procedure on the prisoners involved.[32]

From the beginning of the T'ang dynasty the emperors adopted this practice of imperial inspection of cases. Ch'en Ku-yüan, without citing any evidence, maintains that the custom was common to all the T'ang emperors, though not noted in the annals. Certainly it occurred with some regularity, and the outcome of these inspections was ordinarily either the reduction of sentences or the freeing of the men involved.[33]

The practice reached its fullest development under the Sung. In the eighth month of 966 the Sung founder, T'ai-tsu, "went to the Hall for the Discussion of Military Affairs *(chiang-wu tien)* and himself inspected the cases [from the capital] of Kaifeng. In all, several tens of men were freed."[34] Under the second emperor this inspection of cases in the capital became a regular practice which occurred (with rare exceptions) at least once a year. All the succeeding rulers seem to have continued this practice, and under some of them, in some years, two or even three inspections might be held.

It was clearly recognized that these inspections had in fact become amnesties, not primarily reviews. In a compilation of Sung laws we are told that "in all cases where [a text] says 'grace' *(en)* this refers [equally] to acts of grace and reductions of sentence. [Where a text] says 'reduction' *(chien)* this [refers] equally to ordinary acts of grace *(te-yin)* and inspections of cases *(su-chüeh)*."[35]

Although most references merely speak of the inspection of cases, there are longer examples which explicitly exclude certain crimes. The most commonly excluded crimes were homicide and the Ten Abominations, followed by certain crimes by clerks and civil or military officials—rapacity, judicial abuse and corruption, and robbery within their areas of jurisdiction. A few orders also excluded those guilty of making counterfeit official seals, arson, aggravated assault, or robbery with violence, as well as those "not spared by ordinary amnesties."[36]

Those included are identified in more general terms. Many orders merely say that "prisoners" had their sentences reduced or were freed *(chien-yüan)*, but enough examples specify what sorts of sentences were to be treated in what ways to indicate the general pattern of grace. Although there are a few cases in which the grants seem not to have included capital criminals (merely reducing the sentences of those subject to exile or less), in the great majority of cases criminals liable for the death penalty as well as those liable for exile or (converted) penal servitude all had their sentences reduced one degree—that is, from death to exile, from exile to penal servitude, and so on. Men liable only for beatings were freed.[37]

In granting grace the responsible Sung officials distinguished their prisoners according to the sentence to which they were liable and the circumstances of the original crime. If these circumstances were deemed serious, a criminal might find his sentence merely reduced while others liable for the same sentence were being freed. If the officials judged the circumstances particularly worthy of pity, a man might be freed while his fellow prisoners were only granted reductions. As with the T'ang Code we are not always given a simple definition of seriousness or lightness, such specifications having been set down in the rules called *ko* in the Sung (now largely lost). However, enough examples of such *ko* remain to indicate that the moral tone of the criminal act as evidenced by its circumstances, as well as the prisoner's age and physical condition, influenced the ruling officers.[38]

In describing their reasons for inspecting cases Sung rulers usually point to exceptional weather conditions—great heat in summer or cold in winter, persistent rain, or drought. These anomalies are indications that the *yin* and *yang* forces are out of balance, thus obstructing the "harmonious ether" *(ho-ch'i)*. At least since Han times it had been widely said that delayed cases or other judicial abuses could result in such natural portents. Thus the rationale for these frequent acts of grace was phrased in traditional terms.[39]

The vast majority of notices which specify a place speak of the emperor inspecting cases for the capital area. Although such reviews were restricted in the area covered, their importance should not be underestimated. Early in the Sung period men sentenced to death were all sent in person to the capital for their regular review.[40] Thus until well into the eleventh century any capital case review would have affected a greatly disproportionate share of those criminals liable for execution. Moreover, throughout the dynasty the capital was not only the largest of the empire's cities but also the home of a majority of officials, clerks, and military officers. Even if the inspection of cases had been confined to this one city the system would have been important. There is also a sizable body of evidence which indicates that such inspections, accompanied by reduction of sentences or liberation of prisoners, were also conducted on a regular basis outside the capital.

During the Southern Sung it seems possible that local inspections were carried out at least once, and possibly twice, a year. Clear references dating from the Northern Sung are rare, but there are indications that even during that period, at least on some occasions, the grace associated with inspections was extended to the whole empire. In 989, after he had inspected cases in the capital, the emperor separately ordered forty-two officials to go and inspect cases throughout the empire. And four years later, after completing his capital inspection, he issued an imperial decree ordering that

> among the currently incarcerated men in the various circuits, excluding those guilty of the four sorts of homicide and officials guilty of being principals in abuse of the law or rapacity, all others if their crimes carried the penalty of death are to have this reduced to exile, and those with exile or lesser [sentences are to have their sentences] reduced one degree. Those [liable for] beating with the heavy rod or less are to be freed.[41]

Half a century later the statesman Ts'ai Hsiang, criticizing the frequency and regularity with which grace was extended, said: "I have noted that in recent years, during the hot summer months, the emperor personally goes to inspect the cases of prisoners held in the capital, [and] orders that those guilty people throughout the empire have their sentences reduced."[42]

The information from the Southern Sung indicates clearly that after 1163 inspection of cases took place annually and affected the whole empire. A decree of 1163 says:

> Every year at the time of great heat there ought to be an inspection of cases. In the prefectures of the various circuits we assign the responsi-

bility for this to the Judicial Intendants, who, during the sixth month, are to go to visit all the places under their jurisdiction, to judge and decide current outstanding cases. Where the circumstances are not serious, in a ordered way, [the men involved] should be released. In the prefectures and subprefectures of rustic and distant places the prefectural [authorities] should assign the responsibility to administrative officers. For the subprefectures the duty should fall on the active prefectural vice-administrator *(t'ung-p'an)*. For each case [the responsible official] should write out a report on the existent circumstances and send this up to the Department of Ministries *(shang shu sheng)*. From this time this was done every year.[43]

In the following year the procedure was modified. The Secretariat-Chancellery *(chung-shu men-hsia sheng)* had expressed concern because the inspection of cases did not begin until the arrival of the order in the local jurisdiction. In far distant areas such as Kwangtung, Kwangsi, and Szechuan the order only arrived after the heat of summer had passed. On their recommendation it was ordered that in these areas the Judicial Intendants proceed with their inspection of cases in the sixth month, even if the order had not reached them from the capital.[44] As in the capital, it seems that those subject to the death penalty or less had this reduced one degree, and those liable only for beating with the heavy rod or less were freed.[45]

When an official expressed his concern that in some distant prefectures Judicial Intendants might seek to escape the burdensome duties involved in such inspections by calling even nearby areas "distant and rustic" (thus passing the buck to their subordinates), the court not only agreed to reiterate its orders to Judicial Intendants but also accepted his suggestion that other intendants be called in to aid their judicial colleagues.[46] The circuit of subprefectures was to take place between the last fortnight of the fifth month and the middle of the seventh month. A record of the dates of the arrival and inspections by the supervisory personnel was to be kept. If these were not the intendants, the intendants were expected to check their subordinates' reports before sending them on to the capital.[47] In the early thirteenth century a winter inspection was added to the summer one, prompting one commentator some years afterward to complain that this merely drove local officials into carrying out summary trials, even by lamp-light, so that no evidence of the procrastination would be left when the inspector arrived.[48]

Inspections of cases began from the opening years of the Southern Sung. In 1132 the emperor personally inspected the cases. From this time on the practice became an established custom which continued into the closing decades of the dynasty.[49] In this sense perhaps we should not say that during the Southern Sung ordinary amnesties were rare, but that they were annual events, masquerading under the title of "inspections of cases."

Even if we assume that these various orders and decrees were not fully enforced, the cumulative effect of the plenitude of acts of grace, local amnesties, and inspections of cases paints a picture of traditional Chinese justice very different from the image set forth, however dim-ly, in most books about China. Dynasty after dynasty released those who had been swept between the millstones of the law. This practice never lacked for critics. K'uang Heng and Wang Fu of the Han were followed by a seemingly endless succession of men who attacked the frequent issuing of acts of grace. Since their diatribes, from first to last, hammer away at the same points, we can let one of the most ar-ticulate stand for them all. The great Northern Sung historian and statesman Ssu-ma Kuang spoke out bluntly, repeatedly, and at length against what he saw as the dangers in the system:

It is my humble opinion that the granting of acts of grace does a great deal of harm and brings few benefits—that it is not good government policy. The *Canon of Shün* says, "Inadvertent offenses and those which might be caused by misfortune were to be pardoned, but those who have offended presumptuously or repeatedly were to be punished with death." This means that if someone caused injury through error or mis-take they are to be pardoned, but if they deliberately persevered in evil they were killed. This most certainly does not reflect a system which liberates both the innocent and the guilty! . . .

Now the rulers of our dynasty have conformed themselves to the in-tent of Heaven. They have been truly devoted to the people, and in is-suing orders and commands have always put first acting humanely. But the evil of frequently giving amnesties has not been stopped. Moreover acts of grace in former times were issued irregularly, and were carefully kept secret until they were issued. Their terms and scope could not be known beforehand. Even so, corrupt people acted outrageously in anticipation of forgiveness. How much worse is the situation nowadays when every three years, without fail, at the time of the Suburban Sacrifice a [great] act of grace is issued, and every single year, in midsummer, there is an inspection of cases?

Treacherous clerks practice corruption on a grand scale, to their great benefit; ruthless people act with obstinate perversity, encroaching on and insulting the good. Only one or two out of hundreds and thousands are destroyed. And if through sheer good luck their crimes are uncovered they all go into hiding. Within a year they always meet with an act of grace or a decrease of sentences and then with calm effrontery come forward and are thereafter treated as common citizens. These acts are so frequently expected that men refer to them as "hot-weather decrees."

Honest men are embittered and made fearful; the evil crowd see their aims fulfilled and their spirit in the ascendant. How could this possibly be in line with the imperial intention of serving as the parents of the people, encouraging the good and repressing the evil? Furthermore, inspection of cases was originally undertaken during the heat of summer out of a concern that in the jails there might be men whose cases had been delayed, or improperly decided without being reported up by officials, so that those affected had no way of protesting. Therefore the emperor, being himself concerned, looked into this in order to straighten it out. Thus the innocent would be pardoned, but the guilty would be punished. Men long imprisoned would find their cases dealt with in a single morning. In this way the evil ethers could be dispersed, and the great harmony be reestablished. It was absolutely not a matter of turning everybody loose without even inquiring about their guilt or innocence.

Under your imperial ancestors there was only one inspection of cases in a single year, as a result of which sentences of death or less were all reduced by one degree. In recent years sometimes there are repeated inspections which completely free people sentenced to penal servitude or less. And during the first five months of this year there have already been two inspections, causing the officials to be disheartened and confused, and the dissolute to be insolently angry.

It may not now be possible to completely get rid of this long-standing problem, but I hope you will send down a special directive informing the Secretariat that from now on there is to be only one inspec-

tion per year, and that this is sometimes to take place early in the year
and sometimes late so that those outside the government will not be
able to anticipate it. Those liable for penal servitude will, in accordance
with the old system, merely have their sentence reduced to beating
with the heavy rod. Furthermore in those years when you perform the
sacrifices in the southern suburb [and hence offer a great act of grace]
you will not additionally conduct an inspection of cases. I hope this can
be made the fixed rule so that evil men will not dare to hope that they
can benefit from your liberality, but shall stand forewarned and fearful.[50]

Ssu-ma Kuang, as Confucian moralist and concerned patriot, spoke
out again and again, in a voice of restrained but fervent outrage,
against a system he could do nothing to abolish and little to change.
It was perhaps his good fortune not to know that the policies he so
eloquently advocated, which were to be the pattern for all the succeeding dynasties of imperial China, were already in use, under the
hated and feared sino-foreign enemy regime of the Khitan Liao.

chapter 5

Late Imperial China:
The Significance of Change

DURING the last half century of T'ang rule a new power had emerged in what is today southern Manchuria. A tribal people, the Khitan, taking advantage of the growing weakness of their Turkish overlords, had established a Chinese-influenced state in the area north of Korea. During the period of division which followed the collapse of the T'ang in 907, the Khitan intervened in the politics of the North China plain at the request of one of the contenders for power there. When, with Khitan help, this contender defeated his opponents, he ceded territory within the Great Wall to his tribal allies. With the region north of Peking and south of the wall as the heart of their Chinese holdings, these tribesmen established a dual sino-foreign kingdom called Liao (907–1125). Their administration, a mixture of T'ang and foreign elements, retained tribal law for tribal peoples and used T'ang law, modified to some degree, in controlling Chinese subjects.[1]

In adopting a (modified) T'ang Code the Liao state was following a pattern which was to be imitated by all its successors. For a millennium dynasty after dynasty copied large sections of the T'ang Code almost verbatim into their own legal compilations. Changes in laws occurred and deserve far more intensive study than they have yet been given, but changes in the codes were less striking than than changes in the ways in which the actual law functioned. In reading late imperial materials, including those on acts of grace, one can for general purposes assume that regulations rather like those of the T'ang were still in force.[2]

Materials for the study of law under the Liao are very limited, but it is nonetheless clear that, like their Chinese neighbors to the south, they promulgated acts of grace in the T'ang manner. What little evidence we have suggests that in terms of rituals and coverage their amnesties faithfully followed T'ang models.[3] But while they retained the external shell of the amnesty system, they radically altered its social and legal role and created a pattern which was to be retained by all their successors down to the end of the empire in the early twentieth century. Without altering the details of the system they transformed its impact by drastically reducing the frequency with which acts of grace were proclaimed. The Sung issued great acts of grace once every twenty months on average; the Liao issued them once every seventy-eight months.[4] One Liao emperor, on the throne for thirteen years, issued only one great act of grace. His immediate predecessor, who had reigned for eighteen years, did not issue a single great act of grace. Nor were the Liao rulers liberal with ordinary amnesties—only twenty-three were issued during the two hundred and eighteen years of Liao rule. Only the Emperor Hsing-tsung (r. 1031–1055) approximated the traditional pattern: he issued eight great acts of grace in twenty-five years.

Is this striking decline in the number of acts of grace due simply to the poverty of our sources? Certainly records for the Liao are far less complete than they are for the T'ang or Sung. Yet they do not seem to be less complete than those for many of the pre-T'ang states from whose very partial records we can still trace the pattern of frequent amnesties.

That the change was real and not illusory is also suggested by the example of the sino-foreign state of Chin, which replaced the Liao in North China during the 1120s. The Chin controlled far more Chinese territory than had the Liao, and its ruling group became far more sinicized. Furthermore, we know that the rites used in issuing Chin amnesties were virtually identical with those used under the Sung.[5] And yet, in the frequency with which they issued amnesties, the Chin proved themselves heirs of the Liao and not imitators of their southern neighbors. Great acts of grace were proclaimed approximately once every five years.[6] Again the pattern was broken only by a single emperor, Hsüan-tsung, who reigned from 1213 to 1224. During the disastrous wars against the Mongols, as Chinggis troops battered the Chin defenses, this emperor issued amnesties with classic liberality, one act every nineteen months. But except for this aberrant interlude, the Chin continued the Liao pattern of making acts of grace in practice what they had always been in theory—extraordinary and unusual grants of mercy.

In the 1230s the Mongols finally destroyed the Chin state, and half a century later they eliminated the last remnants of the Sung. For the first time in imperial history the whole empire had fallen victim to outside invaders. During the first period of their rule the Mongols continued to use the laws and legal practices of the Chin in controlling their Chinese subjects. But in the late thirteenth century Chinese officials in the Mongol administration began pressing for the compilation of a new code. The new compilations which eventually were produced drew heavily on T'ang law as well as on the codes of Chin and Sung.[7]

Though the Mongol rulers drew on the T'ang and Sung for some of their laws, they maintained the Liao–Chin pattern in their acts of grace. Between the accession of Qubilai in 1260 and the fall of the dynasty in 1368, great acts of grace were issued on average once every seventy-six months. If we carry the record back to the time when the Mongols first entered North China during the reign of Chinggis, then the average falls to one every hundred and two months. (The few Yüan rulers who do not fit this pattern all had brief reigns.)[8]

In 1368 this succession of sino-foreign states was displaced by a native Chinese dynasty: the Ming. Proudly conscious of their Chinese heritage, Ming authorities sought to emphasize their ties with the native dynasties of the past. And yet in many ways they were the heirs of the sino-foreign dynasties of North China. Their military system, their civil administration, and their legal structure all bore traces of foreign influence. For their laws the Ming drew heavily on T'ang patterns, but they arranged their codes in a manner reminiscent of Yüan compilations. And in their amnesty policies they carried on the pattern of their immediate predecessors and did not hark back to the T'ang or Sung. During the two hundred and seventy-six years from 1368 to 1644, Ming emperors issued only thirty-four great acts of grace—one every ninety-seven months.[9] Again we see repeated the pattern of the Yüan: the only emperors to issue amnesties with any frequency were men who reigned for relatively brief periods.

Eight Ming emperors had relatively short reigns of ten years or less. Collectively they sat on the throne for only forty-four of the Ming dynasty's total of two hundred seventy-six years, yet they issued almost a third of the great acts of grace recorded for the Ming. This pattern, where frequency of amnesties is inversely related to length of reign, is revealed even more strikingly by the long-reigning monarchs. Shen-tsung, the longest-reigning Ming emperor, who held the throne for forty-eight years, did not issue a single great act of grace (and issued only six ordinary acts of grace). The Emperor Shih-tsung, who reigned for forty-five years, issued only three great acts of grace, and the Ming founder, on the throne for thirty-one years, also issued only three *ta-she*.

Like their immediate predecessors, the Ming rulers were sparing in their use of ordinary acts of grace, issuing only twenty-five during the whole of the dynasty. Even in the seventeenth century, when they were beset by domestic unrest and foreign wars, Ming rulers did not become more liberal in their policies.

The rapid decay of Ming administrative efficiency during the seventeenth century prevented effective repression of banditry and contributed to the rapid increase in the power and prestige of a newly founded sino-foreign state centered in southern Manchuria. During the 1620s the rulers of this state adopted the name Ch'ing for their dynasty. In 1644, when Chinese rebels captured Peking, Ch'ing armies were able to seize their opportunity and gain control of North China. Although forty years were to pass before Ch'ing rulers were in complete control of China, they had begun, even before the conquest of 1644, to borrow Chinese imperial policies.

The first man to rule inside the Great Wall, the Shun-chih Emperor (r. 1644–1662), temporarily reversed the late imperial trend toward a restrictive issuing of amnesties. Empirewide amnesties were issued in nine of the eighteen years he was on the throne (and in two of these years he issued two separate acts). Although this policy continued during the early years of his successor K'ang-hsi (while that ruler was under the domination of the regent of Oboi), when K'ang-hsi assumed personal control of affairs the flow of acts of grace was drastically reduced. Empirewide amnesties were issued in four of K'ang-hsi's first six years on the throne. Then, in 1667, Oboi fell from power. Only seven empirewide amnesties were issued during the last fifty-six years of K'ang-hsi's reign—an average of one every ninety-six months. His successor, the Yung-cheng Emperor (r. 1723–1736), issued amnesties only during the year of his accession, and the long-lived Ch'ien-lung Emperor (r. 1736–1796) issued only eleven acts of grace in his sixty-year reign. This restrictive pattern, originating during the troubled early years of K'ang-hsi, continued through the peace and prosperity of the mid-Ch'ing and extended on through the increasing disorders of the late Ch'ing, unaffected by the changing fortunes of the dynasty.[10]

This reluctance to issue empirewide amnesties does not mean that Ch'ing rulers were not aware of policies governing acts of grace. Ch'ing sources on amnesties are amazingly rich. The Ch'ing Code contains many dozens of references to the effects of amnesties, including long lists of crimes covered and excluded. The General Principles section of the *Conspectus of Legal Cases (Hsing-an hui-lan)* is filled with references to the implementation of acts of grace. Together with materials from the *Veritable Records* and such compilations as the *Ta Ch'ing hui tien,* these sources deserve a separate volume. They demonstrate that in the Ch'ing there was an abiding concern with the amnesty system, but they also indicate that these acts were issued relatively infrequently.[11]

The impact of this less liberal policy on those involved in the criminal process was to some extent offset by the system of case reviews and (restricted) reductions of sentence that were called the "assizes" *(shen).* Assizes could not wholly take the place of the amnesty system, however, since many of them only affected capital criminals. And in any event none of them could provide relief to criminals as yet uncaught or to criminals already serving their sentences.

The origin of these assizes is sometimes traced to 1459, when Ming authorities "ordered that every year, after the 'Frost Descends' [*shuang-chiang,* approximately October 23 to November 6], the Three Legal Offices *(san-fa ssu)* should meet together with the nobles to review serious [that is, capital] cases. This was called the Court Assizes *(ch'ao-shen).* Successive reigns then honored this practice."[12]

In fact the system is directly descended from the Han practice of "inspection of cases" *(lu-ch'iu)*. This Han practice had passed by way of the T'ang not simply to the Sung but also to the sino-foreign Liao state. According to the Liao History, on twenty-three occasions during the two hundred and eighteen years of Liao rule inspections of cases were conducted.[13] In recording these inspections the annals of the Liao History almost always note merely that "there was an inspection of cases *(lu-ch'iu)*." In only one case does it report that "criminals sentenced to death for miscellaneous crimes, and those sentenced for lesser crimes, were freed." Two of the reports indicate that, on occasion, inspections could take place in local areas as well as the capital. In light of T'ang practice it seems probable, though unprovable, that such inspections during the Liao were mostly confined to the capital, involved the participation of the emperor, resulted in reductions of sentence for many criminals, and freed those liable for minor punishments.[14]

The Chin (1115–1234) apparently were reluctant to adopt this practice from their Liao predecessors or their Sung contemporaries. A decree found in the Treatise on Law of the *Chin History* says:

> The court each year repeatedly sends out reviewing and inspecting officials *(shen-lu kuan)*. Originally this was done out of concern that the people might be suffering from judicial abuse and delays, yet those sent out frequently do not have their hearts in their work, and merely write out documents. Officials charged with reviewing and inspecting must not only inquire concerning [cases calling for] heavy punishments, but in all cases, and pliants must study them to see if the facts are true or false. If those in prison ought not to be held then they should be freed.[15]

However, the first instance of this practice recorded in the annals occurred in 1164, almost half a century after the founding of the Jurchen state. The next such entry in the annals comes only in 1196.[16] After this, during the last three decades of the dynasty's life, such reviews are noted as occurring every few years.

This scattering of Chin references provides the bridge which links the assizes of later times with the case inspections of preceding dynasties. This transition is reflected in the general term for the officials involved *(shen-lu kuan)*—officials for "inspecting" *(lu)* as in "inspecting cases" but also for "reviewing" *(shen)*, the same character which in later dynasties is translated "assizes." Furthermore references in the annals (presumably drawn largely from the *Chin Veritable Records*) are phrased almost identically with references to Ming assizes recorded in the *Ming Veritable Records*.[17]

In the early thirteenth century this Chin state was first raided and then overrun by the armies of Chinggis Khan and his successors. Although the brief annals of these first Mongol leaders do not mention any such inspections of cases, these begin again from early in the reign of Qubilai (r. 1260–1295). In 1262 it was ordered that in the various circuits officials "carefully examine and rule on *(hsiang-chüeh)* law cases involving judicial abuse," and two years later "officials were dispatched to various circuits to inspect cases *(lu-ch'iu).*" Five more times during Qubilai's reign, and on almost a dozen occasions during the first quarter of the fourteenth century, the authorities ordered such inspections. Some of these inspections dealt with cases in the capital, but the phrasing of the annals entries suggests that the majority involved the dispatching of commissioners to the circuits. Apparently inspections usually resulted in a triage of cases—the most serious criminals were punished after the review, but those whose offenses were less grave had their sentences reduced, and petty crimes calling for beatings were pardoned.[18]

Within half a century of Qubilai's death the Yüan dominions were wracked by internal disorder. From the middle of the fourteenth century on, the Mongols suffered a succession of defeats at the hands of Chinese rebels, who soon became less concerned with destroying the remnants of Mongol power than with fighting one another. The Mongols had become of minor significance militarily, but their dynastic institutions provided a model for the Chinese pretenders to the throne. When Chu Yüan-chang succeeded in defeating the other claimants and founded the Ming dynasty, he largely maintained the institutions and practices of his Mongol predecessors.

Chu Yüan-chang and his heirs further developed the inspection process, which for the first time was consistently referred to as a system of "assizes" *(shen)*. It is said that during the opening years of the dynasty the emperor himself participated in the interrogation of those involved in major cases. But by the early 1380s this involvement apparently had become impractical (perhaps because the abolition of the post of prime minister in 1380 had increased the general administrative burden on the emperor). In the tenth month of 1381 the Hung-wu Emperor decided that he would participate in the interrogations only if they involved military officers liable for the death penalty. He dispatched censors to the local areas to review and judge legal cases. Criminals liable for the death penalty were to be sent to the capital where their cases would be tried by the chief legal officials, who would render a judgment and submit their work for review by other officials. The deliberations of this reviewing body would in turn be sent to the emperor. (Similar procedures were followed in the winter of 1382 and the autumn of 1383.)[19]

In these instances from the reign of the Ming founder the emphasis seems clearly to have been on the rendering of strict but fair justice. The Hung-wu Emperor is reported to have remarked that "in inspecting cases *(lu-ch'iu)* what is most important is really to get the facts, and have the punishment correspond to the crime."[20]

The third Ming ruler, the Yung-lo Emperor (r. 1403–1425), not only continued his father's practice of holding assizes in winter but occasionally called for assizes in the autumn and began the practice of the Hot Weather Assizes *(je-shen)*. In the fourth month of 1404 he said to his chief legal officials:

> The weather is still hot. Those who have been in jail for a long time will certainly become ill. [If] those who become ill are not given help they will certainly die. Thus those who committed [capital] crimes where the circumstances were not grave will still die. How does this differ from killing through abuse of legal power?

He ordered the high legal officials to review all capital cases within the next few days and to divide them into two groups—those charged with grave offenses were to be held in jail until autumn and then executed; those whose crimes were less serious were to be exiled after judgment. Three years later, in the autumn of 1407, he broadened the scope of review by freeing men sentenced to exile or less. Although this act of 1407 was exceptional in that it freed men sentenced to exile, it did set a precedent for the review of noncapital cases; under later emperors this review often resulted in such men having their sentences reduced at the time of the Hot Weather Assizes.[21]

This pattern of sentence reduction (which might be granted at either the Hot Weather Assizes or the Autumn Assizes) appears first under the Hsüan-te Emperor (r. 1426–1436). Those guilty of certain grave capital crimes (such as rebellion or banditry) were to be executed "according to statute." Those guilty of the lesser capital crimes would ordinarily have their sentences reduced to exile at the frontiers. Men sentenced to exile or penal servitude might be allowed to commute their penalties to money payments, and those merely liable for beatings were freed.[22]

These Ming assizes were a halfway house between the case inspections of the Sung and the practices of the Ch'ing. Like their Sung antecedents, they affected all levels of criminals and resulted in most cases in the granting of some benefits. But the term used for them (shen) and related terminology were to be taken up by the Ch'ing. And, as under the Ch'ing, great stress was laid on the importance of dividing capital cases into two groups—those deserving immediate execution (li-chüeh) and those not deserving it. Furthermore there is some evidence that these Ming assizes occurred at least in part out of doors, most often at one of the gates of the capital, highlighting their similarities to both the Ch'ing assizes and the traditional acts of grace.[23]

During the Ming the timing of these assizes varied widely. The Yung-lo Emperor is credited with originating the annual Hot Weather Assizes, which (depending on the source cited) occurred either prior to the calendrical period called "Grain Fills" (hsiao-man) (approximately May 21 to June 6) or during the following ten days. The Spring Assizes, which occurred in the second month, were started under the Hsüan-te Emperor (r. 1426–1436). The T'ien-shun Emperor (r. 1457–1465) began the Court Assizes (ch'ao-shen), which took place during the autumn following the period "Frost Descends" (shuang-chiang)—approximately October 23 to November 6. In 1481, under the Ch'eng-hua Emperor, a system called the Great Assizes (ta-shen) began. These were to be held every five years. And finally, only a few years before the collapse of the dynasty, the authorities drew on precedents from the reigns of the early Ming emperors to justify the beginning of Winter Assizes (tung-shen).[24] In addition to all these reviews in the capital (and in part associated with them in time), the authorities sometimes dispatched commissioners to local areas to review cases or assigned that task to active local officials.

An examination of material in the *Veritable Records* for several dozens of years scattered through the Ming leaves the impression that the most commonly held assizes, the Hot Weather Assizes, were held during most years of the fifteenth century, but they were not always held during the sixteenth or early seventeenth centuries. The Court Assizes were held less regularly than the Hot Weather Assizes, and the other assizes apparently even less often than the Court Assizes. Moreover, other sources report explicitly that in certain periods the assizes did not occur, and emperors on occasion refused to agree to the conducting of the reviews. In short, although it seems that an assize of some sort was conducted during most years of the Ming dynasty there were also numerous years where no review at all occurred.[25]

Ch'ing (1644–1912) legal policies and institutions were patterned after Ming prototypes. In borrowing the general Ming pattern for reviewing cases the Manchu conquerors also took over the assize system, including both the Hot Weather Assizes and the Autumn Assizes. In 1651, seven years after the Manchu armies came through the Great Wall, the emperor issued a decree reviving the Hot Weather Assizes. In his explanation he said:

> The weather is still hot. For days on end there have been winds and dust storms, and no rain. Former dynasties had a regular substatute *(li)* on Hot Weather Assizes. The Ministry of Justice *(hsing-pu)* must thoroughly investigate criminal cases. The offices of the five capital wards, of Shun-t'ien Prefecture, and of the capital districts each should investigate cases. Those [prisoners] not [themselves personally] involved [who have been brought in because they were] connected [with a case] are to be released immediately. [Criminals liable for the punishments of] the heavy or light rod, penal servitude or exile, are in a graded way to have their punishments reduced or forgiven. [As to those capital criminals] the circumstances of whose crimes are pitiable or doubtful, an imperial ruling may be requested on their cases.[26]

A further ruling several years later indicates that at each assize the provincial authorities were expected to submit to the Ministry of Justice a report on cases under their jurisdiction which called for reduction, so that the ministry could solicit imperial authorization.[27] During the Shun-chih period (1644–1662) and the early years of K'ang-hsi (r. 1662–1723) these reviews seem to have been conducted at least in part by special "Officials for Relieving Punishments" *(hsü-hsing kuan)* commissioned by the Ministry of Justice. A decree of 1669 indicates that these special officials were no longer being appointed; as a result, responsibility for the Hot Weather Assizes fell on the local officials, who were to follow the same substatutes used in the capital in assessing and reducing punishments.[28] Apparently later in the reign of K'ang-hsi the Hot Weather Assizes were abandoned, for in the first year of his reign the Yung-cheng Emperor (r. 1723–1736) "revived the substatute on Hot Weather Assizes." These summer reviews and reductions of sentence continued well into the reign of the Ch'ien-lung Emperor (r. 1736–1796), but they seem to have been abandoned in the nineteenth century.[29]

Perhaps because the Hot Weather Assizes were no longer being held when Westerners first began studying the Ch'ing legal system, these summer reviews have been largely ignored, although from the viewpoint of the great mass of prisoners held for lesser crimes they must have been of far more moment than the annual reviews of capital cases. Had they been held regularly, they would have reduced the penalties of innumerable convicts.

The Hot Weather Assizes have been overshadowed in descriptions of the Chinese judicial system by the much better known, and more spectacular, reviews of death sentences sometimes held in the Ch'ing capital in the autumn. Two assizes were to be held. The Court Assizes *(ch'ao shen)* handled cases originating in the capital itself where the sentence called for execution after the assizes rather than immediate execution. The Autumn Assizes handled such cases when they originated outside the capital. As described by Bodde and Morris:

> The Autumn Assizes were scheduled for a day within the first ten days of the eighth lunar month (sometime during September in Western reckoning, by which time, according to the Chinese calendar, autumn was already about half over). Their locale was not far south of the T'ien-an men or Gate of Heavenly Peace, along the west side of the

broad *Ch'ien pu lang* or Esplanade of a Thousand Paces which leads southward from the T'ien-an Square toward the main south gate of Peking.

Although the walls flanking the east and west sides of the Esplanade were each lined on their inner face by a row of small cell-like rooms, it would seem from the wording of the sources that the assizes were not held in these rooms at all (which would have been too small), but in the open air in front of them. There, on the appointed day, several tens of tables, topped by red cloth coverings, were set forth for the participating jurists, who included prominent officials from the Nine Chief Ministries (*chiu ch'ing,* that is, the six boards together with the Court of Revision, the Censorate, and the Office of Transmission), as well as other dignitaries such as the tutors of the imperial heir apparent.

This mixed body examined the "after the assizes" cases and confirmed or altered their provisional classifications. From the *Ta Ch'ing hui-tien* (53/2a) we learn that the various stages of the proceedings were reported in a loud voice and "listened to by the multitude of the humble"—statements indicating that these highest judicial proceedings, like those in the lowest district court, were open to the public. The whole description carries a strongly archaic flavor, reminiscent of the tradition, as described by van Gulik, of "the Priest-King of hoary antiquity, holding court in the open, in the shade of a tree." We may strongly suspect that in the overwhelming majority of cases, the judgments reached in public by this ad hoc body during its one-day session were little more than *pro forma* ratifications of the decisions already privately reached by the officials really professionally concerned. The Court Assizes were the same as those of autumn save for the added feature that their condemned criminals, being all from Peking itself, were allowed to appear in person in order to utter a final plea for themselves.[30]

Cases were classified in decreasing order of seriousness: (1) those where the circumstances called for execution *(ch'ing-shih);* (2) those where the final judgment should be deferred, which meant in practice that the convicted person was to be held in prison for another year *(huan-chüeh);* (3) those where the circumstances were either pitiable or doubtful *(k'o-chin k'o-i);* and (4) those where the criminal might remain at home to care for his parents *(liu-yang).* Bodde and Morris continue:

Following the conclusion of the Autumn and Court Assizes, the results of the classifications then arrived at were submitted to the emperor so that he might examine them prior to a final climactic ceremony at which he confirmed the disposition of the various categories. For the Autumn Assizes this ceremony took place some sixty days before the winter solstice or around October 21, and for the Court Assizes some ten days before the solstice or around December 11. At dawn on these two days, high officials, including presidents or vice-presidents of the nine ministries mentioned earlier, representatives of the Grand Secretariat (a kind of inner cabinet), and others, assembled in the Hall of Earnest Diligence *(mou-ch'in tien)* located in the northern part of the Forbidden City. To mark the solemnity of the occasion, all wore funeral garb of plain undecorated white, the Chinese color for mourning. Our sources describe in great detail each move that followed. We can summarize by saying that the sub-chancellor, kneeling, placed the lists of the condemned on a table in front of the dais on which the emperor was sitting. Apparently the lists included the names of all those placed in the three categories leading to reduced punishment, as well as the fourth category of "circumstances deserving of capital punishment." It was only for the latter, however, that the ceremony was of crucial importance.

Having received the lists, the emperor inspected them and indicated his approval either by marking them himself with his vermillion brush or having a grand secretary do this on his behalf. In particular, with regard to the list of persons in the category of "circumstances deserving of capital punishment," he checked off *(yü kou,* "gave a hook to") the names of those actually destined to die.

Curiously, the Chinese sources, despite their specificity on the steps leading up to this crucial moment, fail to explain how the checking itself was done. For this we have to turn to two of our English-language sources which, though differing slightly, obviously represent a common tradition. Alabaster states that the names of the condemned were written on a large sheet (more probably it was several sheets) "not alphabetically, or by chance, but so that the names of those prisoners who are, in the opinion of the board, less guilty than the others are placed either at the corners or in the center. The list is then submitted to the Emperor who, with a brush dipped in vermillion, makes a circle on it at seeming, and to some extent real, hazard, and the criminals whose names are traversed by the red line are ordered for execution. The others remain on the list until the next year."

Chang Yü-chüan writes somewhat differently that "on the day fixed, the Emperor held a Court, and ordered a Grand Secretary to use the vermillion pen and make a bracket on the list of the capital offenders. . . . Those whose names were enclosed within that bracket were to be executed forthwith, while those whose names were outside the bracket remained in prison and were again brought back to try their luck the following year."

Chang's account seems more probable than Alabaster's, since the procedure described by Alabaster would allow all names not actually touched by the brush to escape execution, and this would probably be an inordinately large number. Be this as it may, it is striking to see the long progression of highly rationalistic procedures in capital cases culminating in a ceremony resting upon magic and the charismatic insight of the emperor.

What happened to those whose names were not checked off? They were kept in prison to reexperience the ordeal a year later. Those guilty of family offenses, if they twice succeeded in escaping the vermillion brush, then had their classification changed to "deferred execution," and their death penalty was reduced to a lower punishment. If, however, the convicted belonged to the subcategories of either officials or ordinary persons, they then had to escape the vermillion brush no less than ten times before achieving the status of "deferred execution." By the law of averages, obviously few persons could thus escape the brush ten times running unless, as seems likely, the names of some were in fact consistently arranged in such a manner as to insure that they would not be checked.[31]

Western writers, and most Chinese commentators, in describing this assize system, speak of it as an annual, spectacular affair. Actual practice was far less simple than this picture suggests. In some years the classic form of assizes, held at the regular time, did take place. Yet a check of events recorded for the autumn months as noted in the *Veritable Records* for a set of years picked at ten-year intervals suggests that this was not always true. In part this discrepancy reflects the Ch'ing practice of setting different deadlines for the review of capital cases in different provinces. These would have been reviewed as they arrived, using the basic assize practices. The *Veritable Records* also contain individual, piecemeal, reviews. Thus in some years the assize processes were no doubt carried out, but in such a way that they are not obvious to the historian. Though this may have been the case in most years where there is no record of the regular assizes, during some years the assizes were suspended as a result of deliberate imperial choice. Early in the Ch'ing assizes were suspended with some regularity: the K'ang-hsi Emperor suspended them on seven occasions during his sixty-two-year reign. Most often this was done shortly after other acts of grace, on the grounds that there were few capital cases left for consideration.[32] Unfortunately the situation for the late Ch'ing is less clear since the compilations that would reveal how often assizes were suspended in the early and middle Ch'ing were not compiled for the nineteenth and early twentieth centuries.

Suspending the execution of criminals, after having finished the assizes, appears to have been much more common than suspending the assizes themselves. This practice was described most succinctly in a ruling from the sixth year of Ch'ien-lung that "the Court Assizes and the Autumn Assizes be carried out in accordance with the substatutes. The 'hooking' and execution of those men really deserving of capital punishment *(ch'ing-shih)* should be suspended."[33]

The reviews themselves were to be conducted. Those who were to benefit would benefit, but in addition those who would have been liable for execution were also permitted to live, at least for another year. During the last forty-five years of the reign of K'ang-hsi death sentences were suspended in twenty-one years. (And in seven other years the assizes themselves were suspended, thus deferring the regular executions.) During the last decade of his reign no regular executions held after the assizes seem to have occurred.

This same pattern was retained by the Yung-cheng Emperor (r. 1723–1736). Executions held after the assizes were suspended in eight of his twelve years on the throne. The Ch'ien-lung Emperor, during the first two decades of his rule, suspended executions after the assizes in ten years. During the last forty years of his reign, however, he abandoned this practice, suspending executions on only two occasions.[34] (Taken together these practices suggest, as Bodde and Morris observed, that long-term imprisonment was a common Ch'ing punishment in fact if not in name.)[35]

In assessing the impact of these policies it should be borne in mind that although Ch'ing review practices did cover certain noncapital cases, the Autumn and Court Assizes were only concerned with those sentenced to die. Moreover, as Bodde and Morris indicate, of crimes punishable by death in Ch'ing China, over forty percent called for immediate execution. Those guilty of such acts could never benefit from the Autumn or Court Assizes. They ordinarily faced only a local trial, the regular review, and a quick death. (Of course, lacking statistics on the frequency with which the different crimes were committed we cannot know what proportion of capital criminals on average this percentage of crimes would have covered.)[36]

Furthermore, particularly during the late eighteenth and nineteenth centuries, some parts of China were under martial law or summary law. This trend toward increased legal violence reached its height during the "eradication campaigns" launched by nineteenth-century local officials in southern China. Current research suggests that in these (admittedly limited) areas summary executions of large numbers of people, after perfunctory trials by locally responsible officials, were not uncommon.[37]

Finally it appears that even when acts of grace were issued they may have reached fewer categories of criminals than they had in T'ang and Sung times. The Ch'ing Code, like the code of the Ming, had a special article entitled "[crimes] not pardoned by ordinary amnesties":

Those guilty of one of the Ten Abominations, of homicide, of stealing state property, of robbery, of theft, of arson, of violating graves, of accepting profit from illicit activities with or without abusing the law, of fraud, of sexual crimes, of kidnapping, of selling kidnapped persons, of seducing and detaining persons, of having illicit liaisons or using deceitful words and spreading false doctrines which cause men to die, of having deliberately convicted an innocent person or deliberately declared innocent a guilty person, of knowingly tolerating or abetting [a criminal], of hiding criminals, of showing them ways to escape, of acting as an intermediary in collecting [criminal] monies, and all other delicts of these sorts which are actual crimes (all these delicts being committed voluntarily and with intent), even if [such criminals] meet with an [ordinary] amnesty they are not to be [wholly] pardoned.[38]

The substatutes which follow this statute in the Ch'ing Code go beyond even this broad list in excluding crimes from being wholly

pardoned by amnesty. In some cases these substatutes are merely clar-
ifications of categories included in the main statute—as when the laws
against heretical sectaries are made explicitly applicable to members
of the White Lotus sect. Other substatutes actually extend the scope
of the groups excluded, as when all cases involving military supplies
and equipment are excluded from amnesty pardons. Finally the
Ch'ing authorities also compiled long lists of unpardonable crimes.
For the most part the individual items in these substatutes merely
spell out the content of the general categories given in the statute—
that is, the rubric "sexual crimes" was meant to include such things as
rape of a girl under twelve years of age, sexual relations with the wife
of a brother, and so on. But some additions are made: commanders
responsible for the loss of fortified positions, both principals and followers in abortion and mutilation, and several more. Perhaps most
striking are the large number of sexual crimes noted and the fact that
a number of crimes specifically concern military personnel.[39]

As in the T'ang and Sung such exclusion appears to have meant
simply that those guilty of the crimes specified were not to be completely pardoned by an amnesty. It did not necessarily mean that they
would not benefit at all. The Ch'ien-lung list says specifically that
"the above are [crimes whose perpetrators] from of old have not been
allowed to adduce [acts of grace] to avoid *(mien)* [punishment]."
There were also, however, a number of substatutes which specified
that for certain crimes amnesties could not be adduced at all or could
not be adduced to reduce punishment.[40]

These lists appear to indicate that the scope of Ch'ing amnesties
was more restricted than that of amnesties issued in the T'ang and
Sung. T'ang and Sung amnesties seem never to have specifically excluded sexual crimes (except those covered by the incest section of the
Ten Abominations or sexual assaults by social inferiors against those of
higher status). Moreover, crimes by military men, such as recidivism
among those deserting while on campaigns, which are included in
Ch'ing lists, rarely appear in earlier sources. Some of these differences
are probably due to flaws in our sources. Still the evidence does raise
the possibility that more crimes were excluded from Ch'ing acts of
grace than from the amnesties granted in the middle period.

How are we to interpret the picture presented by all these facets of the late imperial system of grace? When the Ch'ing materials have been subjected to the intensive study they deserve, the implications of the materials noted above may have to be modified, but at our present stage of studies they do seem to suggest that any criminal who fell into the hands of the law was less likely to benefit from official acts of grace than his predecessors in crime during the period of the Han through the Sung. For some reason the authorities in this later era found themselves able to, or felt compelled to, treat criminals less leniently (at least as far as acts of grace were concerned) than had been the case in earlier times. This transformation leaves us with two critical questions. Why did governments in the earlier period let their criminals go? And why did governments in the later period abandon this policy?

chapter 6

The Uses of Amnesty

DURING the first millennium of the Chinese empire the system of acts of grace was a most striking aspect of traditional Chinese justice. The sources set before us the spectacle of a great empire which opened the gates of its jails every few years, forgave those uncaught, wiped all outstanding cases from the books, dismissed those in process of trial, pardoned men sentenced to death, and often sent home its exiles. Even if we assume, as we should, that the system never worked perfectly, the materials available to us nonetheless make clear that the system worked to an astonishing degree most of the time. In his *Oriental Despotism* Karl Wittfogel paints a grim caricature of the traditional Chinese state. We are told that ancient China was (to borrow the heading of one of his chapters) "Despotic Power—Total and Not Benevolent."[1] Without in any way prejudging the motives of the Chinese emperors I think we must say that in practice, from the viewpoint of those most directly affected by it, the traditional Chinese judicial system was often astonishingly benevolent. This tradition of grace was most marked from the Han through the Sung. Then, around the end of the first millennium A.D., a new and stricter tradition grew up. Appearing first under the sino-foreign state of Liao, this tradition was passed on through the Chin, Yüan, and Ming to the last of the imperial dynasties, the Ch'ing. We must not forget that even in late imperial China acts of grace continued to be issued on a scale which in other areas of the world would have been startling, but compared to the earlier imperial era they came few and far between. How are we to explain the earlier practice and its metamorphosis?

In justifying the issuing of amnesties the records themselves, of course, stress the role of the ruler's will, his concern for the welfare of those unjustly accused or imprisoned, his merciful benevolence. We obviously should not be so fatuous as to accept such assertions at face value, and yet we should not be so cynical that we deny them all meaning—surely occasional Chinese rulers were disturbed by injustice practiced against the ruled.

I have also tried to demonstrate that this amnesty system can be seen as a reflection of the belief that the emperor had the power to cleanse individuals of their taint and reintegrate them into the social body. Obviously late imperial emperors did not wholly reject this belief, since they continued to issue amnesties, albeit less frequently than their predecessors. Perhaps their reluctance to issue amnesties frequently reflects a changed attitude toward the use of undoubted imperial powers—a new attitude consonant with both the northern tribal view of the imperial role, with its emphasis on the ruler as military leader, and that expounded in the writings of the neo-Confucians, with its stress on unqualified obedience.

A related ideological phenomenon is the connection of these acts with portentous events. It is obvious that many members of the elite in Han times, and some in later times, sincerely believed the proposition that human misbehavior (of certain sorts, on the part of certain types of people) could produce ill omens and natural disasters. Miscarriages of justice, and justice too long delayed, were often said to be responsible for disturbances of the harmonious blending of natural forces.[2] Again, without overestimating the weight of such beliefs as causes, we should not discount their role in prompting emperors to issue acts of grace.

Short-run political considerations are another factor of obvious importance. Newly enthroned rulers might wish to reassure potential enemies; men on shaky thrones might wish to strengthen their position. In times of external danger rulers might see amnesties as acts which could contribute to the fullest possible mobilization of national support against the enemy.

Yet such explanations can only be partial. The system of regular amnesties seems only to have appeared with the founding of the empire. But short-term political considerations are always with us. They were surely no less pressing in preimperial times than under the empire. And the emperor's role as a grantor of grace also preceded the unification under the Ch'in. These factors existed *before* the policy began. By contrast the belief that miscarriages of justice caused natural disasters became widespread during the era when the policy of frequent amnesties was developing, yet that policy continued long after such beliefs had lost their hold on the elite.

Another explanation—partial, tentative, and hypothetical—may be found in the fact of empire itself. Perhaps it is not fortuitous that the policy of granting frequent amnesties blossoms almost from the beginning of the unified state. But how could the mere fact of empire contribute to the rise of such a policy? One answer may be sought in the changed possibilities for mobility and escape. Before the unification of the empire people accused of crimes could, and did, flee from one kingdom to another. Geographical movement provided them with the opportunity for a new beginning. But with the founding of the empire such escape became more difficult. There was no place that was not the empire (except the lands of the barbarians). Those in trouble with the law could, and did, flee to the mountains and marshes, but the outlaw life in such havens can hardly have been as pleasant as the life of a nonservile person in a feudal state.

Thus the pressures that could be relieved in preimperial times by flight into another feudal state now needed some other release. Periodic grants of grace could provide that release. A man sought for a crime, or in process of trial, or serving a sentence, could know that his predicament was not hopeless. Sometime soon the state would act to relieve his situation. Behavior which might have been born of desperation was in this way aborted. Those not yet caught might be induced to avoid further, more serious, crimes in the hope of imminent pardon. Those serving sentences might be less tempted by possibilities for escape or feel less driven to revolt when they could foresee future relief.

Such a conjecture is difficult to support and impossible to prove. Even added to the other factors already noted it still leaves the system only half explained. The true key to its growth and maintenance is rather to be sought in a set of institutional constraints which bounded the traditional Chinese state.

Historians dealing with the government of China in traditional times run the constant danger of being spellbound by its elaborate formality. There is a great temptation to forget that the government was tiny—tiny, that is, when its manpower is measured against the numbers of the governed and the size of the territory controlled. The magnitude of the problem can perhaps be indicated by noting that during the Southern Sung, when there were between fifty and sixty million people under Sung rule, the civil service seems to have numbered only about twelve thousand officials.[3] Although the size of the population varied (as did the size of the government staff) the general proposition remains nonetheless true—the traditional Chinese government was simply too small to govern in an intensive manner. And yet, despite this constraint, the government still claimed to be the locus of authority. Private justice was, in theory and usually in practice, antithetical to the state's pretensions.

One result of this disparity between means and professed ends was a policy followed by all dynasties of restricting the state's role in the adjudication of many matters falling under what we would call civil law. The authorities reserved much of their judicial attention for problems we would label criminal. But even under this self-imposed limitation the state's official resources were overextended. In the Southern Sung when there were about twelve thousand members of the civil service, approximately two-thirds worked in the capital. The officials acting outside the capital were thinly spread in three organizational levels: the circuits, the prefectures, and the subprefectures or districts. Only the eight hundred or so subprefectures, on the lowest of these three levels, had direct daily administrative contact with the populace. Here we have a situation in which some eight hundred judges of courts of first instance (subprefects) were bound in law to handle the criminal problems (and some civil problems) arising among fifty to sixty million people. Even this reckoning understates the absurdity of the situation, for these judges, as administrators of their districts, were responsible not only for legal matters but for all other phases of local government.

Even if by some miracle these magistrates had succeeded in processing the criminal cases that accumulated, the state lacked sufficient facilities for controlling large numbers of long-term prisoners. Except during limited periods there were no prisons per se: detention was not a form of punishment. There were only jails designed to hold people before trial, during trial, and prior to punishment.[4] At places of exile or penal servitude, security facilities were rarely adequate. (Local officials often complained about the threat to good order posed by large numbers of convicts in their jurisdictions.) With rare exceptions (such as sea islands or army posts in distant frontier areas) people who really wanted to flee could do so with relative ease. If they remained "in exile" they did so in part because it seemed the prudent or safe course, not the only course.

In practice the state's personnel and facilities were grossly inadequate to hold, process, and punish (through detention) a large number of criminals. But the attitudes of Chinese rulers were heavily influenced by the ideas of the legalists who placed great emphasis on the state's swift and implacable punishment of wrongdoers. To preserve this prerogative of the ruler, the judicial and penal functions were in theory and to a large degree in practice reserved to the officials. The police function, embodying mere instrumental authority, was widely disseminated in order to facilitate the capture of a significant proportion of criminals. Indeed to some extent every man was his brother's keeper, responsible in part for his misdeeds and charged with detecting and reporting his crimes. Moreover the state appointed large numbers of commoners to serve without pay in positions which had police functions.[5] The military establishment was also used to deal with serious breakdowns of social order. One result of this imbalance between the development of the police power and that of the judicial and penal systems was an unmanageable burden of cases and prisoners.

Prior to the establishment of the unified empire the difficulty of controlling prisoners for long terms had been dealt with by corporal punishment. Men had their feet or noses cut off or were otherwise mutilated. Having exacted its retribution the feudal kingdom could be less concerned about the problem of confining criminals.[6] In later times too these "flesh punishments" were a favorite nostrum suggested by advocates of a harsh judicial system. Their reinstitution was rarely attempted, perhaps because the truly critical problem of the legal system was elsewhere—in its underdeveloped capacity for processing cases. Not wanting to surrender the prerogatives of its sovereignty, and understandably chary of simply permitting criminal behavior to go unapprehended, the state authorities were forced into a peculiar dilemma. They escaped it by retaining a relatively effective police system which could apprehend (and thus in theory frighten) a sizable number of criminals, and then obviating the judicial pressure by periodically purging the apparatus.

The problem was thus in outline a simple one. Fifty million people could commit far more crimes than eight hundred judges could handle. Even if the judges were faced with only a tiny fraction of the misdeeds of a population this size they would be overwhelmed. Some safety valve had to be designed to relieve the pressure of business. We should not expect that authorities compelled to clear accounts in this way would blatantly say they were doing so because they had no choice. Many officials do not seem ever to have been wholly clear about the roots of the problems. Even if the system was understood, people would certainly shy away from discussing it candidly. Chinese officials were politicans, men finely attuned to the art of making unavoidable decisions seem the products of subtle and wise choice. To admit that they were coerced by circumstances would be to demean their worth, to throw into doubt their capacity to rectify affairs through the exercise of personal, moral, intelligent choice. Since their right to power was founded on their claim to a capacity to rule, such an admission would have struck at the roots of their own self-justification. It is therefore all the more startling when we find a man who says bluntly, unblushingly, and for the record that in his day the general opinion among officials was that the amnesty system was forced on the state by the government's inability to handle the flood of cases in any other fashion.

Liu Sung was Commandant of Justice *(t'ing-wei)* during the early years of the Chin dynasty (280–420). Like many officials active in judicial matters he was an advocate of a revival of "flesh punishments," but when his advice was ignored he went farther than most in his harsh condemnation of current practices:

> In antiquity punishments were used to eliminate punishments; now the situation is the opposite. All the serious criminals who escape, if

their hair has grown back out to be more than three inches long, suddenly [on being recaptured] are again shaved bald—this is using punishment to give birth to punishment. [Their sentences] are increased by
a year. This is using penal servitude to give birth to penal servitude.
Those who escape are a multitude; prisoners still held have accumulated in great numbers. Those who discuss it say, "As for those in custody, there is no way but for us to amnesty them." Repeatedly [their
counsel] is followed and men are pardoned. . . . [After the decline of
the Chou] there were many troubles and for this reason [criminals]
were pardoned and released. This was practiced provisionally and was
certainly not a way of being kind to criminals! Arriving at the present it
is constantly considered that crimes are piled up and cases are numerous. Amnesties are used to disperse them. Therefore amnesties are ex-
cessively numerous and yet the jails are stuffed full. If this is not soon
stopped it will be beyond help.[7]

Obviously a recognition that the amnesty system was an unavoidable by-product of the accumulation of prisoners was widely current
among Liu Sung's colleagues. When speaking for the record and for
posterity they quite understandably phrased their appraisal of the
amnesty system in terms of sovereign grace. We need not assume they
were so pious as to believe what they were saying.

Certain institutional imbalances posed a problem for Chinese rulers. The amnesty system was the solution they often chose. In this
limited sense the amnesty system was the outcome of the relations of
institutions and might be expected as a possible response to similar
situations in other cultures. But the system did not grow in an intel-
lectual vacuum. Other solutions might have been tried. Some, such
as a return to mutilating punishments, were periodically suggested.
Were there beliefs and values that led Chinese rulers to prefer the use
of amnesties? On the most trivial level the answer is obviously yes.
Amnesties reflected well on the benevolence of the reigning emperor.
His role as the father and mother of the people was embodied in con-
crete acts. On a more profound level the history of amnesties reveals
some of the changes and some of the continuities in Chinese values.
Even in pre-Confucian writings we find a deep-seated belief in the
role of the ruler as model. If the ruler is merciful his subordinates will
be merciful. If he is harsh they will be harsh. Perhaps we should call

this recognition rather than belief. Thoughtful parents soon come to see that their children will do as they do, not as they say; the Chinese ruler, standing *in loco parentis*, had to be a model for imitation, not simply a source of moral exhortation.

In the early writings that emphasize the importance of the ruler as a model there is no hint of magical coercion. The ruler by being merciful does not compel his subordinates to be merciful. They will pattern themselves after him because it is the nature of people to imitate their superiors. In late classical times (from the fourth century B.C. on) several strands of early Chinese speculation began to blend into a view of the world which postulated the effective causal interaction of man and nature. The harmony of natural processes could be maintained by individuals, and most particularly the emperors, only if they behaved in appropriate ways at appropriate times. For every thing there was a season. For each season there was a fitting behavior. Spring was the time of birth and mercy. The emperor not only had to wear the colors fitting to the season and eat its foods; he also had to extend the mercy of the time to those under his dominion. By doing so he harmonized the order of nature. If he chose not to do so he would distort the processes of the world.

This spring of hope was coupled with an autumn of despair. The mercy of one season was complemented by the stern punishments of the other. From its beginnings the Chinese cultural tradition included a strand of belief in complementary opposites, symbolized by the monad of *yin* and *yang.* True justice, achieved over time, could only be reached by the proper measures of benevolence and strictness, of amnesty and punishment. The ruler held the two handles, reward and punishment, the power to cleanse or to chastise. He could not hope to govern well without employing both.

What I am suggesting is that the system of frequent amnesties which begins with the rise of the empire and continues for more than a thousand years was one solution to a problem created by an imbalance of institutions. The imbalance was the root problem. The solution was suggested by Chinese beliefs and supported by political sagacity. The system served as a demonstration of the emperor's role as the intermediary between heaven and man and also his power to cleanse people of their misdeeds just as heaven might cleanse him.

But such beliefs were not necessary for the system to continue. Even a cynical ruler might find it useful. Recognizing the effective functioning of the system does not oblige us to credit the ruling group with "benevolent" intentions—merely with the good sense to grasp an imminent administrative problem and the political acumen to clothe its unavoidable response in humane dress. Given the ruling group's commitment to the proposition that all justice should be state justice, so long as the capacity of the police apparatus to capture criminals exceeded the capacity of the judicial apparatus to process cases and control convicts, the authorities would be faced with a perennial overload. Under these conditions it was of course possible for individual rulers to suspend the system for considerable periods.[8] In so doing they merely increased the problems of their successors.

The main function of the amnesty system was to relieve this pressure, but it also played important subsidiary roles. Those with judicial and police functions in traditional China worked within certain time limits set by law. Criminals were supposed to be captured, and cases decided, within given periods. Failure to complete the tasks assigned within the limits would in theory result in punishment for the officials involved. By closing outstanding cases and clearing out those on a court docket, the amnesty system spared judicial personnel the welter of fines and administrative punishments they would otherwise have suffered.

The system also functioned in lieu of a statute of limitations. Traditional Chinese codes and other legal rulings generally lack provisions saying that cases could not be raised after a specified length of time.[9] With the amnesty system such provisions were not necessary. No case concerning incidents more than a few years in the past could be raised, since intervening acts of grace precluded prosecution. The extraordinarily astute Sung official Chang Fang-p'ing took explicit note of this phenomenon:

I have noted that in recent years officials in the censorate and intendant inspectors frequently raise cases against men which stem from many years past and memorialize and impeach concerning them. In a disorderly way they ask that such men not be allowed to use the acts of grace or reductions of sentence to free themselves or have their punishments reduced. To apply such law against the poor is certainly not the way of good government. The texts of acts of grace say that he who speaks of acts which occurred prior to the amnesty will be considered guilty of the crime named in his accusation. . . . Among men of middling capacity who is able to be wholly without fault? If because of one delict a man be liable throughout his whole life than I fear that in the whole world there will not be a single person unpunished! On meeting with acts of grace men are given the chance to renew themselves. If you suddenly pursue them again and prosecute them, who in the future will feel himself personally secure? In giving way to a momentary flash of petty anger the great trust of the world will be lost.[10]

An analysis of the uses and functions of the amnesty system may help to explain its origins and its continued use, but it also poses a further question. If the amnesty system was not simply an incidental feature of the Chinese judicial system during the first millennium of the empire, but was rather an unavoidable outcome of Chinese state structure and the beliefs of rulers, how are we to explain the change that occurred during late imperial times? Acts of grace were still promulgated with a scope and at a rate unprecedented in other cultures, but there was nonetheless a definite decrease in the liberality of the system.

How could late imperial rulers succeed in reducing the number and scope of acts of grace when their predecessors had failed? If we accept the proposition that in the earlier period the frequency with which amnesties were granted resulted basically from the pressure put on the judicial system by accumulations of prisoners, then we must also say that the apparatus in later times was less burdened. But why? Surely the 275 million Chinese alive in 1779 did not commit fewer crimes than their 60 million ancestors during the Southern Sung?[11] Indeed, we should assume that the absolute number of crimes increased greatly as the population quintupled. Yet the number of judges of courts of first instance (most often district magistrates) did not increase proportionately. The judicial system's caseload should have been far greater than in earlier times. We would expect amnesties to be more frequent, not less so.

A variety of explanations of this conundrum suggest themselves.

Raising them tentatively may at least serve to focus attention on the problem. Perhaps late imperial judges disposed of cases more rapidly, and the penal complex had so changed that it could handle more convicts. If so, the case pressure would have been reduced. However, the studies currently available do not seem to indicate any increase in the speed of the judicial process. Nor, in the absence of adequate studies of traditional Chinese penal practices, can we know whether measures for controlling convicts had improved. The only change which does seem apparent is the rise of long-term imprisonment as a punishment stemming incidentally from the assize process. Late imperial officials do not seem to have been concerned about this side effect of their review system. Possibly this indicates a greater ability to control prisoners.

One factor that in some periods, in limited areas, reduced the judicial burden was the resort to irregular procedures in dispensing justice. At times, particularly in the nineteenth century, the central authorities tacitly or actively gave powers of summary justice to local officials, both civil and military, on a temporary basis. When this summary power prevailed, justice was swift, terrible, and not overly delicate in discriminating the truly guilty from those hapless people swept into the net of responsibility.[12] For late imperial times as a whole, however, this was no doubt a minor factor.

It is also possible that the later imperial judicial apparatus was burdened with a smaller caseload because the police system was either less efficient or less concerned with certain crimes. Lesser efficiency might have resulted from a more widespread use of criminals and military personnel for police duties than appears to have been characteristic of earlier dynasties. It has also been suggested that late imperial mutual security systems such as the *pao-chia* were relatively ineffective. Taken together these factors may have rendered police work more difficult while at the same time creating conditions conducive to disorder. Banditry, always endemic in traditional China, was particularly serious during late imperial times. Not only did it repeatedly burgeon into major rebellions but there were also areas (such as some mining districts in southwestern China) where the state did not even try to exert more than minimal control. Furthermore it is in the Ming and Ch'ing that we see the rise of those massive affrays called *hsieh-*

tou which involved dozens and sometimes hundreds of participants in armed conflicts.[13] Under such conditions the official law enforcement agencies may have focused their attention on controlling large-scale violence, leaving them less time for other aspects of police work. Those involved in such disorders were likely to be accused of crimes calling for immediate execution. Thus they would not long be a burden to the judiciary.

Another change, perhaps the most significant one, was that the late imperial state was less concerned to defend its prerogative as the dispenser of all justice. In all societies at all times the overwhelming bulk of potentially litigable disputes are settled without resort to formal judicial proceedings. Traditional China was no exception to this rule. Indeed Western commentators on traditional Chinese law, insufficiently informed about how disputes are handled in their own civilization, have frequently singled out traditional China as peculiar for the degree to which legal problems were handled without appeal to the courts. There can be no question that in traditional China the bulk of the potential legal disputes were always dealt with informally, but I would suggest that the proportion of cases so handled was even greater during late imperial times than it had been during the first millennium of the empire.[14]

As the population increased without a corresponding expansion of the judicial apparatus or improvement in legal techniques, the potential delays involved in formal state justice and the costs associated with them increased greatly. Government courts became more and more places to be shunned. Great pressure was put on other social organizations—guilds, clans, secret societies—to dispense their own justice to their own members. And great pressure was put on these members to accept this new dispensation. Even so, the increase of population was so large that the courts were overwhelmed. It is from late imperial times that we begin to hear officials, and emperors, say that the courtroom should be made such a frightful and expensive place that all but the most hardened or foolish would seek to avoid it. In the Sung, families often went to law over such minor matters as disputes over tax assessments; such behavior would be far less probable in Ch'ing times.[15]

The late imperial state was able to reduce its dependence on the amnesty system because it suffered less pressure from prisoner over-load. It suffered less pressure principally because it had forced other social units to handle an increasing share of the judicial burden, be-cause it did not attempt to deal (or simply could not deal) with lesser crimes as effectively as had been the case under the early empire, and because to some truly serious criminals it meted out a justice that was swift and final.

Population growth may be one factor involved in the evolution of these aspects of the legal system in the Ming and (most particularly) in the Ch'ing. It cannot, however, account for the origins of the pol-icy of restricting amnesties under the Liao, Chin, and Yüan. Perhaps in seeking an explanation we should look at three key traits of these states—they were ruled by non-Chinese, they were born out of wars, and they kept control of major territories beyond China's borders. The latter fact distinguishes these states from the foreign-dominated states of the period from the Han to the T'ang. These earlier states ex-isted wholly on Chinese soil and were thereby committed much more fully to ruling in Chinese fashion. The rulers of the three later states retained territories beyond the Great Wall and thus remained more in touch with the non-Chinese world out of which they had come. It is no doubt significant that, among these three later states, the Chin dynasty, with the bulk of its domains within the Great Wall, became more sinicized than either the Liao or the Yüan.[16] It should also be remembered that these tribal groups shared a different conception of rule. The idea of Chinese-style hereditary kingship was foreign to them. The concept of the emperor as heaven's cleansing intermediary must have seemed even more strange.

Moreover, these later states (as well as the Ming and the Ch'ing) came to power only after protracted military struggles. The control-ling elements in their elites were initially military men. Military atti-tudes and concerns exercised great influence during the critical forma-tive periods of these states. Their harsh judicial systems may reflect this heritage.[17]

Finally the rulers of these three states were foreigners. Because they were aliens they had to be concerned first and foremost with a popu-lation always potentially and at times actively hostile. The people were the enemy. The mistrust of the rulers necessarily also extended to the Chinese officials through whom their rule was exercised. The loyalty of these servants of the state might in theory be presumed, but in practice it could not be presumed upon. Elaborate safeguards came to be used to prevent Chinese officials from gaining excessive power. Thus the attention of these alien rulers was of necessity focused on two problems—preventing major armed resistance among the people and exercising complete control over the bureaucracy.

The first problem was military rather than judicial. Crimes that did not threaten to grow into insurrection were, relatively speaking, of lesser concern to these states than to Chinese ruled states. Native Chinese dynasties might be concerned about preserving traditional Chinese culture and social order; foreign dynasties not willing to accept full acculturation had to focus their attention on the problem of keeping political power in the hands of a numerically and culturally inferior tribal group. Preserving Chinese culture could not be an end in itself to these states; it was merely a means to the preservation of their power. Given these concerns the alien states had less capacity for handling other administrative tasks, including the dispensing of justice. I suspect that future research will show an increase, in late imperial times, in the proportion of criminal matters dealt with by agencies other than the state.

Alien mistrust of Chinese officials accelerated a trend toward imperial autocracy already evident in the Chinese Sung dynasty. The discretionary authority of officials was more and more restricted in late imperial times as their legal and other privileges decreased. Late imperial officials were subjected to harassment and abuse to a degree quite inconceivable in the T'ang or Sung, and they were surrounded by a growing wall of regulations which made it difficult for them to do their jobs without committing misdemeanors. Since almost everyone committed infractions, a man became beholden to both his superiors and his subordinates. If they chose to draw attention to his failings they could inflict financial hardship or status losses on him and might even injure his career chances.[18]

Hence a government theoretically based on rules became in practice a government based on personal understandings. The long-run result was to stifle initiative. By and large, government officials were tempted to act only when inaction was impossible, and then only in the most cautious manner.[19] Late Chinese governments became increasingly concerned with the problem of stimulating bureaucrats to work actively. The degree of the state's concern, and the persistent attempts to legislate systems that would provoke activity, are perhaps the best indicators of the pervasiveness of the tendency to avoid initiative. One predictable result was the decreasing involvement of the government in the life of the Chinese people. Private groups became largely responsible for many activities, such as public works, welfare, and education, which in earlier times had been at least in part the responsibility of the state. Socially, this transformation is mirrored in the rise of the "gentry" system—a configuration under which the government no longer sought to perform social functions itself but concentrated on using the examination system to certify the ideological reliability of nonofficial agents. The "privatization" of much judicial business is merely one aspect of this general process.

Paradoxically, in later imperial times, as the government became more autocratic in its internal workings, its hold on the society it supposedly ruled grew weaker and weaker. Rulers might be aware of the problem. They were prevented from attempting any radical solution of it (through the dissemination of authority) by their own insecurity. Instead they reacted as authorities frequently do when they feel their power slipping away: they increased the severity of the law. Late imperial law was harsher than early imperial law not only in its less frequent use of grace but also most particularly in its legalization of previously forbidden tortures. Reduction in the frequency with which amnesties were issued also increased the severity of the law by lengthening the time within which criminal cases could be prosecuted (the "statute of limitation") and increased the likelihood that local officials would suffer administrative punishment because of their failure to solve crimes within the set time limits. While his minions meted out this harsher justice to fewer criminals, the emperor exercised more and more control over less and less.

The line of developments hypothesized here never had the chance to work itself out. The armed intrusion of the Western powers in the nineteenth century changed the terms of the equation. With the collapse of the imperial order in 1912, the two thousand year old amnesty system came to an end. But we should not be misled into thinking that the general problem of imbalance in judicial institutions, to which the traditional Chinese amnesty system was one response, has forever disappeared. Even in our own day judicial authorities, facing overcrowded institutions, have been forced at times to open prison gates, however grudgingly.[20]

Reasonable people, facing intractable problems, accept the choices forced upon them. The genius of traditional Chinese statesmen is to be sought not in their solution but in the brilliant legerdemain with which they transformed inevitable and distasteful acts into the quintessence of benevolent free will.

A Note
on Previous Studies

ANY study of amnesties in traditional China should begin with a reading of the "Investigation of Amnesties" in Shen Chia-pen's collected works. The great and indefatigable late Ch'ing scholar has assembled here in chronological order notices of amnesties culled from works of the classical period, as well as from the standard histories and some other sources for imperial times. Shen's searching of the sources he used was very thorough. He did not attempt to use all the relevant materials, and he frequently abbreviates those he does cite, but the sources he did consult were searched carefully. His work is not, properly speaking, an investigation, since he does not really attempt to analyze the data he compiles, but he does provide the interested reader with lists of amnesties in easily accessible form. Equally valuable are his occasional comments on the materials.

Aside from Shen's work surprisingly few studies have been devoted exclusively to the amnesty system. The only book which has come to my attention is the brief and superficial *Chung-kuo ta-she k'ao* by Hsü Shih-kuei. More recent, but even briefer and more superficial, is an article in *Hsing-shih fa tsa-chih* (1969) by Ch'eng Pi-lien entitled "Li-tai she-tien kai-shu." Some years ago Werner Eichhorn published an article called "Bemerkungen über einige nicht amnestierbare Verbrechen im Sung-Rechtwesen" in *Oriens Extremus* (1961). As his title indicates, Eichhorn was concerned with only one aspect of the amnesty process, and even with regard to this he used only a limited number of sources.

Easily the best study of amnesties in any Western language is the chapter devoted to them in A. F. P. Hulsewé's *Remnants of Han Law* (vol. 1). Hulsewé made a careful study of virtually all the important Han materials. Because of the nature of the sources themselves, however, many intriguing questions had to be left unanswered.

In Chinese, Tai Yen-hui's *T'ang-lü t'ung-lun* contains an interesting section on amnesties. However, since this work is devoted to the code it presents an incomplete picture of the T'ang amnesty system. The brief piece on T'ang amnesties in Niida Noboru's *Chūgoku hōsei-shi kenkyū* (vol. 1, pp. 256–263) is also well worth reading.

General histories of Chinese law also slight amnesties. Perhaps the best of the traditional Chinese studies, Yang Hung-lieh's *Chung-kuo fa-lü fa-t'a shih,* mentions amnesties only incidentally. Far better is the all too brief but very perceptive work of Ch'en Ku-yüan called *Chung-kuo fa-chih shih.*

All these works taken together have only scratched the surface of a large topic. With the exception of the Han, so ably analyzed by Hulsewé, no period has been at all well explored. It is to be hoped that this study, though not focused on one period, may provoke interest in the making of more intensive analyses.

Notes

ABBREVIATIONS

BMFEA	*Bulletin of the Museum of Far Eastern Antiquities*
HCP	*Hsü tzu-chih t'ung-chien ch'ang-pien*
KCHP	*Ku chin ho pi shih-lei pei-yao*
LTHFC	*Li-tai hsing-fa chih*
LTMCTI	*Li-tai ming-ch'en tsou-i*
SHT	*Sung hsing t'ung*
SHY	*Sung hui-yao chi-kao*
SS	*Sung shih*
TCLL	*Ta Ch'ing lü-li*
TFSL	*Ch'ing-yüan t'iao-fa shih-lei*
TFYK	*Ts'e-fu yüan-kuei*
TLSI	*T'ang-lü shu-i*
TPYL	*T'ai-p'ing yü-lan*
TTCLC	*T'ang ta-ch'ao ling-chi*
WHTK	*Wen hsien t'ung k'ao*

INTRODUCTION

1. Amnesties in the Chinese fashion were issued in both Japan and Korea. For Japan see Marinus W. Visser, *Ancient Buddhism in Japan,* pp. 202 ff. Some comments on Korean practices are given in William Shaw, "The Neo-Confucian Revolution of Values in Early Yi Dynasty Korea and Its Implications for Law and Social Order."

2. G. Srinivasa Murti and A. N. Krishna Aiyangar, transl., *Edicts of Asoka,* p. 109.

3. C. Pharr, transl., *The Theodosian Code and Novels.*

4. Theodore Mommsen, *Römisches Strafrecht,* pp. 457–458.

5. *Code Penal Suisse,* item 81, no. 1; *Turkish Criminal Code,* item 97; *Quattro codici per le udienze civile e penali,* item 151, nos. 1–4. For the practices of medieval England see Naomi D. Hurnard, *The King's Pardon for Homicide before* A.D. *1307.*

6. I have chosen to translate the word *she* as amnesty rather than pardon because in English amnesty has connotations of a more general forgiveness of larger groups of offenders, whereas pardon frequently refers to the forgiving of individuals or limited groups. In Chinese practice the forgiving of individuals or limited groups was also referred to as *she,* but I am not concerned here with acts of this limited nature. The *she* to which I make reference involve large numbers of men or at least groups of indeterminate size. So for our purposes *amnesty* is the more appropriate rendering.

Under the empire (221 B.C.–A.D. 1912) the use of the term *she* was standard. Prior to the unification of the third century B.C., acts which forgave criminals were also referred to by the terms *yu, mien,* or *ssu.* Many of the sources for this ancient period have been translated. The words in question have been variously rendered. Translators, following the Chinese commentators, tend to equate *she, mien,* and *ssu* as "to pardon," apparently meaning to forgive completely. Many of them distinguish *yu* as meaning "to treat leniently," implying some residual punishment. Yet in some instances leading scholars have translated *yu* as "to pardon." Where the standard translations do not seem to me to distort the implications of the Chinese I have not substituted *amnesty* for *pardon.* Where the translations are misleading I have altered them or substituted my own translations. In all cases I have included the romanization of the Chinese term after the translated word.

CHAPTER 1: ANCIENT CHINA

1. This anthropological perspective was suggested to me by the very interesting work now being done by Katrina McLeod, as reflected in her "Law and Symbolism of Pollution: Some Observations on the Ch'in Laws from Yün-meng."

2. "Oh Feng, be careful and enlightened in regard to your punishments. If somebody has committed a small offense, if it is not an offense through mishap but a persistence and he himself has done what is unlawful according to his set purpose, even if his offense is small then you cannot but kill him. If he has a great offense, if it is not a persistence but an offense by mishap, done by chance, when you have justly probed to the end of his guilt, then you cannot kill him. . . . All people who draw guilt upon themselves, being robbers and thieves and villains and traitors, who kill and destroy and go for spoil, and are forceful and do not fear death, there are none who do not detest them. The king said, Feng, when the primary evil-doers are [thus] greatly detested, how much the more then the unfilial and the unbrotherly? . . . If we are kind to these [unfilial and unbrotherly] and they are not considered as offenders by us the rulers, the norms given by Heaven to our people will be greatly brought into disorder. I say may you speedily follow [the rules of] punishment [of your father] King Wen, and punish these without pardon *(wu-she).*"

See Bernhard Karlgren, "The Book of Documents," and James Legge, *The Chinese Classics,* vol. 3: *The Shoo King,* pp. 388 ff. The translation follows that of Karlgren in all essentials, though I have taken the liberty of making a few very minor changes in wording to make it read more smoothly. In citing translations which are accompanied by a Chinese text such as those of Karlgren or Legge I will not ordinarily provide citations to the original Chinese sources in separate editions. On the date of these texts and the identity of their participants see Herrlee G. Creel, *The Origins of Statecraft in China*, vol. 1, pp. 444 ff.

3. Legge, *Shoo King*, pp. 38–59.

4. Karlgren, "Book of Documents," p. 46. See also Legge, *Shoo King*, pp. 413 ff. This speech fits well with the later tradition that King Wu, after he had conquered the Shang, freed those held in prisons. See Edouard Chavannes, transl., *Les Mémoires historiques de Se-ma Ts'ien*, vol. 1, p. 237.

5. Karlgren, "Book of Documents," p. 64; Legge, *Shoo King*, pp. 493 ff.

6. Karlgren, "Book of Documents," p. 51; Legge, *Shoo King*, p. 431.

7. James Legge, *The Chinese Classics*, vol. 5: *The Ch'un Ts'ew with the Tso Chuen*, pp. 102, 183, 282, 711, 802. See also *Chan kuo ts'e* (SPTK ed.), 7/62a; J. I. Crump, Jr., *Chan-kuo Ts'e*, p. 448, for a somewhat later period.

8. Legge, *Tso Chuen*, p. 409. Legge here translates *she tsui li* as "dealt gently with offenders," but I see no reason why we should not follow his translation of this phrase from p. 655, "pardoning offenders." This interpretation is supported by the description of this accession given in *Kuo yü* (T'ien-sheng ming-tao edition), 13/1b. C. de Harlez, *Koue-Yü: Discours des Royaumes*, vol. 2, p. 141, gives a rather misleading rendering of this passage.

9. Legge, *Tso Chuen*, pp. 348, 440, 649, 655. Not everyone was forgiven, however, since the perverse and bad were still investigated. Pardons might be used more directly for military ends also. Kuan Chung supposedly advised Duke Huan at one point that he should "lighten [the punishments for] crimes and transfer [the resulting funds] to the military. . . . For the death penalty, commute it to one set of leather armor. For lesser penalties use one shield of mottled leather. For petty crimes commute to payments in metal, and treat indulgently *(yu)* crimes with doubtful circumstances." See *Kuo yü* 6/8b–9b; C. de Harlez, *Discours des Royaumes*, vol. 2, p. 19.

10. James Legge, *The Chinese Classics*, vol. 1: *The Confucian Analects*, p. 263. Note the same sentiments repeated in *Ta tai li chi* (SPTK ed.), 8/4b.

11. James Legge, *The Chinese Classics*, vol. 2: *The Works of Mencius*, pp. 135, 157, 195.

12. *Chou li* (SPPY ed.), 2/3a; Edouard Biot, transl., *Le Tcheou-li*, vol. 1, p. 25; *Chou li* 26/10b; Biot, *Tcheou-li*, vol. 2, p. 117.

13. *Chou li* 26/10b; Biot, *Tcheou-li*, vol. 2, p. 117.

14. *Chou li* 10/5b, 10/9b, 35/7b; Biot, *Tcheou-li*, vol. 1, pp. 208, 218; vol. 2, p. 332.

15. *Chou li* 4/9b, 36/1b; Biot, *Tcheou-li*, vol. 1, pp. 300–301; vol. 2, p. 355.

16. *Chou li* 35/3b; Biot, *Tcheou-li*, vol. 2, p. 323. See also James Legge, *Li Ki*, vol. 1, p. 236; S. Couvreur, transl., *Li Ki*, vol. 1, pp. 304 ff.; *Li chi hsün-tsuan* (SPPY ed.), 6/8a ff.

17. *Chou li* 35/9b–11a; Biot, *Tcheou-li*, vol. 2, pp. 337–342.

18. *Mo tzu* 5/19/89, 15/63/340, 15/70/357, 15/70/359. The quoted translation is from Y. P. Mei, *The Ethical Works of Motse*, p. 69.

19. J. J. L. Duyvendak, transl., *The Book of Lord Shang*, p. 206; *Shang tzu* (SPTK ed.), 2/1a.

20. Duyvendak, *Lord Shang*, p. 284; *Shang tzu* 4/8a.

21. Duyvendak, *Lord Shang*, pp. 203, 210, 278–279, 283–284, 287; *Shang tzu* 1/13b, 2/2b, 4/6a, 4/7b, 4/8a, 4/9b. Identical sentiments are found in the *Han Fei Tzu*. See W. K. Liao, transl., *The Complete Works of Han Fei Tzu*, vol. 1, pp. 29, 123–124, 128, 168, 292, 298; vol. 2, p. 284; *Han fei tzu* (SPPY ed.), 1/9b, 4/14b, 4/15a, 4/16b, 5/11b, 9/7b, 9/10a, 19/4a.

22. Wang Hsien-ch'ien, *Hsün-tzu chi-chieh*, in *Chung-kuo ssu-hsiang ming-chu*, 5/9/94. I have used the translation of Burton Watson, *Basic Writings of Mo Tzu, Hsun Tzu, and Han Fei Tzu*, p. 34, but I have translated *she* as "pardon" rather than "mercy." See also Homer H. Dubs, *Hsuntze: The Moulder of Ancient Confucianism*, p. 122.

23. *Hsün-tzu chi-chieh* 5/12/157. Hsün Tzu here quotes a section of the *Book of Documents*, which can be found in Legge, *Shoo King*, p. 166. This section is from the "Old Text" version and is therefore, taken as a whole, a late forgery, but Hsün Tzu's citation at least indicates that this particular passage occurred in a book he knew as the *Documents* in the third century B.C.

24. *Kuan tzu* (SPPY ed.), 1/12a–15b. Parts of this section are translated in Lewis Maverick (ed.), *Economic Dialogues in Ancient China*, pp. 40–45. The strictures against officials tampering with the orders of the ruler are repeated in *Kuan tzu* 5/10b. The concept of forgiving first and second offenses and punishing third offenses may have been borrowed from the *Kuo yü* 6/7b, where it refers to errors by officials. The especially severe punishment of officials who break orders is also advocated in other works such as *I chou shu* (SPPY ed.), 3/8b, and Legge, *Shoo King*, pp. 165–166. Unfortunately, it is not possible to date the *I chou shu* passage. That in the *Documents* existed at least as early as the third century B.C.

25. *Kuan tzu* 6/1b–3b. I am using the excellent translation of W. Allyn Rickett, *Kuan Tzu: A Repository of Early Chinese Thought*, pp. 91–93.

26. *Kuan tzu* 6/3b; Rickett, *Kuan Tzu*, p. 94.

27. *Kuan tzu* 5/7a.

28. *Kuan tzu* 3/16b; see also 8/9a.

29. *Kuan tzu* 8/3a; see also 16/7b.

30. Legge, *Li Ki*, vol. 1, pp. 235–238; Couvreur, *Li Ki*, vol. 1, pp. 304 ff.; *Li chi hsün-tsuan* 5/19a ff.

31. *Kuan tzu* 14/5b, 17/4a, 17/10a, 24/22a. For renderings see Maverick, *Economic Dialogues*, pp. 89, 98, 102, 211.

32. Legge, *Li Ki*, vol. 1, pp. 259–304; Couvreur, *Li Ki*, vol. 1, pp. 339 ff.; *Li chi hsün-tsuan* 6/8a ff.

CHAPTER 2: THE EARLY EMPIRE

1. Pan ku, *Ch'ien Han shu* 23/12a; A. F. P. Hulsewé, *Remnants of Han Law*, vol. 1, p. 333. As a careful reading of this chapter will show, I have made extensive use of

Hulsewé's excellent study. His chapter on amnesties is one of the few thorough investigations of amnesty practices, and in substantial part I have merely rearranged and
reanalyzed material originally described by him. He was also kind enough to read my
first draft of this chapter and offer many valuable suggestions.

2. Pan Ku, *Ch'ien Han shu* 1A/23b; Homer H. Dubs, transl., *The History of the
Former Han Dynasty*, vol. 1, p. 74; Ssu-ma Ch'ien, *Shih chi* 8/20a; Chavannes, *Mémoires historiques*, vol. 2, p. 226; Hulsewé, *Remnants of Han Law*, p. 226.

3. Ssu-ma Ch'ien, *Shih chi* 6/47a, 43/25b; Chavannes, *Mémoires historiques*, vol.
2, p. 241; vol. 5, p. 89. For the reforms of Shang Yang see J. J. L. Duyvendak, *The
Book of Lord Shang*.

4. Ssu-ma Ch'ien, *Shih chi* 5/12a–b; Chavannes, *Mémoires historiques*, vol. 2,
pp. 32–33. For this story see J. Prusek, *Chinese Statelets and the Northern Barbarians*, pp. 130 ff.

5. Ssu-ma Ch'ien, *Shih chi* 5/29a–b, 33a; Chavannes, *Mémoires historiques*, vol.
2, pp. 84–86, 96.

6. Ssu-ma Ch'ien, *Shih chi* 6/12a; Chavannes, *Mémoires historiques*, vol. 2,
p. 130.

7. Ssu-ma Ch'ien, *Shih chi* 6/33a; Chavannes, *Mémoires historiques*, vol. 2, p.
205; Sun K'ai, *Ch'in hui-yao*. *Shih chi* 15/48b dates this amnesty to 209 B.C.

8. Pan Ku, *Ch'ien Han shu* 1A/23b; Dubs, *Former Han Dynasty*, vol. 1, p. 74.

9. Shen Chia-pen, *Shen chi-i hsien-sheng i-shu*, she-k'ao 2/1a ff. Shen's study of
amnesties is the best general introduction to the amnesty system. For the most part
Shen lists amnesties from various dynasties (and hence has been used as the basis of
many of the statistical calculations in later chapters) and does not analyze the material, but his incidental comments are extremely valuable.

10. The most convenient listings of Han amnesties are to be found in Hsü T'ien-
lin, *Hsi Han hui-yao*, chap. 63; Hsü T'ien-lin, *Tung Han hui-yao*, chap. 36; and
Shen, *Shen chi-i hsien-sheng i-shu*, chaps. 2, 3. The statistics given in this chapter are
drawn from these sources and from the annals sections of the two Han histories unless
otherwise stated. For the Former Han, see also Dubs, *Former Han Dynasty*, vol. 1,
pp. 74, 81, 99, 104, 121, 125, 129, 136, 141; Chavannes, *Mémoires historiques*, vol.
2, pp. 336, 384, 393. On p. 99 and at several other points Dubs translates the passage
as involving the pardoning of those guilty of less than capital punishment. His renderings in these cases cannot be accepted, and indeed at other places he accurately
gives the phrase involved as meaning the pardoning of those guilty of capital or lesser
crimes. There is, moreover, one other minor problem with some of his translations of
these passages. He renders the phrase *shu-ssu* as "irrevocable death sentences." Although there are differences in interpretation among the commentators on this
phrase, it seems clear that those who make it equivalent to beheading are correct.
This is indicated by an amnesty dated A.D. 82 in which those merely sentenced to
death had their sentences reduced one degree and were sent to the frontier as guards.
Those sentenced to *shu-ssu* were castrated. Clearly *ssu* and *shu-ssu* are not the same.
Equally clearly *shu-ssu* was not an irrevocable sentence. It seems most logical to assume that *shu-ssu* specifically referred to beheading. See Shen, *Shen chi-i hsien-*

sheng i-shu, 3/2b. Hulsewé has indicated in a personal communication that *shu-ssu* unquestionably meant "to behead."

11. Dubs, *Former Han Dynasty,* vol. 1, pp. 182, 265; vol. 2, pp. 49, 93, 96–97, 101, 118, 215. Amnesties on the changing of reign titles were particularly common in the Latter Han. See Shen, *Shen chi-i hsien-sheng i-shu,* 2/6a–10a.

12. Dubs, *Former Han Dynasty,* vol. 2, p. 93.

13. Ibid., pp. 228–229.

14. Ibid., p. 385.

15. *Chou i* (Shih san ching chu-shu ed.), 25/40/hsiang. The translation is based on Z. D. Sung, *The Text of the Yi King,* pp. 171–172.

16. Pan Ku, *Ch'ien Han shu* 36/7a. The translation is from Hulsewé, *Remnants of Han Law,* pp. 107–108. Hulsewé has also assembled other references to this practice in Han times.

17. Wang Ch'ung, *Lun heng* (SPTK ed.), 14/7a. The translation is after A. Forke, *Lun-heng of Wang Ch'ung,* vol. 1, p. 281. In later times, when the Han view had lost some of its currency, these beliefs lived on in imagery. "The words of a ruler," we are told by Liu Hsieh, "are lofty and laden with meaning. . . . Therefore . . . in giving pardons *(ssu-she)* they should be as gracious as the dews in the Spring." See Liu Hsieh, *Wen hsin tiao lung* (SPPY ed.), 4/23b. The translation is from Vincent Y. C. Shih, *Literary Mind and the Carving of Dragons,* p. 114.

18. See for instance the *Wang-ch'i ching,* the *Feng chüeh shu,* and the *Huang-ti chen* as quoted in the Li Fang, *T'ai-p'ing yü-lan,* 652/9b (hereafter cited *TPYL*).

19. Ssu-ma Ch'ien, *Shih chi* 27/42a; Chavannes, *Mémoires historiques,* vol. 3, pt. 2, p. 411.

20. Fang Hsüan-ling, *Chin shu,* 11/19a. See Gustav Schlegel, *Uranographie chinoise,* p. 516.

21. *TPYL* 652/9b.

22. Ch'iu Han-p'ing, *Li-tai hsing-fa chih,* p. 586 (hereafter cited *LTHFC*).

23. Fan Yeh, *Hou Han shu,* chaps. 1–9. These amnesties are also listed in Hsü T'ien-lin, *Tung Han hui-yao,* chap. 36.

24. Shen, *Shen chi-i hsien-sheng i-shu,* she-k'ao 3/16b.

25. Dubs, *Former Han Dynasty,* vol. 3, p. 62.

26. Hulsewé, *Remnants of Han Law,* p. 245.

27. Ibid., p. 238.

28. Pan Ku, *Ch'ien Han shu,* chap. 1A–12 passim; Fan Yeh, *Hou Han shu,* chaps. 1–9 passim; Hulsewé, *Remnants of Han Law,* pp. 209–214.

29. Fan Yeh, *Hou Han shu* 38/2a. The translation is from Hulsewé, *Remnants of Han Law,* p. 91.

30. Pan Ku, *Ch'ien Han shu* 71/2a–b.

31. Hulsewé, *Remnants of Han Law,* pp. 247–248.

32. Legge, *Li Ki,* p. 259; Couvreur, *Li Ki,* vol. 1, p. 339; *Li chi hsün tsuan* 6/8a.

33. See for instance Fan Yeh, *Hou Han shu* 3/6a, 6/11b.

34. Fan Yeh, *Hou Han shu* 6/3a–b.

35. Wei Hung, *Han chiu i,* pu-i B/7b; Hulsewé, *Remnants of Han Law,* p. 247.

36. Liu Hsieh, *Wen hsin tiao lung*, 4/22a; Shih, *Literary Mind*, p. 110.

37. Hulsewé, *Remnants of Han Law*, pp. 238–239. This conclusion is also supported by several other cases. In 87 B.C., when the authorities were looking for the great-grandson of the Emperor Wu so that they might execute him, he was protected by Ping Chi. Then "there was a great act of grace. [Ping] Chi hence sent the great-grandson in a carriage to the home of his [deceased] grandmother." See Dubs, *Former Han Dynasty*, vol. 2, p. 201. And in A.D. 21, when numerous bandit groups had arisen, an amnesty was issued. The guilty ones assumed that they would be included, but we are told that when they received the order of amnesty "and wanted to disband and scatter some on the contrary were prevented [from returning home] and attacked." See Dubs, *Former Han Dynasty*, vol. 3, p. 420. Another incident, recorded in the *Tung kuan Han chi*, reports an amnesty which did not include fugitives or those whose crimes had not come to light at the time of the amnesty; but here again it is strongly implied that this exclusion is irregular and a deviation from proper practice. See *Tung kuan Han chi* (SPPY ed.), 18/3b–4a.

38. The translation is based on Dubs, *Former Han Dynasty*, vol. 3, pp. 62–63, but has been amended at the suggestion of Hulsewé to indicate that the phrase *i pu-tao lun* ought properly to be rendered "condemned them (or sentenced them) for impiety."

39. The *History of the Former Han* says that in 83 B.C. the "Empress née Shang-kuan was established [as empress]. An [ordinary] amnesty was granted to the empire, and plaints (*tz'u-sung* or civil suits) [which dated from] before the second year of Hou-[yüan] [87 B.C.] all were to be dismissed." Since an ordinary amnesty has just been granted in 86 B.C., the specific order dismissing plaints prior to 87 B.C. would seem superfluous if ordinary amnesties dismissed current cases. My translation here is based on Dubs, *Former Han Dynasty*, vol. 2, p. 157. See also Hulsewé, *Remnants of Han Law*, p. 239. As Hulsewé has kindly brought to my attention, Dubs's rendering of *tz'u-sung* as "accusations and legal cases" is incorrect: only civil matters are covered by the term. Hulsewé had already said this in *Remnants of Han Law*, p. 48, and noted it again in a personal communication in which he also indicated that he still believed that the prohibition of raising cases probably began earlier in the Former Han and that the evidence I cite here does not indicate a distinction between ordinary and great acts of grace.

40. Hulsewé, *Remnants of Han Law*, pp. 239–240.

41. The earliest instance occurred in 196 B.C. when the Emperor Kao issued an ordinary amnesty which covered "all under Heaven who were guilty of capital crimes or less and ordered that they all be taken into the army." See Dubs, *Former Han Dynasty*, vol. 1, p. 136. Many similar amnesties are recorded for the Latter Han. These later decrees do not include the word *she*. Typically they merely order officials to "reduce the world's capital sentences by one degree and exile [the men thus spared] to the borders." See Hulsewé, *Remnants of Han Law*, pp. 245–246; Shen, *Shen chi-i hsien-sheng i-shu*, 3/9b–10b.

42. For a more detailed description of various Han penal practices, including this one, see Hulsewé, *Remnants of Han Law*, pp. 102 ff.

43. Ordinary amnesties greatly reduced the punishments of those sentenced to

penal servitude. It seems improbable that they would thereafter willingly enter the army, though perhaps they might have been compelled to do so.

44. In *Remnants of Han Law,* pp. 244–245, Hulsewé wrote that there was a fact which "makes it impossible to assume that a plain amnesty did not include persons condemned to capital punishment. This fact is the existence of quite a number of amnesties expressly restricted to the *t'u,* the hard labor convicts." His conclusion, then, is that "when *t'u* are mentioned expressly, capital cases are excluded, whereas a 'plain' amnesty did include them." Personal communication.

45. Dubs, *Former Han Dynasty,* vol. 2, p. 200, n.4; Hulsewé, *Remnants of Han Law,* pp. 240–241.

46. Hulsewé, *Remnants of Han Law,* pp. 275–276.

47. See the lists in the Hsü T'ien-lin, *Hsi Han hui-yao,* chap. 63, and Hsü T'ien-lin, *Tung Han hui-yao,* chap. 36.

48. Wei Hung, *Han chiu i,* A10b; Hulsewé, *Remnants of Han Law,* p. 247. That great acts of grace pardoned those involved in rebellious activities would also seem to be indicated by the events of 87 B.C. when Ping Chi prevented the seizure of the imprisoned grandson of the rebellious heir-apparent. Then, after there had been a great act of grace, Ping Chi apparently no longer feared for the boy's safety, for he "sent the [imperial] great-grandson in a carriage to the home of his [deceased] grandmother." See Dubs, *Former Han Dynasty,* vol. 2, p. 201. The citation of the act preserved to us does not mention pardoning those involved in rebellion, but Ping Chi obviously knew that the boy had been absolved. A *ta-she* issued in 16 B.C. also says nothing about pardoning those jointly adjudicated for greatly refractory acts, but the brothers and sisters of the Marchioness of An-p'ing, who had attempted to bewitch pregnant women in the emperor's harem, were all freed (though they had to return to their home commandaries). See Pan Ku, *Ch'ien Han shu* 97B/6b; Hulsewé, *Remnants of Han Law,* pp. 167, 239.

49. The suggestions made here are tentative. Hulsewé, the leading authority on Han law, has expressed grave doubts about the possibility of distinguishing great acts of grace from ordinary amnesties in the Han period. Personal communication.

50. Pan Ku, *Ch'ien Han shu* 81/3a–b.

51. Hsü T'ien-lin, *Tung Han hui-yao* 36/9a.

52. Wang Fu, *Ch'ien fu lun* (SPPYed.), 4/6a.

53. Ts'ui Shih, "Cheng lun," in *Ch'ün shu chih yao* (SPTK ed.), 45/13b–14a. He also remarks in passing (8b) that if crimes were not pardoned or commuted then officials would be careful in their work.

54. Hsün Yüeh, *Shen chien* (SPTK ed.), 2/14b. See also *Shen chien* 1/9b.

55. Hsün Yüeh, *Ch'ien Han chi* (SPTK ed.), 22/8a. For an extensive discussion of the Three Laws see Hulsewé, *Remnants of Han Law,* pp. 368 ff., n. 143.

CHAPTER 3: ACTS OF GRACE IN MEDIEVAL CHINA: A.D. 220–907

1. Wang Ch'in-jo, *Ts'e-fu yüan-kuei,* pp. 976–977 (cited hereafter as *TFYK*). This great Sung dynasty encyclopedia is the most convenient and fullest source for the acts of grace of the period covered by this chapter. It is, however, flawed in one respect: it

systematically ignores the reign of the Empress Wu (r. 684–705). For this period one must consult Shen Chia-pen, *Shen chi-i hsien-sheng i-shu*, she-k'ao, 4/24b–25a.

In one incident in A.D. 530 a variant of the practice of announcing amnesties from elevated places occurred when the emperor (apparently) issued an amnesty from atop the earthen altar. It also seems possible that in this case the variation is only apparent, however, and results from the abbreviation of the original description. See *TFYK*, p. 977.

2. Ch'ang-sun Wu-chi, *Sui shu* (SPTK ed.), 25/12b. See also Étienne Balazs, *Le Traité juridique du "Souei-choux*," p. 62; Uchida Tomoo, "Zui-sho keihō-shi," pt. 4, *Do-shisha hōgaku* 88(1965):173. Feng Yen, *Feng shih wen chien chi*, 4/3a–b, indicates that the use of the golden cock was a post-Han development. For a translation of this passage see Robert des Rotours, *Traité des fonctionnaires et traité de l'armée*, vol. 1, p. 364, n. 1.

3. *TFYK*, pp. 989–990; *LTHFC*, p. 341. Uchida Tomoo, "Kyu Tō-sho keihō-shi," pt. 3, *Do-shisha hōgaku* 18/3(1967):140; Karl Bünger, *Quellen zur Rechtsgeschichte der T'ang-zeit*, p. 92.

4. The composite and somewhat simplified picture drawn here is based mainly on the descriptions given in Cheng Chü-chung et al., *Cheng-ho wu li hsin i*, 83/2b–6a, 28/2b–6a, 100/4b–8a, 33/3a–6b. See also the brief descriptions in T'o T'o et al., *Sung shih*, 117/9b–10a (cited hereafter as *SS*); Wang Ying-lin, *Yü hai*, 67/4a. There were a few minor differences in detail between T'ang and Sung rites. See Ou-yang Hsiu, *Hsin T'ang shu*, 48/27a; Feng Yen, *Feng shih wen chien chi*, 4/3a–b; Wang Tang, *T'ang yü lin*, 5/128. See also des Rotours, *Traité*, vol. 1, pp. 363–364, 462. Rites under the sino-foreign state of Chin (1115–1234) appear to have been the same as those in the Sung. See Chang Wei, *Ta Chin chi li*, 24/1a ff.

5. Jan Jacob Maria de Groot, *The Religious System of China* (Leiden: E. J. Brill, 1892–1910), vol. 6, pp. 965–971. It should be remembered that in traditional China "death" referred to any traumatic loss of consciousness.

6. *SS* 117/8a, 10a. The association of amnesties with the Hall of Light goes back to Han times. See Hsieh Wei-hsin, *Ku chin ho pi shih-lei pei-yao*, 25/4b–5a (hereafter cited as *KCHP*). In the early T'ang the documents apparently were sent by horse post in the care of specially designated commissioners. Because of problems created by this system in the ninth century a new system of urgent dispatch was inaugurated. Horse post was also used in the Sung. See Niida Noboru, *Tōryo shui*, p. 798; *LTHFC*, p. 341; Uchida Tomoo, "Kyu Tō-sho keihō-shi," pt. 3, *Do-shisha hōgaku* 18/3(1967): 140; Bünger, *Quellen*, p. 92; Chang P'u, *Li-tai ming-ch'en tsou-i*, 218/9b–10a (cited hereafter as *LTMCTI*); Sung Ch'i, *Ching wen chi* (TSCC ed.), 85/959; Hsieh Shen-fu, *Ch'ing-yüan t'iao-fa shih-lei*, p. 228 (hereafter cited as *TFSL*).

7. *SS* 98/5b. Such worship was also sometimes done in T'ang times. See *TFYK*, p. 1006. For examples of letters of congratulation see, for the T'ang, Liu Tsung-yüan, *Liu ho tung chi* (SPPY ed.), 39/9a–b; for the Sung, see Sung Ch'i, *Ching wen chi*, 85/959, and Wang Feng, *Wu ch'i chi*, 16/10b–12a. See also Ch'ang-sun Wu-chi, *T'ang-lü shu-i*, 2/91 (cited hereafter as *TLSI*).

8. Edwin Reischauer, transl., *Ennin's Diary*, pp. 180–182. Unfortunately we do

not seem to have for this early period the detailed descriptions of the receipt of acts of grace by local officials which we have for Ming times. See *Ming hui-tien* 74/1742 ff.; *Hung-wu li-chih* 7/6b; *Chieh-hsing shih-li* 20/1a.

9. *LTHFC*, pp. 171, 175, 201, 224, 249. Although one hundred days was the generally used figure, there are a few examples of fifty or thirty-day limits. In the theoretical texts which discuss amnesties in terms of astronomical and other portents, a variety of limits are set according to magical considerations. To my knowledge such magically determined limits were never employed in practice. See *LTHFC*, p. 204; *TFYK*, p. 983; *TPYL* 652/9b (citing the *Feng chieh shu* and the *Wang ch'i ching*).

10. *TLSI* 2/13, 14, 15. Go-betweens and guarantors involved in illegal marriages or sales were not to be tried even though they had let the deadline pass without confessing.

11. *TLSI* 2/13. This provision, according to the commentary, applied to crimes ranging from detaining someone or holding them through peaceful enticement down to private possession of forbidden materials—that is, it would not have applied to serious crimes. The sources from the Sung dynasty are a little ambiguous on this point, but it seems that in Sung times a man who did not confess and whose crimes were discovered during the amnesty grace interval was to be prosecuted. There does not seem to be any indication that such prosecution was limited to specified crimes. See Li Tao, *Hsü tzu-chih t'ung-chien ch'ang-pien*, 73/10b–11a (cited hereafter as *HCP*).

12. *TFYK*, p. 980.

13. *TFYK*, p. 1007. This decree indicates clearly that such acts of grace had major political and economic aspects. Several writers have taken special note of the Ch'ing remissions of taxes, as if this were in some way an unusual practice. The data from acts of grace suggest rather that the late imperial dynasties were unusual only in that they forgave taxes so infrequently, whereas in earlier times this was done every few years. Some of these acts even canceled private debts. See Hung Mai, *Jung chai sui-pi* (TSCC ed.), fifth collection, p. 75. The general continuity in types of criminal provisions may perhaps best be indicated by giving a Ch'ing dynasty example. A decree from the reign of Hsüan-tsung says in part: "Officials, clerks, military men, or the people who have committed crimes, with the exception of those guilty of Plotting Rebellion, Treason, or Sedition, sons and grandsons who plot to kill grandfathers and grandmothers or fathers and mothers, those guilty of incest, wives who kill their husbands, slaves who kill the masters of their households, those who in one family kill three members none of whom were guilty of capital crimes, those who commit abortions and cause injury, those who commit premeditated or deliberate homicide, and actually take men's lives, those involved in ku-poison black magic, those who commit homicide using poison, violent bandits, heretics, and others guilty of one of the Ten Abominations, those who have seized military equipment, or hidden fugitives, all others, prior to dawn of the twenty-seventh day of the eighth month of the twenty-fifth year of Chia-ch'ing, whether already discovered or not, whether their cases have already been completed or not, are to be freed. Those who bring cases concerning affairs which happened prior to the amnesty are to be guilty of the crime noted in their

plaint. Those men subject to military exile in each province, those who are found on investigation to have been in exile for three years during which they have been well behaved and have not broken the law, as well as those who are seventy years old, may be freed to return to be registered [as ordinary commoners]. . . ." See *Ta-Ch'ing Hsüan-tsung Ch'eng huang-ti shih-lü* 3/18a–b. For a Ming sample of similar acts see Fu Feng-hsiang, *Huang Ming chao ling* (Taipei: Ch'eng Wen Publishing Co., 1967), 1/7b.

14. Specific grants to religious groups were not unknown, however. See the *ta-she* of A.D. 711 (*TFYK*, p. 998) and A.D. 738 (*TFYK*, p. 1013). The only dynasty where Buddhist influence on pardons is evident is the Yüan. See *LTHFC*, pp. 466–467.

15. There are occasional puzzling exceptions to this general rule. In A.D. 305 there was a Chin great act of grace granted to a group of six prefectures. See *TFYK*, p. 969. In A.D. 684 there was a decree granting the benefits of a great act of grace to Lo prefecture and those of an ordinary act of grace to the rest of the empire. See *TFYK*, p. 955. Another apparent example is entitled a great act of grace for the capital and surrounding areas. In this case, however, the words *ta-she* do not occur in the text of the decree as we have it but only in the heading, and the wording is similar to that in some ordinary acts of grace. It seems probable that this is a simple case of mislabeling. See Sung Min-ch'iu, *T'ang ta chao ling chi*, 84/483 (cited hereafter as *TTCLC*). For another example of a *ta-she* confined to the capital see *TFYK*, p. 973. But these exceptions are so few when measured against the many hundred *ta-she* which applied to the whole empire that they hardly affect the general argument.

16. Again there are puzzling exceptions to this general rule, for a few of what purport to be *ta-she* provided lesser benefits. In two of these cases the words *ta-she* appear only in the headings of their entries in the *TTCLC* and not in the text of the decrees themselves. In the longer versions of these decrees found in the *TFYK* there is no mention of *ta-she*. Thus they would seem to have been ordinary acts of grace, mislabeled. This appears to have been the opinion of Shen Chia-pen, for he notes them but does not label them *ta-she*. See *TTCLC* 482, 485; *TFYK*, pp. 1053, 1055; Shen Chia-pen, *Shen chi-i hsien-sheng i-shu*, she-k'ao 4/17b. One case, however, is more problematical. The *TTCLC* 104 preserves a decree of *ta-she* supposedly associated with the selection of an heir apparent in A.D. 805. In this case the words *ta-she* appear in the text, which rather than freeing all criminals merely reduced sentences for all those with penalties heavier than beating. Those liable for beating were freed. Unfortunately the *TFYK* does not contain this decree.

The absence of this decree from the most comprehensive listing of T'ang acts of grace should serve as a reminder that our catalog of such acts is incomplete, and that we are stating *minimum* levels of judicial grace by relying on those documents which have been preserved to us. See also *Huang Ming chao ling* 1/76; *Ta-Ch'ing Hsüan-tsung Ch'eng huang-ti shih-lü* 3/18a–b for the Ming and Ch'ing.

17. Hsü Ching-tsung, *Wen kuan tz'u lin*, p. 666; *LTHFC*, p. 223; Yao Ssu-lien, *Ch'en shu*, 2/35–36; *TFYK*, p. 980, chap. 84 passim. This was still the practice under later dynasties. See also *Huang Ming chao ling* 1/7b; *Ta-Ch'ing Hsüan-tsung Ch'eng huang-ti shih-lü* 3/18a–b.

18. *TLSI* 1/38. The best English language introduction to these general topics is Wallace Johnson, *The T'ang Code: General Principles*, vol. 1. In this chapter I have adopted from his work the translations of a number of legal terms. He has also compiled an index to the T'ang Code which made far easier the task of preparing the material for this chapter. See Wallace Johnson, comp., *T'ang-lü shu-i yin-te*. See also *Ta-Ch'ing Hsüan-tsung Ch'eng huang-ti shih-lü* 3/18a–b.

19. *LTHFC*, p. 219; *TFYK*, p. 980; the same stipulation was also used in later times. See *Huang Ming chao ling* 1/7b; *Ta-Ch'ing Hsüan-tsung Ch'eng huang-ti shih-lü* 3/18a–b.

20. *LTHFC*, pp. 171, 223, 231; Hsü Ching-tsung, *Wen kuan tz'u lin*, p. 666; Chang P'u, *Li-tai ming-ch'en tsou-i*, 218/2b; Yao Ssu-lien, *Ch'en shu*, 2/35–36; *TFYK*, p. 980. For the continuation of this provision in later dynasties see, for example, *Huang Ming chao ling* 1/7b.

21. *TLSI* 3/78.

22. Hsiao Tzu-hsien, *Nan Ch'i shu*, 2/32. Other examples occur in later decrees from the Liang dynasty. See *LTHFC*, pp. 217, 231.

23. *LTHFC*, p. 272.

24. *TLSI* 4/6, 7; *TFYK*, p. 1055 et passim. An incident from the Liu Sung (A.D. 455) indicates that cases of Depravity *(pu-tao)* and Lack of Filial Piety *(pu-hsiao)* could be raised after an intervening amnesty. See *LTHFC*, p. 188. For the continuation of similar rules under later dynasties see, for the Liao, Shimada Masao, *Ryōsei no kenkyū*, p. 266; for the Sung, see Chang Fang-p'ing, *Lo ch'uan chi* (SPPY ed.), 20/14b–15a; for the Ming, see *Huang Ming chao ling* 1/7b; for the Ch'ing, see *Ta-Ch'ing Hsüan-tsung Ch'eng huang-ti shih-lü* 3/18a–b and *Ta Ch'ing lü-li* 1/309 (hereafter cited *TCLL*). For a French translation of this last passage see P. L. F. Philastre, *Le Code annamite*, vol. 1, p. 159.

25. *TLSI* 4/81. During the Ming such officials were considered guilty of "having deliberately convicted an innocent man." See *Ta Ming lü* (Huang Ming chih-shu ed.), 14/237b–238a.

26. *LTHFC*, pp. 249–250; *TLSI* 1/52; Johnson, *Code*, pp. 154. Those sentenced for crimes that called for exile despite amnesty could not benefit from this statute. Such permission continued to be granted by later dynasties, but sparingly. See Tou I, *Sung hsing t'ung* 3/5b (hereafter cited *SHT*); *Ta Ming lü chih-chieh*, p. 54; *Huang ch'ao wen hsien t'ung k'ao* (Chiu-t'ung ed.), 210/23b, 43a.

27. *LTHFC*, p. 157.

28. Hao I-hsing, *Pu Sung shu hsing-fa chih* (TSCC ed.), 8, 18. The examples cited involved those guilty of killing junior relatives and officials. This was not merely a policy but was written into the laws. At this time these people were to be transported two thousand *li*. See *LTHFC*, pp. 181–182. Such practices continued to be followed throughout imperial times. See *TCLL* 4/2866; Philastre, *Code annamite*, vol. 2, p. 373.

29. *TLSI* 3/54; see also 3/49. This policy was also followed in later times. For the Sung see *TFSL*, pp. 228, 518–519. A *li* was approximately one third of a mile.

30. *TLSI* 2/9, 10; see also 2/99. For an example of this policy from Northern Chou

(A.D. 558) see *LTHFC*, p. 273; Ch'eng Shu-te, *Chiu-ch'ao lü-k'ao*, p. 420. For the commutation provisions see Niida, *Tōryo shui*, p. 788. Similar rules were followed during the Sung; see *TFSL*, pp. 227, 544. For the Ming see *Ta Ming lü chih-chieh*, pp. 63–67. For the Ch'ing see Philastre, *Code annamite*, vol. 1, pp. 194–204. The T'ang rules on this point are curiously similar to an amnesty of the Anglo-Saxon King Athelstan, who pardoned all thefts committed within a certain period, but on condition that the thieves confess their crimes before a set date and make amends. See Hurnard, *King's Pardon*, p. 4.

31. *TLSI* 4/35.

32. *TLSI* 2/14, 15.

33. *TLSI* 4/84. Post-Sung rules were more severe. See *Ta Ming lü* 14/237b; *TCLL* 5/3721; Philastre, *Code annamite*, vol. 2, pp. 714–716.

34. *TLSI* 3/2, 3, 5, 6, 8. These mandatory divorces occurred when either of the parties to the marriage committed certain serious crimes within the family—for example, if they beat or killed members of their spouse's family or had sexual intercourse with certain relatives. See Ch'ü T'ung-tsu, *Law and Society in Traditional China*, pp. 122–123. For the Sung continuation of this practice see *HCP* 73/10b and *TFSL*, p. 227. For the Ming see *Ta Ming lü chih-chieh*, p. 214. For the Ch'ing see *TCLL* I/309, II/1092; Philastre, *Code annamite*, vol. 1, pp. 159, 545; Gui Boulais, *Manuel du code chinois*, p. 301; G. T. Staunton, *Ta Tsing Leu Lee*, p. 120.

35. *TLSI* 2/109.

36. Johnson, *Code*, p. 29; Ou Koei-hing, *La Peine d'après le code des T'ang*, pp. 57–60. Such provisions had been, and continued to be, characteristic of Chinese law. See Hulsewé, *Remnants of Han Law*, pp. 298 ff.; Karl Bünger, "The Punishment of Lunatics and Negligents According to Classical Chinese Law"; *SHT*, 4/2b ff.; *TCLL* I/409 ff.; Philastre, *Code annamite*, vol. 1, pp. 184 ff.; *Ta Ming lü* 13/54a–b.

37. *TLSI* 2/37. No mention is made of the treatment of women who were unable to pay the redemption fees, so we must assume that they were sent into exile.

38. *TLSI* 1/25 ff.; Johnson, *Code*, p. 83; Ou, *La Peine*, pp. 67–68; Tai Yen-hui, *T'ang lü t'ung lun*, pp. 216 ff. For the early history of this system see Hulsewé, *Remnants of Han Law*, pp. 285–298; Balazs, *Le Traité*, p. 145, n. 185; Ch'eng Shu-te, *Chiu-ch'ao lü-k'ao*, p. 245. The Eight Deliberations and other privileges for officials continued to be copied into the codes of later dynasties. See Shimada Masao, *Ryōsei no kenkyū*, pp. 141 ff.; *SHT* 2/1a ff.; Paul Ratchnevsky, *Un Code des Yüan*, pp. 17 ff.; *Ta Ming lü chih-chieh*, p. 28 ff.; *Ta Ming ling* (Huang Ming chih shu ed.), 1/37b ff.; *Ta Ch'ing lü-li* 3/1a ff. It should be noted, however, that the Yung-cheng Emperor in the Ch'ing remarked that "the old text statutes and substatutes have an item on the Eight Deliberations which has been handed down for a long time through successive dynasties, but in our dynasty, although we have this text, in reality we do not practice it." See *Huang ch'ao t'ung chih* (Chiu t'ung ed.), 76/15a.

In my account of T'ang privileges (and the same description would hold generally true for later dynasties) I have simplified the criteria for membership in the privileged groups. In actual practice the value of rank depended in some cases on whether it was substantive or honorary, posthumously rewarded or awarded to a living official, and so forth. It should also be borne in mind that in late imperial times the effects of these privileges on the treatment of officials seems to have been less than it was in the T'ang and Sung.

The treatment of officials stands in sharp contrast to that accorded certain other groups. During the Latter Wei one functionary complained that whereas officials guilty of Plotting Sedition might be pardoned by a small act of grace, clerks guilty of even minor crimes were excluded from amnesties. See Ch'eng Shu-te, *Chiu-ch'ao lü-k'ao*, pp. 381–382. For an excellent description of the legal position of T'ang officials and their privileges, see Tai Yen-hui, *T'ang lü t'ung lun*, especially pp. 241–280.

39. Ch'eng Shu-te, *Chiu-ch'ao lü-k'ao*, p. 245. Another incident, from A.D. 275–280, indicates that those guilty of corruption were to be barred from office *(chin-chih)* despite an intervening amnesty; ibid., p. 263. For a general description of these sanctions during this era see Balazs, *Le Traité*, pp. 114–115, n. 82, p. 166, n. 233.

40. *LTHFC*, p. 246.

41. The rulings concerning the Latter Wei do not explicitly say that the rules involved were to apply to officials within their spheres of jurisdiction, but from the general tenor of the material I think we can assume that to have been the case. See *LTHFC*, pp. 246, 248–249; Ch'ang-sun Wu-chi, *Sui shu* 25/17b; Balazs, *Le Traité*, p. 75; Uchida, "Zui-sho," pt. 6, p. 115; *TLSI* 1/37–40, 4/76; Johnson, *Code*, passim, especially pp. 133 ff.

42. *Hsü t'ung tien* (Chiu-t'ung ed.), 117/1b; *TFYK*, pp. 977–978; *TTCLC* 392. Ex-officials who died in exile might be posthumously "reinstated" in their old offices. See *TFYK*, p. 1075 et passim.

43. Fan Yeh, *Hou Han shu*, 2/17b, 3/16a, 6/10b.

44. For the Wei see the *Hsien-ti chuan* cited in the annotation of Ch'en Shou, *San kuo chih* (Erh shih ssu shih ed.), 2/15b; See also *LTHFC*, p. 279. Codes in late imperial China had a special article called "those not to be spared by ordinary amnesties." See *Ta Ming lü* 13/51a–b; *TCLL* 1/307.

45. *LTHFC*, p. 255; Hsü Ching-tsung, *Wen kuan tz'u lin*, p. 666; *TFYK*, p. 979 et passim. Rules of amnesty coverage were also used in certain situations to determine eligibility for individual pardons. Under T'ang law a criminal who captured (or in some cases killed) and turned over to the authorities someone guilty of a crime more heavily punished than his own, or captured half or more of a gang of criminals, was to be pardoned. However, if his crime was one not forgiven by an ordinary amnesty he could not be pardoned. See *TLSI* 2/20–21.

46. *TFYK*, pp. 981–1097.

47. *TFYK*, p. 1012.

48. *TLSI* 2/21.

49. *TLSI* 1/16; Johnson, *Code*, pp. 66. My renderings of the names of these Ten Abominations are taken from Johnson's work. Some of the crimes included in the Ten Abominations are mentioned in Han materials. See Hulsewé, *Remnants of Han Law*, pp. 156–204. During the post-Han era the practice of grouping particularly horrible crimes together appeared. See Balazs, *Le Traité*, pp. 142–145, n. 184. The name Ten Abominations with the list of crimes that were later to be covered by that

term first appeared during the Sui. From the Sui it was taken over by the T'ang and later dynasties. For translations of the relevant materials see (in addition to Johnson) Ou, *La Peine*, pp. 99, 102; Bünger, *Quellen*, p. 88; Raymond Deloustal, "La Justice dans l'ancien Annam," pp. 97–98; Paul Ratchnevsky, *Un Code des Yüan*, p. 13; Philastre, *Code annamite*, vol. 1, pp. 122–124. Contumacy continued to be a crime not pardoned by ordinary amnesties, because, as the Ch'ing Code says, "It is a crime which severs the moral ties created by Heaven." See *TCLL* 4/2938; Philastre, *Code annamite*, vol. 2, p. 401.

50. *TLSI* 4/85, 73. Apparently men in jail awaiting execution often asked their relatives or dependents to kill them so that they might be spared the horrors of official execution. See Philastre, *Code annamite*, vol. 2, pp. 652 ff.

51. *TLSI* 4/84–85.

52. Fan Yeh, *Hou Han shu*, 2/17b, 6/10b.

53. The properties of those who had been living with the principals but who were not liable for joint adjudication were not to be confiscated, nor were the properties of those who were liable to be jointly adjudicated but who had not been living with the principals. See *TLSI* 3/41.

54. *TLSI* 4/84–85.

55. *LTMCTI* 218/3a, 4b.

56. *TLSI* 2/3, 6–8, 3/41.

57. *TLSI* 2/8.

58. Edward H. Schafer, *The Vermillion Bird*, p. 102.

59. *TLSI* 1/50, 56–57, 3/51. For the continuation of these rules in later times see *SHT*, 18/2a ff.; *TCLL* IV/2491; Philastre, *Code annamite*, vol. 2, p. 205; *Ta Ming lü chi-chieh*, p. 429.

60. Ch'eng Shu-te, *Chiu-ch'ao lü-k'ao*, p. 317; Ch'ang-sun Wu-chi, *Sui shu* 25/5b; Balazs, *Le Traité*, p. 42; Uchida, "Zui-sho," pt. 2, p. 66.

61. *TLSI* 4/85. See, for example, *Ta Ming lü* (Huang Ming chih-shu ed.), 14/237b–238a, *TCLL* 5/3727 ff.

62. *TFYK*, pp. 981–1094.

63. *TTCLC* 397, 489.

64. This general rule seems to be indicated by a statement in the commentary to the T'ang Code which says that if the letter of amnesty said that "without distinction of light or heavy all are to be freed," but did not say that "those not to be benefited by ordinary amnesties are to be benefited," then this latter group of persons was not within the scope of the grant of complete liberation. See *TLSI* 4/85. By contrast it is indicated in some other passages of the commentary that crimes not specifically mentioned might be included by implication from other provisions of the amnesty. Thus the commentary says that "[when] the amnesty letter determines the names of the crimes one should follow the lighter [interpretation]. It is not permitted to cite the statutes and by analogy seek a heavier [penalty]. Commentary: for example the act of grace of Chen-kuan 9/3/16 [A.D. 635] forgave those guilty of capital crimes or less. The scope of the amnesty did not include those not spared by ordinary amnesties, those guilty of the Ten Abominations, heretics who misled the multitudes, or those guilty of Plotting Treason when overt acts had occurred. According to the amnesty

those guilty of the Ten Abominations were not to be pardoned. Plotting Treason is one of the Ten Abominations. [But] the amnesty especially allows the pardoning of those involved in Plotting Treason when no overt acts had occurred [that is, by specifically indicating exclusion of cases where overt acts had occurred]." See *TLSI* 4/85. The implications of this are made explicit in Sung Law. It was acknowledged that a decree of amnesty did not exhaustively catalog the crimes to be forgiven. Officials were to classify other crimes by "analogy" as falling within the grant.

65. *TLSI* 1/50–51; Johnson, *Code*, pp. 213–214. Those who had not set out on the road because it was not the proper season for traveling were also freed. See *TLSI* 1/52; Niida, *Tōryō shui*, p. 770. Such provisions were part of the legal rules both before and after T'ang times. See Ch'eng Shu-te, *Chiu-ch'ao lü-k'ao*, pp. 381–382; Hsü Ching-tsung, *Wen kuan tz'u lin*, p. 666; *SHT* 3/4a–5a; Hsü Sung, *Sung hui-yao chi kao*, hsing-fa 4/29a–b (hereafter cited *SHY*); *HCP* 393/21a.

66. This is the opinion of both Shen Chia-pen and Tai Yen-hui. See Shen Chia-pen, *Shen chi-i hsien-sheng i-shu*, Ming lü mu chien 1/12a–b; Tai Yen-hui, *T'ang-lü t'ung-lun*, p. 330.

67. *TLSI* 1/51; Johnson, *Code*, p. 152.

68. *TLSI* 1/49; Johnson, *Code*, p. 147.

69. *TFYK*, pp. 968, 980; *LTHFC*, pp. 171, 173, 201, 204, 208, 224, 231; Hsü Ching-tsung, *Wen kuan tz'u lin*, p. 666; Shen Yüeh, *Sung shu* (Erh shih san shih ed.), 3/26; Balazs, *Le Traité*, p. 114, n. 79. The phrase used in this pre-T'ang period for release of "perpetual" exiles was *yüan-ch'ien* and not the *fang-huan* of T'ang times.

70. *TTCLC* 11, 106, 373, 381, 389–390, 439, 486, 492.

71. *TFYK*, pp. 981–985. Kao-tsu actually issued four *ta-she*, but one was issued on his accession and hence could not result in freeing men convicted during his reign. See also the decree of T'ien-pao 6 (A.D. 747) which resulted in the transfer of men exiled prior to A.D. 742, and this despite *ta-she* in 742 and 744. See *TFYK*, pp. 1016–1019.

72. *KCHP* 25/9a.

73. *Hsü t'ung tien* (Chiu T'ung ed.), 117/2a.

74. *TTCLC* 401.

75. *SHT*, 3/8b; *Hsü t'ung tien* 117/1b. In late imperial China men in exile were also sometimes (but not always) freed to return by amnesties. See Chiang Ch'ao-po, *Shuang chiu yao lü* (TSCC ed.), 2/17; *Ta-Ch'ing Hsüan-tsung Ch'eng huang-ti shih-lü* 3/18a–b.

76. *TTCLC* 401. Some of these men serving exile *(liu)* might be officials, particularly those originally sentenced to death but spared and sent to serve *liu*. This much is clear from the text of this decree. (It was quite common to sentence officials to death and then commute this penalty to exile through a special individual imperial act of grace.) However, it is also clear that not all those affected by measured transfer were officials. See, for example, a decree which speaks of "miscellaneous criminals sentenced to exile who have already been transferred to nearer jurisdictions"; *TTCLC* 439. For other examples of this process see *TTCLC* 11, 29, 105–106, 373, 381, 385, 390, 393, 439, 492.

77. *TTCLC* 492. "If [such men] have already been transferred on two occasions then free them." Although this is the only example I know of such a provision being explicitly included in our corpus of acts of grace, I suspect that it reflects a common practice. For "reranking" see *TFYK*, p. 1094. Such reranking was generally granted after a number of measured transfers; see *TFYK*, chaps. 84–91 passim.

78. Lu Chih, *Chu lu hsüan kung tsou-i*, 11/4a ff.

79. Shen, *Shen chi-i hsien-sheng i-shu*, she-k'ao 4/23b–25a. Shen lists no empire-wide ordinary acts of grace for the Empress Wu, but this is hardly surprising since during her twenty-year reign she issued twenty-nine great acts of grace.

80. Wu Ching, *Chen-kuan cheng-yao* (SPPY ed.), 8/12b–13a. Other versions of this statement can be found in several places including *LTMCTI*, 118/6b, and Wang P'u, *T'ang hui-yao* (TSCC ed.), 40/728.

81. The editors of the *Hsü t'ung tien* remark that "from the reign of T'ai-tsung such a thing had rarely been seen. For petty faults officials were censured and could no longer be listed for appointment. When Shun-tsung ascended the throne [in 805] he for the first time allowed them to be transferred by stages *(liang-i)*." See *Hsü t'ung tien* 117/1a. There are other expressions of similar sentiments later in the T'ang, but they seem not to have affected practice. See also Wang P'u, *T'ang hui-yao*, for a document from A.D. 836.

82. *TFYK*, pp. 982–1094. See also Shen, *Shen chi-i hsien-sheng i-shu*, she-k'ao 4/25a, for the situation under the Empress Wu.

83. The figures for these calculations were taken from Shen, *Shen chi-i hsien-sheng i-shu*, she-k'ao. To double-check the accuracy of Shen's work I also consulted the annals of the *New T'ang History*. Shen had noted every amnesty. For the pre-T'ang period, several states usually were in power at the same time in different parts of China; in calculating averages for the whole group I therefore took the average of the averages of each calculated separately.

CHAPTER 4: ACTS OF GRACE IN SUNG CHINA

1. The *Sung hsing t'ung* consists of the T'ang Code, amended in some minor ways, plus currently relevant decrees issued by emperors of the T'ang or the Five Dynasties subsequent to the publication of the edition of the T'ang Code used. Parts of our current version were in fact copied from the T'ang Code by twentieth-century editors. See Makino Tatsumi and Niida Noboru, "Ko Tō-ritsu sogi seisaku nendai ko," *Tōhōgakuhō* (Tokyo), 1(1931):70–158, 2(1932):50–226.

2. The best of the Southern Sung annals, Li Hsin-ch'uan, *Chien-yen i-lai hsi nien yao lu*, covers only the early part of the Southern Sung, and at that is less detailed than the *Rough Draft*. The useful annals known as the *Sung shih ch'uan-wen hsü tzu-chih t'ung-chien*, by an unknown author, cover the whole dynasty but contain far more material on the reign of Kao-tsung (1126–1162) than on the reigns of later emperors. In addition to these annals, the *Rough Draft*, and the *Chien-yen i-lai hsi nien yao lu*, I also made use of the *Sung shih*; Wang Ch'eng, *Tung tu shih lüeh*; *Sung ta-chao ling-chi*; *Huang Sung chung-hsing liang ch'ao sheng cheng*; Ma Tuan-lin, *Wen hsien t'ung k'ao*; Ch'en Chün, *Huang ch'ao pien-nien kang-mu pei-yao*; Hsüeh

Ying-ch'i, *Sung Yüan t'ung-chien;* Li Ch'ih, *Huang Sung shih ch'ao kang yao;* Li Hsin-ch'uan, *Chien-yen i-lai ch'ao-yeh tsa-chih;* and Pi Yüan, *Hsü Tzu-chih t'ung-chien* (Blockprint edition, 1801).

3. The best examples of Sung acts of grace are to be found in Li Yu, *Sung ch'ao shih shih.*

4. The theoretical penalties are set down in the General Principles section of the Sung Code, but Sung penal practice seems to have deviated more from the supposed legal prescriptions than that under any other dynasty. No adequate study of Sung penal practice exists in any language. Despite this great variation of practice from the impression conveyed by the code, the Sung authorities continued to subject prisoners to the same sorts of punishments as earlier and later states.

5. The statistics used here are based on the annals and other materials cited in note 2 above.

6. In counting these ordinary amnesties I have included only acts which affected all criminals, including those sentenced to death. In addition there were a dozen empirewide acts of grace which reduced the sentences of all men subject to exile or less but did not affect capital sentences. During the Sung ordinary amnesties were referred to as *te-yin.* This term was also used in the T'ang.

7. See Miyazaki Ichisada, "Sō-Gen jidai no hōsei to saiban kikō," pp. 136 ff.; Hsü Dau-lin, "Sung-lü chung te shen-p'an chih-tu," pp. 18–28; Tseng Kung, *Lung p'ing chi,* 3/5a; *SHY* hsing-fa 3/51a, 4/57a–b. See also Hsü Dau-lin, "Fan-i piehk'an k'ao," pp. 20–28; Hsü Dau-lin, "Sung-ch'ao te hsien-chi ssu-fa," pp. 19–28.

8. *SHY* hsing-fa 3/51a.

9. *SHY* hsing-fa 6/63a.

10. David C. Buxbaum, "Some Aspects of Civil Procedure and Practice at the Trial Level in Tanshui and Hsinchu from 1789 to 1895."

11. See Miyazaki Ichisada, "Sō-Gen jidai no hōsei to saiban kikō," p. 141. But see *SHY* hsing-fa 4/57a–b; Tseng Kung, *Lung p'ing chi,* 3/5a. See also *SHY* hsing-fa 4/69 ff.

12. In practice, apart from frequent amnesties, other factors sharply reduced the proportion of capital criminals who were executed—one official estimated that only about ten percent actually were killed. See *SHY* hsing-fa 6/44a.

13. *TFSL,* p. 227; *SHY* hsing-fa 4/1a–b, hsing-fa 4/51a, hsing-fa 4/24b, hsing-fa 4/38a–b. In later times it appears that men already in exile were usually not freed to return. See *Ta Ming ling* 1/46b; *TCLL* 1/312–313; *Huang ch'ao wen hsien t'ung k'ao* 210/52b.

14. T'o T'o, *Sung shih* 15/6a–b. This practice continued under some later dynasties. For the Ch'ing see *Huang ch'ao wen hsien t'ung k'ao* 210/5a.

15. *TLSI* 1/52; *SHT* 30/11b.

16. *SHY* hsing-fa 4/59a. Even those men "exiled" and registered in the army (whose terms of service were indeterminate) were no worse off than ordinary soldiers. See Sogabe Shizuo, "Sōdai no shihai ni tsuite."

17. See *SHY* hsing-fa 6/65a–66a for some figures on this problem. See also *TFSL,* p. 512.

18. See, for example, *SHY* hsing-fa 4/46b; *LTHFC,* p. 415.

19. *LTMCTI* 218/24a.

20. I am indebted to Hoyt Tillman of the University of Arizona for bringing to my attention the case of Ch'en Fu-liang's father. See also *SHY* hsing-fa 4/48a–b.

21. Under the Sung, failure to comply completely with enforcement was apparently considered the crime of "breaking regulations" *(wei-chih)*. See *KCHP* 25/7b. During the Ch'ing the problem was covered by special rules. If officials delayed ten days in freeing those due for release under an amnesty, the officials were to be demoted. If officials thought the case was suspicious and the criminal should not be freed, they were to memorialize. See *TCLL* 4/3522–3523.

22. *LTMCTI* 218/10b.

23. *HCP* 180/17a. See also *HCP* 73/7b. Apparently it was hard to keep the news of such grants from leaking out unofficially. See Li Hsin-ch'uan, *Chien-yen i-lai hsi nien yao lü*, p. 423.

24. *HCP* 78/12a, 86/11b, 91/13b, 122/11a et passim; *TFSL*, pp. 227–228; *WHTK* 173/1495; *KCHP* 25/7b.

25. *WHTK* 173/1496; Li Ch'ih, *Huang Sung shih ch'ao kang yao*, 1/14a.

26. *WHTK* 173/1495; *LTHFC*, pp. 423–424.

27. *LTHFC*, p. 425; Chuang Chi-yü, *Chi lei pien* (TSCC ed.), chung p. 53.

28. *SHY* hsing-fa 4/39b; *TFSL*, p. 229.

29. *TFSL*, p. 228.

30. Cheng K'o, *Che yü kuei chien* (TSCC ed.), p. 66.

31. There are various references to breakdowns in the system. See *HCP* 380/17a, for example, about officials in exile still being held despite several amnesties. See also *SHY* hsing-fa 4/45a.

32. *LTHFC*, pp. 219, 231, 259, 274; Ch'ang-sun Wu-chi, *Sui shu* 25/6a, 9b, 19a; Balazs, *Le Traité*, pp. 43, 53, 78.

33. *LTHFC*, pp. 339, 357; *TFYK*, p. 991 et passim; Ch'en Ku-yüan, *Chung-kuo fa-chih shih*, p. 313.

34. *SHY* hsing-fa 5/1a.

35. *TFSL*, p. 226. There is a variety of terms for inspections of cases which by Sung times were synonyms. Most commonly such inspections were called *lu-ch'iu* (錄囚), but in the T'ang they were at times called *lu-ch'iu* (慮囚) and in the Sung they are occasionally called *su-chüeh* (疎決). Shen Chia-pen, *Shen chi-i hsien-sheng i-shu*, wen-tsun ch'iu 9a–10a, explains the root meanings behind *lu-ch'iu* (錄囚) and *lu-ch'iu* (慮囚).

36. *SHY* hsing-fa 5/3b, 4b, 5/4a–b, 5b–6a, 6b, 8a–b, 10a, 10b, 11a–b, 12a, 40a–b. Although it is not so specified in all cases, it seems clear that the exclusions were to apply in most cases to all of the "four homicides" *(ssu-sha)*: premeditated murder *(mou-sha)*, deliberate murder *(ku-sha)*, homicide in an affray *(tou-sha)*, and killing during banditry *(chieh-sha)*. Several of the order also specify that the victim must have in fact died. Those guilty of attempted murder were not excluded.

37. *SHY* hsing-fa 5/1a ff., see especially 7b, 9a, 9b. There is even one instance in which coverage did not extend to exile: only those liable for sentences of penal servitude had their sentences reduced (ibid., 5b). But this is an anomaly in light of the general practice.

38. Occasionally some guidance is given, as when we are told that assaults and homicides which result from them are to be distinguished by whether the assailant was armed, and with what, as well as where the assailant struck the victim. See *TFSL*, p. 230.

39. For this set of beliefs see Hsü Dau-lin, "Crime and Cosmic Order"; *SHY* hsing-fa 5, 14a, 39a, 39b–40a, 40a, 40b, 40b–41a, 41a, 41a–b, 42a, 44a–b, 45b, 46a. There are occasional exceptions to this rule, as in the inspection of A.D. 1101 which purports to be connected with the sickness of the empress dowager; ibid. 10b–11a.

40. This procedure was halted ostensibly because of deaths among those being moved to the capital. See *LTHFC*, p. 383.

41. *SHY* hsing-fa 5/3b. See also examples dating from 1006 (*HCP* 48/13a) and 1075 (*HCP* 12507/1a).

42. Chao Ju-yü, *Chu ch'en tsou-i* 100/2a.

43. *SHY* hsing-fa 5/39a.

44. *SHY* hsing-fa 5/39b.

45. *SHY* hsing-fa 5/40a–b.

46. *SHY* hsing-fa 5/42b–43a; see also 45b.

47. *SHY* hsing-fa 5/46b.

48. *SHY* hsing-fa 3/88a, 5/46b, 47a–b, 47b.

49. *SHY* hsing-fa 5/11a ff.

50. Ssu-ma Kuang, *Wen kuo wen cheng Ssu-ma kung wen-chi* (SPTK ed.), 18/7a–8a. I have rendered this passage somewhat freely in an attempt to preserve the feeling of the original for an English-speaking audience. Also found, with some errors in text, in *HCP* 12429/4a–b. The translation of the quote from the *Book of Documents* is from Legge, *Shoo King*, p. 39. For other samples of this sort of criticism see *LTHFC*, pp. 291, 423; Hsü t'ung tien 117/2a; Ma Tuan-lin, *Wen hsien t'ung k'ao* 1495–1496; *HCP* 180/17a; Wang P'u, *Wu-tai hui-yao* (TSCC ed.), 119; Chao Ju-yü, *Chu ch'en tsou-i* 100/3a; *LTMCTI* 218/2b, 10a–b, 11a–b, 11b–12b, 116b; Hung Mai, *Jung chai sui-pi* (fifth collection), pp. 62, 147; Wang P'u, *T'ang hui-yao* 40/728–729.

CHAPTER 5:
LATE IMPERIAL CHINA: THE SIGNIFICANCE OF CHANGE

1. The only substantial English-language work on the Liao state, Karl A. Wittfogel and Feng Chia-sheng, *The History of Chinese Society: Liao,* does not deal with Liao law as a major topic, but see pp. 465–467. Much more informative is Shimada Masao, *Ryōsei no kenkyū.*

2. A brief description of this evolution of Chinese codes from the T'ang on is given in Derk Bodde and Clarence Morris, *Law in Imperial China,* pp. 55–63.

3. Shimada Masao, *Ryōsei no kenkyū,* pp. 140, 266–267.

4. For these Liao statistics see Shen Chia-pen, *Shen chi-i hsien-sheng i-shu,* she-k'ao, 5/12a–14a.

5. Chang Wei, *Ta Chin chi li* (Pai pu ts'ung-shu chi-ch'eng ed.), 24/1a ff.

6. According to the figures given by Shen, *Shen chi-i hsien-sheng i-shu,* she-k'ao

5/14b–16a, the average was once every sixty-five months. The *Hsü wen hsien t'ung-k'ao* (Chiu T'ung ed.) adds several other acts, giving an average of once every fifty-four months.

7. For a description of this process see Paul Heng-chao Ch'en, *Chinese Legal Tradition under the Mongols: The Code of 1291 as Reconstructed.*

8. Shen, *Shen chi-i hsien-sheng i-shu,* she-k'ao 5/16a–18b. The short reigns of Wu-tsung (r. 1308–1312), Ying-tsung (r. 1321–1324), Wen-tsung (r. 1330–1333), and Ning-tsung (r. 1333) were periods of internal political struggle. As often happened under such conditions, acts of grace were issued frequently, perhaps as part of a desperate search for political support. Wu-tsung issued four in five years on the throne; Ying-tsung two in three years; and Wen-tsung three in five years. Of these acts, however, one for each emperor came on his accession to the throne, a more or less standard practice prior to the Ming dynasty. So it might be more meaningful to say that Wu-tsung issued three more amnesties than he might have been expected to; that Ying-tsung issued one more; and Wen-tsung two more. In any case the reigns of these men, totaling less than 14 out of the 108 years of Yüan rule in China, are only a minor exception to the general pattern.

9. Shen, *Shen chi-i hsien-sheng i-shu,* she-k'ao 5/18b–21b.

10. I am deeply indebted to Dr. Fu-mei Chen for her comments on this work and most particularly on the Ch'ing section. Her advice saved me from committing a number of egregious errors. I should stress, however, that the arguments which follow in Chapter 6, and especially the more speculative interpretations of the late imperial materials, do not necessarily reflect her views. These hypotheses rather represent a first attempt to come to grips with the implications of the changes in the frequency of amnesties. Because the Ch'ing sources are so rich and varied, it was not realistically possible for me to deal with them except in a highly selective and incomplete manner. They really deserve a separate and thorough study by a specialist in late traditional law. Such a study might well result in more adequate hypotheses about the meaning of the basic change with which I have been concerned.

Nevertheless, even the limited survey I was able to make does seem to show without qualification that the number of acts of grace declined in the late imperial period. Some idea of the number of amnesties can be gained from such works as Chao Erh-sun, *Ch'ing shih kao,* chaps. 1–25, and from *Huang ch'ao wen hsien t'ung k'ao* (Chiu-t'ung ed.), chap. 210. (In addition to their notices of amnesties the *Ch'ing shih kao* annals also take note of many grants of goods, ranks, and so on; these grants might be called acts of grace but were not amnesties since they contained no criminal provisions. These grants seem never to have been labeled *she.*)

11. *Ta Ch'ing lü-li hui t'ung hsin tsuan,* 5 vols., passim, but see especially vol. 1, pp. 307 ff. This is a reprint of the 1873 version of the Ch'ing Code. See also *Hsing-an hui-lan hsü-pien* (Taipei: Wen Hai Publishing Co., 1970), *ming-li* section; *Ta Ch'ing hui-tien shih-li* (Kuang-hsu ed.), 729:1–731:14.

12. *LTHFC,* p. 588; Chang T'ing-yü, *Ming shih* (Po-na ed.), 12/4a.

13. See Wakashiro Kujiro, *Ryō-shi sakuin.* Given the poverty of Liao sources we should probably assume that inspections of cases happened on other unrecorded oc-

casions, but unfortunately we have no way of estimating how often they may have taken place.

14. T'o T'o et al., *Liao shih*, 3/3b, 3/8a, 6/6b, 7/1b, 13/5a, 13/5b, 13/8b, 13/9b, 14/1b, 15/6a, 15/7b, 15/12a, 16/2a, 16/4a, 16/6a, 24/1b. See also *LTHFC*, p. 430. Since the Liao borrowed the Chinese aspects of their legal institutions from the T'ang, T'ang practices are more relevant than those of the contemporary Sung.

15. *LTHFC*, p. 440.

16. We do have indirect evidence that inspections had taken place between these two dates. A decree preserved in the *Hsü t'ung chih* (Chiu t'ung ed.), 146/8b, makes reference to those *shen-lu kuan* who had failed to impeach guilty officials and clerks.

17. T'o T'o et al., *Chin shih* (Po-na ed.), 6/13b, 10/12a, 11/4a, 12/1b, 14/6b, 15/11a, 15/13a, 15/13b, 16/5a, 17/3b. On the sources for the Chin history see Chan Hok-lam, *The Historiography of the Chin Dynasty: Three Studies*, pp. 22–23. This picture—the belated adoption of the inspection system and its transformation during the last part of the dynasty into a fairly frequent though irregular part of the judicial process—probably reflects accurately the actual course of events. The *Chin History*, like the histories of the Liao and the Sung, was compiled by a commission a little more than a century after the collapse of the Chin. The paucity of reviews recorded for the Liao may well reflect the poor quality of the sources transmitted from the Liao to the Yüan by the intervening Chin state. But the Mongols overran the Chin and in large measure adopted its personnel and practices in ruling China. Moreover, soon after the conquest devoted officials who had served Chin set about the task of collecting and preserving Chin historical records. The Yüan compilers thus had available to them adequate Chin records, and we know from the example of the Sung history that the compilers included notices of case inspections in the imperial annals when these were noted in their sources.

18. Sung Lien, *Yüan shih* (Po-na ed.), 5/4b, 6/6b, 6/19a–b, 12/16a, 13/11a, 13/16b, 14/15b, 20/14b, 21/15b, 22/14b, 22/22b, 23/7a, 24/23b, 26/18b, 27/1b, 30/2b, 30/15a–b.

29. *LTHFC*, pp. 587–588; Chang T'ing-yü, *Ming shih*, 2/18a; *Ming T'ai-tsu shih-lü* 139/6b, 149/3a, 155/4a.

20. *Ming T'ai-tsu shih-lü* 149/3a.

21. *LTHFC*, pp. 587–588; *Ming Ch'eng-tsu shih-lü* 28/6b, 36/3a, 70/1b, 157/3a, 219/2a.

22. *Ming Hsüan-tsung shih-lü* 23/5b, 17/1a, 28/5b, 29/4a–b, 39/9a, 43/3b, 106/1b; *LTHFC*, p. 588.

23. See, for example, *Ming Ch'eng-tsu shih-lü* 36/3a; *LTHFC*, p. 587.

24. *LTHFC*, pp. 588–589; *Ming Ch'eng-tsu shih-lü* 28/6b; Chang T'ing-yü, *Ming shih*, 12/4a, 14/3b; *Hsü t'ung Chih* 149/6a; *Ch'in ting hsü wen hsien t'ung k'ao* (Chui t'ung ed.), 136/32b.

25. *LTHFC*, p. 588; *Ch'in ting hsü wen hsien t'ung k'ao* 136/32b; *Ming T'ai-tsu shih-lü* 136, 149, 163, 209; *Ming Ch'eng-tsu shih-lü* 36, 70, 101, 157, 219; *Ming Jen-tsung shih-lü* 37/3a; *Ming Hsüan-tsung shih-lü* 10, 17, 23, 28–29, 39, 42–43,

45, 54, 59, 81, 87, 91, 99, 106, 110; *Ming Ying-tsung shih-lü* 28, 55, 68, 116, 176; *Ming Wu-tsung shih-lü* 191, 197, 213, 242, 250.

26. *Ta Ch'ing shih-tsu chang huang-ti shih-lü* 55/6b; *Huang ch'ao t'ung-chih* (Chiu t'ung ed.), 87/2b. See also *Huang ch'ao wen hsien t'ung k'ao* (Chiu t'ung ed.), 210/2a.

27. *Huang ch'ao wen hsien t'ung k'ao* 210/2b.

28. *Huang ch'ao wen hsien t'ung k'ao* 210/3b, 2b. The reports of these local officials still had to be processed through the Ministry of Justice.

29. *Huang ch'ao wen hsien t'ung k'ao* 207/2a, 210/45a; a check of the material during the appropriate months in the *Veritable Records* for ten-year intervals during the nineteenth century showed no example of the Hot Weather Assizes.

30. Bodde and Morris, *Law in Imperial China*, pp. 136–137.

31. Ibid., pp. 139–140.

32. *Huang ch'ao wen hsien t'ung k'ao* 210/11b–29a.

33. Autumn Assizes were in theory to be held on a day within the first ten days of the eighth lunar month. I checked the *Veritable Records*—not only for this period but for several weeks before and after this period—at ten-year intervals for the nineteenth century. Frequently there were no references to the assize process. Moreover, several references that did mention the review process implied that it was being conducted on a piecemeal basis province by province. Dr. Fu-mei Chen assures me that this was general Ch'ing practice. To comb out all the relevant material would thus require an inordinate labor for the purposes of this study. In attempting to assess the role of assizes in creating de facto sentences of long-term imprisonment we should also take note of an edict from the reign of K'ang-hsi which specified that men spared death were to be sentenced to three months wearing the wooden stocks called the cangue, whipped one hundred blows, and exiled to Heilungchiang, rather than simply kept in jail. In the present primitive state of our knowledge about Chinese penal practices we cannot know how effectively this ruling was enforced or for how long. See *Huang ch'ao wen hsien t'ung k'ao* 210/6a.

34. *Huang ch'ao wen hsien t'ung k'ao* 210/40a.

35. Bodde and Morris, *Law in Imperial China*, p. 140.

36. See Bodde and Morris, *Law in Imperial China*, pp. 140–141. On occasion, however, even "immediate" executions were deferred. See T'ao Hsi-sheng, *Ch'ing-tai chou-hsien ya-men hsing-shih shen-p'an chih-tu chi ch'eng-hsu*, p. 68. The figures cited by Bodde and Morris were drawn from the late nineteenth-century edition of the *Ch'ing hui-tien*. Harry Lamley has brought to my attention the remarkable increase in the number of statutes and substatutes that called for capital punishment—from 375 in the *Shun-chih lü-li* to 840 by the late Ch'ing. On this point see Sano Manabu, *Sano Manabu chosaku shu*, vol. 4, p. 58.

37. Harry Lamley, "Feud-Strife: The Hsieh-tou Phenomenon in Taiwan and Southeastern China."

38. *TCLL* 1/307; Philastre, *Le Code annamite*, vol. 1, pp. 156–157; Staunton, *Ta Tsing Leu Lee*, p. 18. This Ch'ing rule is virtually identical with that current in the Ming. See *Ta Ming lü chih-chieh*, pp. 48–49.

39. *TCLL* 1/322–327. See also *TCLL* 1/328, 4/3430, 1/309.

40. *TCLL* 4/3405–06, 4/3430, 1/309, 1/310.

CHAPTER 6: THE USES OF AMNESTY

1. Karl Wittfogel, *Oriental Despotism*.

2. Hsü Dau-lin, *"Crime and Cosmic Order,"* pp. 111–126. After reading many of the sources involved, my impression is that Hsü was quite right in saying that Western students of Chinese law (with the notable exception of A. F. P. Hulsewé) have overdrawn the Chinese conception that misdeeds lead to natural disasters.

3. For the population figures see Kato Shigeru, *Shina keizai-shi kosho*, vol. 2, p. 319. Since Kato's figures are for households, I have multiplied them by a factor of four and five to arrive at a rough estimate of numbers of individuals. The civil service size is taken from E. A. Kracke, Jr., "Family versus Merit in the Chinese Examination System," p. 120.

4. Perpetual imprisonment was, however, occasionally used in late imperial times. See Thomas A. Metzger, *Internal Organization of Ch'ing Bureaucracy*, p. 263.

5. Hsiao Kung-ch'üan, *Rural China: Imperial Control in the Nineteenth Century;* Philip Kuhn, *Rebellion and Its Enemies in Late Imperial China*.

6. I would argue that corporal punishments in less developed societies (including preimperial China) did not necessarily reflect any lesser sensitivity to the brutality of physical punishments but rather were at least in part a mere recognition that the state lacked the capacity for population control needed for punishments requiring detention of large numbers of criminals. This is of course merely the obverse of the argument presented above regarding the importance of the possibility of flight in preimperial China.

7. *LTHFC*, pp. 162–163.

8. The most often cited example of this suspension was the era when Chu-ko Liang dominated affairs in Shu. See Hsü Chien, *Ch'u hsüeh chi*, p. 471. Chu-ko Liang's case was noted in later times.

9. There were rules limiting the raising of certain property suits. See Hsü Dau-lin, "Sung-lü i wen chi-chu," p. 19.

10. Chang Fang-p'ing, *Lo ch'uan chi* (SPPY ed.), 20/14b–15a.

11. This population estimate is from Ho Ping-ti, *Studies in the Population of China*, p. 64. There were more districts in Ch'ing China than in Sung China, and therefore more judges, but the few hundred more judges were faced with a quadrupled or quintupled population.

12. Harry Lamley, "Feud-Strife: The Hsieh-tou Phenomenon in Taiwan and Southeastern China."

13. Ibid.

14. Of course we are talking here of proportions. Even in Ch'ing China local officials might handle a substantial number of civil disputes. See David C. Buxbaum, "Some Aspects of Civil Procedure and Practice at the Trial Level in Tanshui and Hsinchu from 1789 to 1895."

15. Lou Yüeh, *Kung k'uei chi*, 26/4b. While it is true that in law all serious crimes were supposed to be reported to the authorities for official investigation, we know that in practice nonofficial groups at times dealt also with such acts. Unfortunately at the present state of our knowledge we do not know how frequently this occurred.

16. For the degrees of sinification involved see particularly Wittfogel, *Oriental Despotism*, especially pp. 219–225; Jing-shen Tao, *The Jurchen in Twelfth Century China*; John W. Dardess, *Conquerors and Confucians*.

17. The compilers of the *Liao History* remark in the Treatise on Punishments that "because the Liao founded their state by force of arms, in suppressing violence and in curbing immorality, they placed nothing before punishments." See *LTHFC*, p. 427.

18. Metzger, *Internal Organization*, especially chap. 4, discusses the Ch'ing system of official surveillance and reports, and he comments on the associated sanctions and rewards in great detail.

19. See Metzger, *Internal Organization*, especially pp. 48 ff.

20. ATLANTA, Ga. (AP)—Dozens of ex-prisoners, many expressing joy and surprise, streamed through Atlanta bus stations today as Georgia began a mass parole program to relieve its crowded prisons. . . . Cecil McCall, chairman of the Pardons and Paroles Board, said that board "realizes this action is contrary to sound parole practice but the hazards of taking such action must be viewed in light of the dangers if we fail to act." See *Honolulu Star-Bulletin* (Monday, October 27, 1975).

Bibliography

ABBREVIATIONS

SPPY   *Ssu-pu pei-yao*
SPTK   *Ssu-pu ts'ung-k'an*
TSCC   *Ts'ung-shu chi-ch'eng*

WORKS IN CHINESE AND JAPANESE

Chan kuo ts'e 戰國策. SPTK edition.

Chang Fang-p'ing 張方平. *Lo ch'uan chi* 樂全集. SPPY edition.

Chang P'u 張溥. *Li-tai ming-ch'en tsou-i* 歷代名臣奏議. Ch'ung-chen woodblock edition, 1635.

Chang T'ing-yü 張廷玉. *Ming shih* 明史. Po-na edition.

Chang Wei 張瑋. *Ta Chin chi li* 大金集禮. Pai pu ts'ung-shu chi-ch'eng edition.

Ch'ang-sun Wu-chi 長孫無忌. *Sui shu* 隋書. SPTK edition.

————. *T'ang-lü shu-i* 唐律疏議. Taipei: Commercial Press, 1970.

Chao Erh-sun 趙爾巽. *Ch'ing shih kao* 清史稿. Taipei: Kuo-fang yen-chiu yüan, 1961.

Chao Ju-yü 趙汝愚. *Chu ch'en tsou-i* 諸臣奏議. Taipei: Wen Hai Publishing Co., 1970.

Ch'en Chün 陳均. *Huang ch'ao pien-nien kang-mu pei-yao* 皇朝編年綱目備要. Tokyo: Seikado bunko, 1936.

Ch'en Ku-yüan 陳顧遠. *Chung-kuo fa-chih shih* 中國法制史. Shanghai: Commercial Press, 1935.

Ch'en Shou 陳壽. *San kuo chih* 三國志. Erh shih ssu shih edition.

Cheng Chü-chung 鄭居中 et al. *Cheng-ho wu li hsin i* 政和五禮新議. Shanghai: Commercial Press, 1933.

Cheng K'o 鄭克. *Che yü kuei chien* 折獄黽鑑. TSCC edition.

Ch'eng Pi-lien 城壁連. "Li-tai she-tien kai-shu" 歷代赦典概述. *Hsing-shih fa tsa-chih*, 13/3, 1969.

Ch'eng Shu-te 程樹德. *Chiu-ch'ao lü-k'ao* 九朝律考. Shanghai: Commercial Press, 1955.

Chiang Ch'ao-po 蔣超伯. *Shuang chiu yao lü* 爽鳩要錄. TSCC edition.

Chieh-hsing shih-li 節行事例. Huang Ming chih-shu edition.

Ch'in ting hsü wen hsien t'ung k'ao 欽定續文獻通考. Chiu-t'ung edition.

Ch'iu Han-p'ing 丘漢平. *Li-tai hsing-fa chih* 歷代刑法志. Taipei: San min shu chü, 1964.

Chou i 周易. Shih san ching chu-shu edition.

Chou li 周禮. SPPY edition.

Chuang Chi-yü 莊季裕. *Chi lei pien* 雞肋編. TSCC edition.

Fan Yeh 范曄. *Hou Han shu* 後漢書. Erh shih ssu shih edition.

Fang Hsüan-ling 房玄齡. *Chin shu* 晉書. Erh shih ssu shih edition.

Feng Yeh 封演. *Feng shih wen chien chi* 封氏聞見記. Taipei: Chi fu ts'ung-shu edition, 1966.

Fu Feng-hsiang 博鳳翔. *Huang Ming chao ling* 皇明詔令. Taipei: Ch'eng Wen Publishing Co., 1967.

Han Fei Tzu 韓非子. SPPY edition.

Hao I-hsing 郝懿行. *Pu Sung shu hsing-fa chih* 補宋書刑法志. TSCC edition.

Higashigawa Tokuji 東川德治. *Shina hō-sei shi kenkyū* 支邦法制史研究. Tokyo: Yuhikaku, 1924.

Hsiao Tzu-hsien 蕭子顯. *Nan Ch'i shu* 南齊書. Peking: Chung hua shu chü, 1972.

Hsieh Shen-fu 謝深甫. *Ch'ing-yüan t'iao-fa shih-lei* 慶元條法事類. Tokyo: Koten kenkyū-kai, 1968.

Hsieh Wei-hsin 謝維新. *Ku chin ho pi shih-lei pei-yao* 古今合璧事類備要. Taipei: Hsin hsing shu chü, 1969.

Hsing-an hui-lan hsü-pien 刑案匯覽續編. Taipei: Wen Hai Publishing Co., 1970.

Hsü Chien 徐堅. *Ch'u hsüeh chi* 初學記. Peking: Chung hua shu chü, 1962.

Hsü Ching-tsung 許敬宗. *Wen kuan tz'u lin* 文館詞林. Shanghai: Commercial Press, 1936.

Hsü Dau-lin 徐道鄰. "Sung-lü chung te shen-p'an chih-tu" 宋律中的審判制度. *Tung-fang tsa-chih*, 4/4, November 1970.

———. "Sung-lü i wen chi-chu" 宋律佚文輯註. *Tung-fang tsa-chih*, 4/3, September 1970.

———. "Fan-i pieh-k'an k'ao" 翻異例勘考. *Tung-fang tsa-chih*, 6/6, August 1972.

———. "Sung-ch'ao te hsien-chi ssu-fa" 宋朝的縣級司法. *Tung-fang tsa-chih*, 5/9, April 1972.

Hsü Shih-kuei 徐式圭. *Chung-kuo ta-she k'ao* 中國大赦考. Shanghai: Shang wu yin shu kuan, 1934.

Hsü Sung 徐松. *Sung hui-yao chi kao* 宋會要輯稿. Taipei: Shih chieh shu chü, 1965.

Hsü T'ien-lin 徐天麟. *Hsi Han hui-yao* 西漢會要. Shanghai: Commercial Press, 1936.

———. *Tung Han hui-yao* 東漢會要. Shanghai: Commercial Press, 1937.

Hsü t'ung chih 續通志. Chiu-t'ung edition.

Hsü t'ung tien 續通典. Chiu-t'ung edition.

Hsü wen hsien t'ung k'ao 續文獻通考. Chiu-t'ung edition.

Hsüeh Ying-ch'i 薛應旂. *Sung Yüan t'ung-chien* 宋元通鑑. Block print edition, 1556.

Hsüeh Yun-sheng 薛允升. *Tu-li ts'un-i* 讀例存疑. Taipei: Chinese Materials and Research Aids Service Center, 1970.

Hsün Yüeh 荀悅. *Ch'ien Han chi* 前漢紀. SPTK edition.

———. *Shen chien* 申鑒. SPTK edition.

Huang ch'ao t'ung chih 皇朝通志. Chiu-t'ung edition.

Huang ch'ao wen hsien t'ung k'ao 皇朝文獻通考. Chiu-t'ung edition.

Huang Sung chung-hsing liang ch'ao sheng cheng 皇宋中興兩朝聖政. Taipei: Wen Hai Publishing Co., 1967.

Hung Mai 洪邁. *Jung chai sui-pi* 容齋隨筆. TSCC edition.

Hung-wu li-chih 洪武禮制. Huang Ming chih-shu edition.

I Chou shu 逸周書. SPPY edition.

Johnson, Wallace, comp. *T'ang-lü shu-i yin-te* 唐律疏議引得. Taipei: Chinese Materials and Research Aids Service Center, 1964.

Kato Shigeru 加藤繁. *Shina keizai-shi kosho* 支邦經濟史考證. Tokyo: Tōyō bunko, 1952–1953.

Ku-liang 穀梁. SPTK edition.

Kuan tzu 管子. SPPY edition.

Kung-yang 公羊. SPTK edition.

Kuo Yü 國語. T'ien-sheng ming-tao edition.

Li chi hsün-tsuan 禮記訓纂. SPPY edition.

Li Ch'ih 李埴. *Huang Sung shih ch'ao kang yao* 皇宋十朝綱要. Lin ching k'an ts'ung-shu edition, 1924–1927.

Li Fang 李昉. *T'ai-ping yü-lan* 太平御覽. Chia-ch'ing woodblock edition, 1812.

Li Hsin-ch'uan 李心傳. *Chien-yen i-lai ch'ao-yeh tsa-chih* 建炎以來朝野雜記. Taipei: Wen Hai Publishing Co., 1967.

———. *Chien-yen i-lai hsi nien yao lu* 建炎以來繫年要錄. Peking: Chung hua shu chü, 1956.

Li Tao 李燾. *Hsü tzu-chih t'ung-chien ch'ang-pien* 續資治通鑑長編. Taipei: Shih chieh shu-chü, 1954.

Li Yu 李攸. *Sung ch'ao shih shih* 宋朝事實. Kuo hsüeh chi pen ts'ung-shu edition.

Liu Hsieh 劉勰. *Wen hsin tiao lung* 文心雕龍. SPPY edition.

Liu Tsung-yüan 柳宗元. *Liu ho tung chi* 柳河東集. SPPY edition.

Lou Yüeh 樓鑰. *Kung k'uei chi* 攻媿集. Wu ying tien chü chen pen ch'uan shu edition.

Lu Chih 陸贄. *Chu lu hsüan kung tsou-i* 註陸宣公奏議. Pai pu ts'ung-shu chi-ch'eng edition.

Ma Tuan-lin 馬端臨. *Wen hsien t'ung k'ao* 文獻通考. Kuo hsüeh chi pen ts'ung-shu edition.

Makino Tatsumi 牧野巽 and Niida Noboru 仁井田陞. "Ko Tō-ritsu sogi seisaku nendai ko" 故唐律疏議製作年代考. *Tōhōgakuhō* (Tokyo), no. 1, 1931; no. 2, 1932.

Ming hui-tien 明會典. Shanghai: Commercial Press, 1936.

Ming T'ai-tsu shih-lü 明大祖實錄; *Ming Ch'eng-tsu shih-lü* 明成祖實錄; *Ming Hsüan-tsung shih-lü* 明宣宗實錄; *Ming Jen-tsung shih-lü* 明仁宗實錄; *Ming Ying-tsung shih-lü* 明英宗實錄; *Ming Wu-tsung shih-lü* 明武宗實錄. Taipei: Chung yang yen-chiu yüan, 1964.

Miyazaki Ichisada 宮崎市定. "Sō-Gen jidai no hōsei to saiban kikō" 宋元時代の法制と裁判機構. *Tōhōgakuhō* (Kyoto), vol. 24, 1959.

Mo tzu 墨子. Chu tzu chi ch'eng edition. Shanghai: Chung-hua shu chü, 1954.

Niida Noboru 仁井田陞. *Chūgoku hōsei-shi kenkyū* 中國法制史研究. Vol. I, "Criminal Law." Tokyo: Tōkyō daigaku shuppankai, 1959.

———. *Tōryō shui* 唐令拾遺. Tokyo: Tōkyō teikoku daigaku shuppankai, 1933.

Ou-yang Hsiu 歐陽修. *Hsin T'ang shu* 新唐書. Erh shih ssu shih edition.

Pan Ku 班固. *Ch'ien Han shu* 前漢書. Wang hsien-ch'ien ch'ien Han shu pu-chu edition.

Pi Yüan 畢沅. *Hsü tzu-chih t'ung-chien* 續資治通鑑. Block print edition, 1801.

Sano Manabu 佐野學. *Sano Manabu chosaku shu* 佐野學著作集. Vol. 4. Tokyo: Chosakushu kankokai, 1957–1958.

Shang tzu 商子. SPTK edition.

Shen Chia-pen 沈家本. *Shen chi-i hsien-sheng i-shu* 沈寄簃先生遺書. Taipei: Yee Wen Publishing Co., 1964.

Shen Yüeh 沈約. *Sung shu* 宋書. Erh shih san shih edition.

Shimada Masao 島田正郎. *Ryōsei no kenkyū* 遼制之研究. Ueda nakazawa insatsu kabushiki kaisha, 1954.

Sogabe Shizuo 曾我部靜雄. "Sōdai no shihai ni tsuite" 宋代の刺配について. *Bunka* 文化, 24/1, 1965.

Ssu-ma Ch'ien 司馬遷. *Shih chi* 史記. Erh shih ssu shih edition.

Ssu-ma Kuang 司馬光. *Wen kuo wen cheng Ssu-ma kung wen-chi* 溫國文正司馬公文集. SPTK edition.

Sun K'ai 孫楷. *Ch'in hui-yao* 秦會要. Taipei: Chung-hua ts'ung-shu edition, 1956.

Sung Ch'i 宋祁. *Ching wen chi* 景文集. TSCC edition.

Sung Lien 宋濂. *Yüan shih* 元史. Po-na edition.

Sung Min-ch'iu 宋敏求. *T'ang ta chao ling chi* 唐大詔令集. Peking: Shang wu yin shu kuan, 1959.

Sung shih ch'uan-wen hsü tzu-chih t'ung-chien 宋史全文續資治通鑑. Taipei: Wen Hai Publishing Co., 1968.

Sung ta-chao ling-chi 宋大詔全集. Peking: Chung hua shu chü, 1962.

Ta-Ch'ing Hsüan-tsung Ch'eng huang-ti shih-lü 大清宣宗成皇帝實錄. Fascimile reproduction of manuscript on red lining paper.

Ta Ch'ing hui-tien shih-li 大清會典事例. Kuang-hsü edition.

Ta-Ch'ing lü-li hui t'ung hsin tsuan 大清律例會通新纂. Taipei: Wen Hai Publishing Co., 1964.

Ta-Ch'ing Shih-tsu Chang huang-ti shih-lü 大清世祖章皇帝實錄. Facsimile reproduction of manuscript on red lining paper.

Ta Ming ling 大明令. Huang Ming chih-shu edition.

Ta Ming lü 大明律. Huang Ming chih-shu edition.

Ta Ming lü chih-chieh 大明律直解 (1395). Chōsen sōtokufu chūsūin, 1936.

Ta tai li chi 大戴禮記. SPTK edition.

Tai Yen-hui 戴炎輝. *T'ang Lü t'ung Lun* 唐律通論. Taipei: Chung hua shu chü, 1964.

T'ao Hsi-sheng 陶希聖. *Ch'ing-tai chou-hsien ya-men hsing-shih shen-p'an chih-tu chi ch'eng-hsü* 清代州縣衙門刑事審判制度及程序. Taipei: Shih-huo ch'u-p'an she, 1972.

T'o T'o 脫脫 et al. *Chin shih* 金史. Po-na edition.

———. *Liao shih* 遼史. Taipei: Yee Wen Publishing Co., 1956.

———. *Sung shih* 宋史. Taipei: Yee Wen Publishing Co., 1965.

Tou I 竇儀. *Sung hsing t'ung* 宋刑統. Taipei: Wen Hai Publishing Co., 1954.

Tseng Kung 曾鞏. *Lung p'ing chi* 隆平集. Taipei: Wen Hai Publishing Co., 1967.

Ts'ui Shih 崔寔. "Cheng lun" 政論. In *Ch'ün shu chih yao*. SPTK edition.

Tung kuan Han chi 東觀漢記. SPPY edition.

Uchida Tomoo 內田智雄. "Kyu Tō-sho keihō-shi" 古唐書刑法志. *Do-shisha hōgaku*, 18/3, 1967.

———. "Zui-sho keihō-shi" 隋書刑法志. *Do-shisha hōgaku*, 6/11, 1964; 88, 1965.

Wakashiro Kujiro 若城久治郎. *Ryō-shi sakuin* 遼史索引. Kyoto: Tōhō bunko gakuin, 1937.

Wang Ch'eng 王稱. *Tung tu shih lüeh* 東都事略. Taipei: Wen Hai Publishing Co., 1967.

Wang Ch'in-jo 王欽若. *Ts'e-fu yüan-kuei* 冊府元龜. Shanghai: Chung hua shu chü, 1960.

Wang Ch'ung 王充. *Lun heng* 論衡. SPTK edition.

Wang Feng 王逢. *Wu ch'i chi* 梧溪集. Chih pu tsu chai ts'ung-shu edition.

Wang Fu 王符. *Ch'ien fu lun* 潛夫論. SPPY edition.

Wang Hsien-ch'ien 王先謙. *Hsün-tzu chi-chieh* 荀子集解. In *Chung-kuo ssu-hsiang ming-chu*. Taipei: Shih chieh shu chü, 1959.

Wang P'u 王溥. *T'ang hui-yao* 唐會要. TSCC edition.

———. *Wu-tai hui-yao* 五代會要 TSCC edition.

Wang T'ang 王讜. *T'ang yü lin* 唐語林. TSCC edition.

Wang Ying-lin 王應麟. *Yü hai* 玉海. Chia-ch'ing woodblock edition, 1806.

Wei Hung 衛宏. *Han chiu i* 漢舊儀. Sun hsing-yen edition.

Wu Ching 吳競. *Chen-kuan cheng-yao* 貞觀政要. SPPY edition.

Yang Hung-lieh 楊鴻烈. *Chung-kuo fa-lü fa-ta shih* 中國法律發達史. Taipei: Commercial Press, 1967.

Yao Ssu-lien 姚思廉. *Ch'en shu* 陳書. Peking: Chung hua shu chü, 1974.

WORKS IN WESTERN LANGUAGES

Balazs, Étienne, *Le Traité juridique du "Souei-choux."* Leiden: E. J. Brill, 1954.

Biot, Edouard, transl. *Le Tcheou-li.* Paris: Imprimerie Nationale, 1851.

Bodde, Derk, and Clarence Morris. *Law in Imperial China.* Cambridge: Harvard University Press, 1967.

Boulais, Gui. *Manuel du Code chinois.* Shanghai: Variétés sinologiques no. 55, 1924.

Bünger, Karl. *Quellen zur Rechtsgeschichte der T'ang-zeit.* Peiping: The Catholic University, 1946.

———. "The Punishment of Lunatics and Negligents According to Classical Chinese Law." *Studia Serica,* 9/1, 1950.

Buxbaum, David C. "Some Aspects of Civil Procedure and Practice at the Trial Level in Tanshui and Hsinchu from 1789 to 1895." *Journal of Asian Studies,* 30/2, February 1971.

Chan Hok-lam. *The Historiography of the Chin Dynasty: Three Studies.* Wiesbaden: F. Steiner, 1970.

Chavannes, Edouard, transl. *Les Mémoires historique de Se-ma Ts'ien.* Paris: E. Leroux, 1895.

Ch'en, Paul Heng-ch'ao. *Chinese Legal Tradition under the Mongols: The Code of 1291 as Reconstructed.* Princeton: Princeton University Press, 1979.

Ch'ü T'ung-tsu. *Law and Society in Traditional China.* Paris: Mouton and Co., 1965.

Code Penal Suisse. Lausanne: Editions Payot, 1975.

Couvreur, S., transl. *Li Ki.* Ho Kien Fou: Imprimerie de la Mission Catholique, 1899.

Creel, Herrlee G. *The Origins of Statecraft in China.* Chicago: University of Chicago Press, 1970.

Crump, J. I., Jr. *Chan-Kuo Ts'e.* Oxford: Clarendon Press, 1970.

Dardess, John W. *Conquerors and Confucians.* New York: Columbia University Press, 1973.

Deloustal, Raymond. "La Justice dans l'Ancien Annam." *Bulletin d'École Francaise d'Extreme Orient,* 9, 1909.

Dubs, Homer H. *The History of the Former Han Dynasty.* Baltimore: Waverly Press, 1938.

———. *Hsuntze: The Moulder of Ancient Confucianism.* London: A Probsthain, 1927.

Duyvendak, J. J. L., transl. *The Book of Lord Shang.* London: A. Probsthain, 1928.

Eichhorn, Werner. "Bemerkungen über einige nicht amnestier bare Verbrecken im Sung Rechtwesen." *Oriens Extremus,* 8, 1961.

Forke, A., transl. *Lun-heng of Wang Ch'ung.* Shanghai: Kelly and Walsh, 1907.

Groot, Jan Jacob Maria de. *The Religious System of China.* Leiden: E. J. Brill, 1892–1910.

Harlez, C. de. *Koue-Yü: Discours des Royaumes.* Louvain: J. B. Istas, 1895.

Ho Ping-ti. *Studies in the Population of China.* Cambridge: Harvard University Press, 1959.

Hsiao Kung-ch'üan. *Rural China: Imperial Control in the Nineteenth Century.* Seattle: University of Washington Press, 1960.

Hsü Dau-lin. "Crime and Cosmic Order." *Harvard Journal of Asiatic Studies,* 30, 1970.

Hulsewé, A. F. P. *Remnants of Han Law.* Vol. 1. Leiden: E. J. Brill, 1955.

Hurnard, Naomi D. *The King's Pardon for Homicide before A.D. 1307.* Oxford: Clarendon Press, 1969.

Johnson, Wallace. *The T'ang Code: General Principles.* Vol. 1. Princeton: Princeton University Press, 1979.

Karlgren, Bernhard. "The Book of Documents." *Bulletin of the Museum of Far Eastern Antiquities,* vol. 22, 1950.

Kracke, E. A., Jr. "Family versus Merit in the Chinese Examination System." *Harvard Journal of Asiatic Studies,* 10/2, 1947.

Kuhn, Philip. *Rebellion and Its Enemies in Late Imperial China.* Cambridge: Harvard University Press, 1970.

Lamley, Harry. "Feud-Strife: The Hsieh-tou Phenomenon in Taiwan and Southeastern China." Paper delivered at the Conference on Taiwan Historical Studies, sponsored by the American Council of Learned Societies, Pacific Grove, California, September 1972.

Legge, James. *The Chiness Classics.* Vol. 1: *The Confucian Analects*; vol. 2: *The Works of Mencius*; vol. 3: *The Shoo King*; vol. 5: *The Ch'un Ts'ew with the Tso Chuen.* Hong Kong: Hong Kong University Press, 1960.

———. *Li Ki.* Oxford: Clarendon Press, 1885.

Liao, W. K., transl. *The Complete Works of Han Fei Tzu.* London: A. Probsthain, 1959.

Maverick, Lewis, ed. *Economic Dialogues in Ancient China.* Carbondale: L. Maverick, 1954.

McLeod, Katrina. "Law and Symbolism of Pollution: Some Observations on the Ch'in Laws from Yün-meng." Paper delivered to the Association for Asian Studies, Chicago, 1978.

Mei, Y. P. *The Ethical Works of Motse.* London: A. Probsthain, 1929.

Metzger, Thomas A. *Internal Organization of Ch'ing Bureaucracy.* Cambridge: Harvard University Press, 1973.

Mommsen, Theodore. *Römisches Strafrecht.* Graz: Akademische Druck–U. Verlagsanstalt, 1955.

Murti, G. Srinivasa, and A. N. Krishna Aiyangar, transl. *Edicts of Asoka.* Adyar, Madras: Adyar Library, 1951.

Ou, Koei-hing. *La Peine d'après le code des T'ang.* Shanghai: Université l'Aurore, 1935.

Pharr, C., transl. *The Theodosian Code and Novels.* Princeton: Princeton University Press, 1952.

Philastre, P. L. F. *Le Code annamite.* Paris: E. Leroux, 1909.

Prusek, J. *Chinese Statelets and the Northern Barbarians.* Dordrecht: Reidal, 1971.

Quattro codici per le udienze civile e penali: Codice penali. Milan: I. di G. Pirola, 1967.

Ratchnevsky, Paul. *Un Code des Yüan.* Paris: E. Leroux, 1937.

Reischauer, Edwin O., transl. *Ennin's Diary.* New York: Ronald Press, 1955.

Rickett, W. Allyn. *Kuan Tzu: A Repository of Early Chinese Thought.* Hong Kong: Hong Kong University Press, 1965.

Rotours, Robert des. *Traité des fonctionnaires et traité de l'armée*. Leiden: E. J. Brill, 1948.

Schafer, Edward H. *The Vermillion Bird*. Berkeley: University of California Press, 1967.

Schlegel, Gustav. *Uranographie chinoise*. Leiden: E. J. Brill, 1875.

Shaw, William. "The Neo-Confucian Revolution of Values in Early Yi Dynasty Korea and Its Implications for Law and Social Order." Paper delivered at the conference on Law and the State in Traditional East Asia, East Asian Legal Studies, Harvard Law School, 1978.

Shih, Vincent Y. C. *Literary Mind and the Carving of Dragons*. New York: Columbia University Press, 1959.

Staunton, G. T. *Ta Tsing Leu Lee*. London: Cadell and Davies, 1810.

Sung, Z. D. *The Text of the Yi King*. Shanghai: Modern Education Co., 1935.

Tao, Jing-shen. *The Jurchen in Twelfth Century China*. Seattle: University of Washington Press, 1977.

Turkish Criminal Code. English translation. Headquarters United States Air Force in Europe, Office of the Staff Judge Advocate, 1960.

Visser, Marinus W. *Ancient Buddhism in Japan*. Leiden: E. J. Brill, 1935.

Watson, Burton. *Basic Writings of Mo Tzu, Hsün Tzu, and Han Fei Tzu*. New York: Columbia University Press, 1967.

Wittfogel, Karl. *Oriental Despotism*. New Haven: Yale University Press, 1957.

Wittfogel, Karl, and Feng Chia-sheng. *The History of Chinese Society: Liao*. Philadelphia: American Philosophical Society, 1949.

Yang Lien-sheng. "Ming Local Administration." In Charles Hucker, ed., *Chinese Government in Ming Times: Seven Studies*. New York: Columbia University Press, 1969.

Glossary

ch'ang-she　常赦

ch'ang-she so pu mien che　常赦所不
　免者

ch'ang-t'u　長徒

ch'ao-shen　朝審

cheng-fa　正法

ch'eng-nu　城奴

chiang wu tien　講武殿

chieh-chieh　結解

chieh-sha　劫殺

chien-men　監門

chien-yüan　減原

ch'ien-pu lang　千步廊

chih-chien yüan　知諫院

chih-shih　制施

ch'ih-hsing　弛刑

chin-ku　禁錮

ch'ing　請

ch'ing hsing-fa　輕刑法

ch'ing-kuan　請官

ch'ing-shih　情實

chiu-ch'ing　九卿

chu fan pu tang te i she　諸犯不當得
　以赦

chu pu ying yu she　諸不應宥赦

chung-shu men-hsia ch'eng-hsiang
　中書門下丞相

chung-shu men-hsia sheng　中書門下省

chü-tso　居作

ch'u ching hsi　出輕繫

ch'u-ming　除名

ch'ü-she　曲赦

en　恩

fang chiu-tsui　放舊罪

fang-huan　放還

fu-tso　復作

fu-t'zu　復資

ho-ch'i　和气

hsi-sung　徙送

hsiang-yen　詳讞

hsiao-kung　小功

hsiao-man　小滿

hsien-tsai　現在

hsing-jen　行人

hsing-pu　刑部

hsü-hsing kuan　卹刑官

hsüan-hui shih　宣徽使

hsün　勳

huan-chüeh　緩決

hui　惠

i　議

i-chüeh　義絶

i-hsiang　移鄉
i pu-tao lun　以不道論

je-en　熱恩
je-shen　熱審

k'ai-fu san-sheng　開府三省
k'ai-shih　開釋
ko-men shih　閤門使
k'o-chih k'o-i　可矜可疑
ku　蠱
ku-sha　古殺
k'uan　寬

li-chüeh　立決
liang-i　量移
lien-tso　連坐
liu　流
liu-jen chi chiang-ssu tsung-liu che i
　chin-ti　流人及降死從流者移近地
lu-ch'iu　錄(慮)囚

mien　免
mien-kuan　免官
mien so chü chih kuan　免所居之官
ming-li　名例
ming-t'ang　明堂
mou ch'in tien　懋勤殿
mou-fan　謀反
mou-p'an　謀叛
mou-sha　謀殺
mou ta-ni　謀大逆

nei-luan　內亂

o-ni　惡逆

pi-ku hsing　畢古刑
pu-hsiao　不孝
pu-i　不義
pu-mu　不睦
pu-she　不赦
pu-she-hsing　不赦刑

pu-she kuo　不赦過
pu tang te she　不當得赦
pu-tao　不道
pu yu kuo　不宥過

san-chien　三監
san fa-ssu　三法司
san-fu　三府
shang shu　尚書
shang shu sheng　尚書省
she　赦
she-kuo　赦過
she-tsui　赦罪
she tsui-jen　赦罪人
she tsui-jen ch'ien-chih　赦罪人遷之
shen　審
shen-k'an　審勘
shen-lu kuan　審錄官
shen-tsung　神宗
shih-erh wei　十二衛
shih hsing-fa　弛刑罰
shih-ting　侍丁
shu-mi shih　樞密使
shu-ssu　殊死
shuang-chiang　霜降
ssu　死
ssu　肆
ssu-sha　四殺
ssu-she　肆赦
ssu-sheng　肆眚
ssu ta-sheng　肆大眚
su-chüeh　疎決

ta chiang chün　大將軍
ta-hsiang　大宰
ta-li ssu　大理寺
ta pu-ching　大不敬
ta-she　大赦
ta-shen　大審
te-yin　德音
t'ing chung ch'iu　挺重囚
t'ing wei　廷尉
tou sha　鬥殺

tso chiang kuan liang-i chin-ch'u　佐降
　官量移近處
t'u　徒
tung-shen　冬審
t'ung-p'an　通判
tz'u-sung　辭訟
tz'u-yu　刺宥

wei-chih　違制
wu-k'u ling　武庫令

wu-she　無赦
wu-sheng chang-kuan　五省長官
yin ta-tu tu ch'ang shih　尹大都督長使
yu　宥
yu-tsui　宥罪
yu tsui-li　宥罪戾
yü-k'ou　予勾
yü-lin chün　羽林軍
yüan-ch'ien　原遣

Index

abduction. *See* kidnapping
abortion, 110, 139n13
abuse toward officials, 56, 141n28
accessories, 63
acts of grace: administrative sanctions and,
55ff, 59, 120; astrology and, 22–23,
139n9; benefits of, 2, 5, 14, 15, 29ff,
45ff, 59ff, et passim; calendrical considerations and, 20–22; Ch'ing dynasty example, 139n13; criticism of, 35, 91–93; definition of, xi; effects on criminals currently
serving sentences, x, 5, 32–33, 44, 45,
67–70, 140n13, 147n13; events involving
the imperial family, 16ff, 25; excluded
crimes, 2, 30, 45, 57, 59, 64–66, 109–
110; frequency of, 24ff, 70–72, 75, 95–
98; groups affected, 5, 16, 28, 57, 109;
localized, 16, 27, 58, 86; military and, x,
4, 15, 16, 28, 45; occasions for issuing, 4,
14ff, 25; outside China, x, 130n1, 130n5;
portents and, 16ff, 25, 34, 113, 139n9;
reasons for issuing, 1ff, 4, 25–27, 113ff;
religious elements and, x, 16ff (*see also*
Buddhist and Taoist clergy); rites associated with, 28, 38ff, 95; role of the
ruler, 3, 6, 15ff; statute of limitations
function, 30, 48, 120–121, 126; sumptuary laws and, 51
adoption, 52ff, 62
adultery, x
age, effect on sentencing, 6, 53, 54, 64
amnesties, definition of, xi. *See also* acts of
grace
analogy, 60, 144n64
appropriate separation *(i-chüeh)*, 53, 62
arson, 87, 109
Asoka, x
assault, 60, 87

assizes *(shen)*, 98ff; suspension of, 103, 108
attendant adult males *(shih-ting)*, 49. *See
also* remaining at home
Autumn Assizes, 102ff

bandits, 64, 84, 139n13, 148n36. *See also*
robbery; theft
battery. *See* assault
beating, punishment of, 46, 51, 53, 58, 59,
82–83, 89, 93, 100ff, et passim
black magic poisoning *(ku)*, 54, 63ff,
139n13
bribery. *See* corruption
Book of Changes (I ching), 21
Book of Documents, 2, 8
Book of Lord Shang, 7
Book of Rites, 9, 10, 28
booty, 50–51
Buddhist and Taoist clergy, 39, 41, 42, 45
Bureau of Policy Critism *(chih chien yüan)*,
84

"Canon of Shun," 2, 91
capital punishment, 1ff, 6, 8, 10, 31, 44,
46, 48, 51, 54, 65, et passim
cases where final judgment should be deferred *(huan-chüeh)*, 105
cases, "light or heavy", 44, 47, 59, 88
cases, with doubtful or pitable circumstances *(k'o-chin k'o-i)*, 9, 105
Chang Fang-p'ing, 120
ch'ang-she. See ordinary acts of grace
ch'ang-she so pu mien che (those not to be
spared by ordinary acts of grace), 57
ch'ang-tu (long-term servitude), 67
ch'ao-shen (Court Assizes), 98
Ch'en (dynasty), 46, 67, 72
Ch'en Ku-yüan, 87

ch'eng-nu (city slaves), 45

Chi'i (dynasty), 71, 72

chiang-wu tien (Hall for the Discussion of Military Affairs), 87

chieh-chieh (preliminary finding), 76

chieh-sha (homicide during banditry), 148n36

chien-yüan (reducing sentence or freeing), 88

Ch'ien Fu Lun, 35

chih chien-yüan (Bureau of Policy Criticism), 84

chih-shu (ordinances), 29

ch'ih-hsing (relaxing of punishments), 32

Chin (dynasty, 280–420), 23, 37, 50, 56, 60, 61, 72, 140n15

Chin (dynasty, 1115–1234), xi, chap. 5 passim, 138n4, 151n17

Ch'in (dynasty), 8, 11, chap. 2 passim

Ch'in Shih-huang, 14

Ch'ing (dynasty), xi, 77, chap. 5 passim

Chinggis, 96, 100

ch'ing hsing fa (lighten punishment), 9

ch'ing-shih (circumstances calling for execution), 105, 108

chiu-sheng (Nine Chief Ministers), 105

chu fan pu tang te i she (all those whose crimes are not liable to receive pardon), 57

chu pu ying yu she (all those who ought not to be treated leniently), 57

Chu Yuan-chang, 100ff

ch'u ch'ing hsi (liberate prisoners guilty of small offences), 10

chung-shu men-hsia sheng (Secretariat-Chancellery), 90

Ch'uan Pu-i, 28

circumstances calling for execution *(ch'ing-shih)*, 105, 108

city slaves *(ch'eng-nu)*, 45

clerks, 84, 87, 89, 92, 139n13, 143n38

codes, xi, 12–13, 15, 43, 55, 94, 98

Commandant of Justice *(t'ing wei)*, 117

Commandant of the Military Storehouse *(wu-k'u ling)*, 38

Commissioner of Imperial Pennants *(hsuan-hui shih)*, 39

Commissioner of Military Affairs *(shu-mi shih)*, 39

commutation, 35, 51, 53ff, 63, 102, 132n9

concubines, 52

confiscation of property, 61, 62

Confucius, 5

Confucianism, 8ff

Conspectus of Legal Cases (Hsing-an hui-lan), 98

Contumacy *(o-ni)*, 52, 60, 144n49

corporal punishments, 5, 116. *See also* beating

corruption, 47, 51, 55, 56, 59, 64–65, 89, 109, et passim

"Counsels of the Great Yü," 2

Court Assizes *(ch'ao-shen)*, 98

crimes: against good morals, 3, 9, 11, 47, 109; against the state, 4, 28, 44 (*see also* rebellion; Great Sedition; Plotting Rebellion; Plotting Great Sedition; Plotting Treason); committed through forgetfulness, 6, 9 (*see also* negligence; inadvertence; mishap); committed through ignorance, 6, 9 (*see also* mishap; negligence; inadvertence); deliberate, 2, 4, 9, 109, 131n2; involuntary, 6 (*see also* mishap; inadvertence; negligence); unpardonable, 4, 44, 60, 64ff

death of prisoners, 82

death penalty. *See* capital punishment

decapitation, 10, 46, 52, 55, 60

degradation, 46, 55ff, 63, 69

deliberately convicting innocent men, 48, 109, 141n25

Deliberation (privilege of) *(i)*, 55

demoted officials, 45, 57, 69. *See also* degradation

Department of Ministries *(shang shu sheng)*, 90

Depravity *(pu-tao)*, 60, 63, 141n24

diminished responsibility (groups), 6, 53ff, 61, 64

Discord *(pu-mu)*, 52, 60

disenrollment *(ch'u-ming)*, 56, 57, 59

Divinations of the Yellow Emperor, 23

double restitution, 51

Duke Mu, 13

Eastern Chou (dynasty), 4ff

Eastern Roman Empire, x

Eastern Wei (dynasty), 46, 66

Empress Lu (Han), 18, 24, 34

Emperors: An (Han), 25; Ch'ang (Han), 25; Che-tsung (Sung), 80; Ch'eng (Han), 17, 20; Ch'eng-hua (Ming), 102; Ch'ien-lung (Ch'ing), 98, 104, 108, 110; Chih (Han), 25; Ching (Han), 18, chap. 2 passim; Chung (Han), 25; Ho (Han), 25; Hsien (Han), 25, 34; Hsing-tsung (Liao), 95; Hsuan (Han), 17, 34; Hsuan-te (Ming), 102; Hsuan-tsung (Chin), 95; Hsuan-tsung (T'ang), 44, 65, 70; Huan (Han), 25; Hui (Han), 16; Hui-tsung (Sung), 40, 78, 80; Hui-tsung (T'ang), 40; Hung-wu (Ming), 101; K'ang-hsi (Ch'ing), 97, 104, 108, 152n33; Kao-tsu (Han), 12, chap. 2 passim, 46; Kao-tsu (T'ang), 68, 71; Kao-tsung (Sung), 75; K'uang-wu (Han), 24, 25; Ming (Han), 25; Ning-tsung (Yüan), 150n8; P'ing (Han), 24, 26, 30; Shang (Han), 25; Shao (Han), 25; Shen-tsung (Ming), 97; Shun (Han), 25, 29; Shun-Chih (Ch'ing), 97, 104; Shun-Tsung (T'ang), 146n81; T'ai-tsu (Sung), 79, 80, 87; T'ai-Tsung (Sung), chap. 4 passim; T'ai-Tsung (T'ang), 68, 70, 71, 146n81; Te-Tsung (T'ang), 71; T'ien-shun (Ming), 102; Wen (Han), 18, 24, 35; Wen-Tsung (Yüan), 150n8; Wu (Han), 16, chap. 2 passim; Wu (Liang), 46; Wu-tsung (Yüan), 150n8; Ying-tsung (Yüan), 150n8; Yüan (Han), 34; Yung-cheng (Ch'ing), 98, 104, 108, 142n38; Yung-lo (Ming), 101, 102

en (grace), 87
enslavement, 61, 62
execution of criminals, suspension of, 108
exile, 29, 32, 33, 45, 46, 48, 49, 51, 52, 53, 54, 61, 79, 81–82, et passim

fa-chia. See legalists
false accusations, 56
false representations, 52
fang huan (freed to return), 67
First Emperor (of Ch'in), 14
fornication, 57
fraud, 48, 51–52, 59, 109
freed to return (from exile) *(fang huan)*, 67
"Frost Descends" *(shuang-chiang)*, 98, 102
Fu Ch'ien, 22
fu-tso (convicts freed of the outward symbols of their status but fulfilling their terms of penal labor), 33
fu-tz'u (reranking, of officials), 55ff, 69
fugitives, 26, 27, 30, 31, 53, 67, et passim

golden cock, 38ff
grace *(en)*, 87
"Grain Fills" *(hsiao-man)*, 102

Grand Minister *(ta-hsiang)*, 6
Great Assizes *(ta-shen)*, 102–103
Great Irreverence *(ta pu-ching)*, 60
Great Sedition *(ta-ni)*, 33, 34, 44, 54. *See also* Plotting Great Sedition

Hall for the Discussion of Military Affairs *(chiang-wu tien)*, 87
Hall of Light *(ming-t'ang)*, 40
Han (dynasty), 15, chap. 2 passim, 38, 58, 99
Han Yü, 68
harboring, 4, 109, 139n13
harmonious ethers *(ho-ch'i)*, 88
heresy, 44, 64–65, 109, 110, 139n13, 149n64
High Court of Justice *(ta-li ssu)*, 76
Historical Records, 13, 14, 22
History of the Former Han, 18ff, 28
ho-ch'i (harmonious ethers), 88
homicide, x, 4, 50, 52ff, 56, 59, 60, 87, 109, et passim; deliberate murder *(ku-sha)*, 148n36; during an affray *(tou-sha)*, 148n36; during banditry *(chieh-sha)*, 148n36; killing of a ruler, 4; premeditated murder *(mou-sha)*, 148n36
Hot Weather Assizes *(je-shen)*, 101ff
hsi-sung (transported), 50. See also *i-hsiang* (shifting the residence)
hsiao-kung (morning degree), 61
hsiao-man ("Grain Fills"), 102
hsien-tsai (current criminals), 43
Hsing-an hui-lan (Conspectus of Legal Cases), 98
hsing-pu. See Ministry of Justice
hsü-hsing kuan (Officials for Relieving Punishments), 104
Hsün Tzu, 8
Hsün Yüeh, 35, 36
Hu Kuang, 28
huan-chüeh (cases where final judgment should be deferred), 105
Hulsewé, A.F.P., x, chap. 2 passim, 129

i pu-tao lun (condemned for impiety), 136n38
i-chüeh (appropriate separation), 53, 62
i-hsiang (shifting the residence), 50, 59
immediate execution *(li-chüeh)*, 102
inadvertence, 2, 4, 9. *See also* mishap; negligence; crimes, committed through forgetfulness, committed through ignorance.

Incest *(nei-luan)*, 60, 139n13
inspection of cases *(lu-ch'iu)*, 28, 86ff, 99ff

je-en (warm grace), 84
je-shen (Hot Weather Assizes), 101ff
jointly adjudicated: for black magic poisoning, 54, 64; for Plotting Great Sedition, 54, 63; for Plotting Rebellion, 33, 44, 45, 54, 56, 61ff; for Plotting Treason, 63
Ju Shun, 22
Judicial Intendants, 90
Judicial Process, 76–77, 122

K'ai-yuan (period), 44, 57, 58
Khitan. *See* Liao
kidnapping, 55, 56, 57, 109
Kings: Chuan-hsiang, 14; Hsiao-wen, 14; Shao-hsiang, 14; Wu, 2, 5
ko, 88
ko-men shih (Palace Postern Commissioners), 40
k'o-chin k'o-i (cases with doubtful or pitiable circumstances), 9, 105
ku (black magic poisoning), 54, 63ff, 139n13
ku-sha (homicide, intentional), 148n36
Kuan Tzu, 8, 10, 35
k'uan (pardon), 6
K'uang Heng, 35
Kwangsi, 90
Kwangtung, 90

labor (penal). *See* penal servitude
Lack of Filial Piety *(pu hsiao)*, 56, 60, 141n24
Latter Chin (dynasty), 69
Latter Chou (dynasty), 73
Latter Han (dynasty), chap. 2 passim, 60, 67, 86
Latter Wei (dynasty), 49, 56, 57, 66, 143n38
legalists, 7ff
li (⅓ English mile), 50, 52, 61, 64, 68, 103, et passim
li-chüeh (immediate execution), 102
Liang (dynasty), 43, 46, 64, 67, 72
liang-i. See measured transfer
Liao (dynasty), xi, 73, 93, chap. 5 passim
Ling-nan, 59
liu. See exile
Liu Chi (Liu Pang), 12ff
liu-jen chi chiang-ssu tsung-liu che i chin-ti (transfer to nearer territory of men in ex-

ile because their original death sentences were reduced), 69
Liu Sung, 117–118
Liu Sung (dynasty), 43, 47, 50, 60, 67, 71, 141n24
local amnesties *(ch'u-sha). See* acts of grace, localized
long term servitude *(ch'ang-t'u)*, 67
Lu Chih, 69–70
lu-ch'iu. See inspection of cases

marriage, 52ff, 139n10
measured transfer *(liang-i)*, 45, 69, 79ff, 145n76, 146n81
Mencius, 5
Meng K'ang, 33
mental incompetence, 6, 53
mien (forgiving punishment), 131n6
military, 9, 28, 45, 87, 89, 110, 139n13
Ming (dynasty), xi, 23, chap. 5 passim
ming-t'ang (Hall of Light), 40
Ministry of Justice *(hsing-pu)*, 46, 68, 76, 103, 104
mishap, 2, 9, 11, 131n2. *See also* inadvertence; negligence; crimes, committed through forgetfulness, committed through ignorance
mitigation, 2, 9. *See also* mishap; negligence; crimes, committed through forgetfulness, committed through ignorance; inadvertence: diminished responsibility
Mo-tzu, 7
Mommsen, x
mou fan. See Plotting Rebellion
mou-p'an. See Plotting Treason
mou-sha (premeditated murder), 148n36
mou ta-ni. See Plotting Great Sedition
mutilating punishments. *See* corporal punishment

negligence, 6. *See also* inadvertence; mishap; crimes, committed through forgetfulness, committed through ignorance
nei-luan (Incest), 60, 139n13
Nine Chief Ministries *(chiu ch'ing)*, 105
Northern Ch'i (dynasty), 38, 71
Northern Chou (dynasty), 47, 57, 71, 141n30
Northern Sung (dynasty), 40, chap. 4 passim
Northern Wei (dynasty), 38, 71

officials, crimes of, 4, 8, 16, 28, 52, 56, 65,

85, 87, 89, 133n24, 139n13, 143n38, 145n76
Officials for Relieving Punishments (hsü-hsing kuan), 104
ordinary acts of grace (ch'ang-she), xi, 44, 57, 61, 75, 95, 97, et passim

Palace Postern Commissioners (ko-men shih), 40
parents, crimes against, 4, 60
patricide, 4, 60, 139n13
penal servitude, 5, 28, 29, 32, 33, 49, 53, 58, 67, et passim
Petition (privilege of) (ch'ing), 54, 55
physical handicaps, and law, 53. See also diminished responsibility
Plotting Great Sedition (mou ta-ni), 54, 60, 62–63, 65, 139n13, 143n38
Plotting Rebellion (mou fan), 16, 33, 34, 44, 60ff, 139n13
Plotting Treason (mou-p'an), 60, 139n13, 144n64
Prefectural Vice-administrator (t'ung-p'an), 90
preliminary finding (chieh-chieh), 76
pu-i (Unrighteousness), 60
pu she (do not pardon), 8, 9
pu she hsing (did not pardon crimes), 7
pu she kuo (do not pardon), 9
pu tang te she (not to be amnestied), 57
pu-tao (Depravity), 60, 63, 141n24
pu yu kuo (not indulgent with transgressions), 7
punishments: seasonal interruption of, 10, 21, 79; types of, 75

Qubilai, 96, 100

rapacity. See corruption
rape, 55, 60
rebellion, 16, 33, 54, 61, 62, 102. See also Plotting Rebellion
recidivism, 3, 47, 110
rectification of status, 48, 53
redemption, 28, 55. See also commutation
Reduction (privilege of) (chien), 55, 63
reductions of punishments, 28, 31, 58
relatives (of wrongdoers), 52, 60–61, 64. See also jointly adjudicated
remaining at home: shih ting, 49; liu-yang (Ch'ing dynasty), 105
reparation. See restitution
replacement (of office), 55

reranking (of officials), 55ff, 69
residual punishments, 49, 56, 64
resignation from occupied office (mien so chü chih kuan), 56, 57, 59
resignation from office (mien-kuan), 56
restitution, 48, 50, 59
review (shen-k'an), 76ff
reviewing and inspecting officials (shen-lu kuan), 99–100
Rites of Chou, 5–6
robbery, 10, 48, 50, 55, 59, 65, 84, 87, 109, et passim
Rome, amnesties in, x

san fa-ssu (Three Legal Offices), 98
seals, 59, 65, 87
seasonal interruption of legal process, 10, 21, 79
seasons and amnesties, 20–22
Second Emperor (of Ch'in), 15
Secretariat-Chancellery (chung-shu men-hsia sheng), 90
servile classes, 48, 53, 56, 60, 139n13
sexual crimes, 55, 60, 109, 110, 139n13, 142n34
shang-shu sheng (Department of Ministries), 90
she, xi, 2, 5, 22, 27, 30, 31, 131n6, et passim; definition of, xi
she kuo (pardon errors), 21
she tsu jen ch'ien chih (amnestied criminals and transported them), 14
she tsui jen (amnestied criminals), 13
she tsui li (pardon criminals), 9, 132n8
shen. See assizes
Shen Chia-pen, 16, 25, 128
shen-k'an (review), 76ff
shen-lu kuan (receiving and inspecting officials), 99–100
shifting the residence (i-hsiang), 50, 59
shih hsing fa (relax punishments), 9
shih ting (attendant adult males), 49. See remaining at home
shu-ssu (decapitation), 134n10
shuang-chiang ("Frost Descends"), 98, 102
slaves. See servile classes
sorcery, x. See also black magic; heresy
Southern Ch'i (dynasty), 43, 47, 67
Southern Sung (dynasty), chap. 4 passim
Spring and Autumn period, 4ff
ssu (pardon), 131n6
Ssu-ma Kuang, 91
ssu-sha (four homicides), 148n36

ssu-she (giving pardons), 135n17
status (and law), 52ff
strangulation, 46, 54, 55, 60, 61, 64
su-chüeh. See inspection of cases
Suburban Sacrifice, 17, 38, 92
Sui (dynasty), chap. 3 passim
summary punishment, 48, 77, 85, 91, 109, 122
sumptuary laws, 51
Sung (dynasty), 40, 57, 69, chap. 4 passim
Sung Collected Documents (Sung hui yao chi kao), 79, 86
Szechuan, 90

Ta Ch'ing hui tien, 98
ta-hsiang (Grand Minister), 6
ta-li ssu (High Court of Justice), 76
ta-ni. See Great Sedition
ta pu-ching (Great Irreverence), 60
ta-she (great act of grace), xi, 13ff, 17, 27, 30, 31, 44, 57, et passim
ta-shen (Great Assizes), 102–103
Taoists. *See* Buddhist and Taoist clergy
tatooing, of criminals, 64
te-yin (ordinary act of grace), 147n6
Ten Abominations, 52ff, 59, 60ff, 87, 139n13, 144n64, et passim
theft, 47, 51, 56, 109
Theodosian Code, x
Three Legal Offices *(san fa ssu),* 98
time limits: for surrender, 43, 51; for transport of prisoners, 66–67, 80
t'ing chung ch'iu (be lenient to those guilty of major crimes), 10
t'ing-wei (Commandant of Justice), 117
tou-sha (homicide in an affray), 148n36
transfer of residence. *See* shifting the residence
Treatise on Law *(Chin History),* 99
Ts'ai Hsiang, 89

tso-chiang kuan liang-i chin-ch'u (demoted and exiled officials transferred in a measured way to nearer jurisdictions), 69
Ts'ui Shih, 35
tung-shen (Winter Assizes), 102ff
t'u (hard labor convicts), 137n44
t'ung-p'an (Prefectural Vice-administrator), 90
tz'u (pardon), 6
tz'u-sung (civil suits), 136n39

Unrighteousness *(pu-i),* 60

Wang Ch'ung, 22
Wang Fu, 35
Wang Mang, 18, 19, 24, 29
Wang Shen, 68
Wang Tsun, 30
warm grace *(je-en),* 84
Warring States period, 4ff
wei-chih (breaking regulations), 148n20
Wei Hung, 29, 34
Western Chou (dynasty), 2ff
Winter Assizes *(tung-shen),* 102–103
Wittfogel, Karl, 112
women, 53, 54, 60, 61, 62, 64
Wu Han, 35
wu-k'u ling (Commandant of the Military Storehouse), 38
wu-she (without pardon), 7ff, 131n2

yang, 40
Yen Shih-ku, 28
yin and *yang,* 40, 88, 119
yu (mitigation, to pardon), 2, 8ff, 131n6, 132n9
yu-tsui (deal gently with crimes), 21
Yüan (dynasty), xi, chap. 5 passim, 140n14
yuan-ch'ien (release of exiles), 145n69

About the Author

BRIAN E. MCKNIGHT completed the PH.D. at the University of Chicago, and is professor of history at the University of Hawaii. He has twice been an associate at the Center for East Asian Legal Studies of the Harvard Law School and was visiting professor of history at Syracuse University in 1978–1979. His principal publications include *Village and Bureaucracy in Southern Sung China* (1971), *The Washing Away of Wrongs: Forensic Practice in 13th Century China* (forthcoming), and various articles on Chinese legal, social, and governmental history.

Production Notes

This book was designed by Roger Eggers
and produced by The University Press of Hawaii.

Composition and paging were done on the
Quadex Composing System and typesetting on the
Compugraphic Unisetter. The text typeface is
Garamond No. 49 and the display typeface is
Benguiat Condensed.

Offset presswork and binding were done by
Halliday Lithograph. Text paper is Glatfelter
Offset, basis 55.